Trust

A History

GEOFFREY HOSKING

OXFORD
UNIVERSITY PRESS

OXFORD
UNIVERSITY PRESS

Great Clarendon Street, Oxford, OX2 6DP,
United Kingdom

Oxford University Press is a department of the University of Oxford.
It furthers the University's objective of excellence in research, scholarship,
and education by publishing worldwide. Oxford is a registered trade mark of
Oxford University Press in the UK and in certain other countries

Published in the United States of America by Oxford University Press
198 Madison Avenue, New York, NY 10016, United States of America

British Library Cataloguing in Publication Data
Data available

Library of Congress Control Number: 2013956956

ISBN 978–0–19–871238–1

Printed in Great Britain by
CPI Group (UK) Ltd, Croydon, CR0 4YY

Preface

This book has been far longer in the making than I had anticipated. Its first fruit was a Royal Historical Society Study Day in 2004, and I am thankful to Jinty Nelson and Martin Daunton for their encouragement in organizing it and publishing some of the results. I owe a great deal to an Elizabeth and J. Richardson Dilworth Fellowship for 2006–7 at the Institute for Advanced Study, Princeton, which provided much-appreciated leisure, model facilities, and lively colleagues among whom to advance my ideas. Jonathan Israel was a thoughtful and helpful organizer of our Institute seminar, and has provided perceptive comments and unfailing support ever since. I have developed and refined my thinking over the years with seminar presentations among historians, economists, social psychologists, and international relations experts, and I have learnt a great deal from those who took part. Some of those seminars were held in various parts of Russia, under the auspices of the Moscow School of Civic Education, and I owe a lot to the participants, and especially to Lena Nemirovskaia and Yury Senokosov, the organizers, for their lively engagement in discussions.

I am especially grateful to Ute Frevert, who found time to read and comment on the whole of a close-to-final draft of the text. David d'Avray read substantial parts of an earlier draft, and offered insight, encouragement, and good cheer at times of low morale. When I was working in Moscow, Liudmila Cherni-chenko provided hospitality and friendly interest; I am indebted to her for helping me to understand what ordinary Russians felt during their crisis of the 1990s. Sections of earlier drafts were also read by David Cannadine, Simon Dixon, Eric Gordy, Ian Kershaw, Alena Ledeneva, Dominic Lieven, Ivana Mar-ková, Jinty Nelson, Lena Nemirovskaia, Onora O'Neill, Robert Putnam, Susan Reynolds, Anthony Seldon, Yury Senokosov, Robert Service, Robert Skidelsky, Steve Smith, Alexei Tikhomirov, and Nick Wheeler—in some cases so long ago that they may have forgotten they did so. But all have contributed to my thinking, and I am grateful to them all. My own failings will be only too evident, despite all they have done.

Several libraries have been indispensable to my work, especially those of University College London, the School of Slavonic & East European Studies, the British Library, the London Library, the Firestone Library of Princeton University, and that of the Institute for Advanced Study, Princeton.

I want to thank Oxford University Press's anonymous reviewers, and especially Christopher Wheeler and his successor, Robert Faber, as editors for their encour-agement, critical support, and perceptive reading of drafts. The final text would have been much weaker without them.

I owe most of all to my wife Anne and my daughters Katya and Janet, for giving me warmth and support through the long years of partial absence from family affairs, as well as a general readers' perspective and at times expert guidance too.

Geoffrey Hosking

School of Slavonic & East European Studies
University College London
April 2014

Acknowledgements

I hereby record my thanks to the publishers who have given me permission to reproduce sections of my previously published works:

Cambridge University Press: 'Trust and Distrust: A Suitable Theme for Historians?', *Transactions of the Royal Historical Society* (sixth series), 16 (2006), 95–116.

Taylor & Francis: 'Trust and Symbolic Systems: Religion and Nationhood', in Ivana Marková and Alex Gillespie (eds), *Trust and Conflict: Representation, Culture and Dialogue*, London: Routledge, 2012, 17–36.

Koninglijke Brill NV: 'Structures of Trust: Britain and Russia Compared', in Masamichi Sasaki and Robert M. Marsh (eds), *Trust: Comparative Perspectives*, Leiden: Brill, 2012, 31–68.

Modern Humanities Research Association: 'Trust and Distrust in the USSR: An Overview', *Slavonic & East European Review*, 91/1 (January 2013), 1–25.

Contents

Introduction

In the western world there is a crisis of trust. Some of the certainties on which till recently we based our lives suddenly seem less certain. In the past we relied on banks to be rocks of financial stability and integrity; but now in the United Kingdom and European Union we have discovered that some of our bankers are greedy and reckless, that they manipulate interest rates to their own advantage, that they knowingly sell customers unnecessary payment insurance policies, and that they are bad at assessing risk, which is supposed to be their speciality. We have learnt to distrust both their competence and their moral sense. We used to trust governments to oversee our financial life and to collect taxes equitably, but it transpires that officials have been averting their gaze from tax havens, which enable the rich to avoid paying their fair share. The personal integrity of those who represent us is a prerequisite of effective democracy, yet the scandal of careless or even fraudulent expenses claims to pad out parliamentary salaries occurred in the United Kingdom, not in some raw and impoverished state.

Sections of the media, with at least the passive approval of some politicians, have been breaking the law to eavesdrop on people's private lives and ferret out confidential information. Some policemen appear to have taken bribes not to investigate the resulting felonies. Other policemen have infiltrated groups exercising legitimate rights of protest, and have then formed sexual relationships with trusting women in those groups; in one or two cases the result has been a family based on deceit. The US and UK security services, supposed to protect law-abiding citizens, have, it turns out, been collecting personal information on a huge scale by tapping internet communications and mobile phones; they have been misusing laws concerning terrorism and official secrets to harass and detain (or attempt to detain) whistleblowers and journalists who could embarrass the government. In all these sensitive areas of life the trust we used to place in our institutions has been significantly weakened in recent years. Newspaper editorials frequently refer to a loss of trust in public life, while politicians appeal, helplessly or speciously, for renewed trust.

In September 2013 only 46 per cent of US citizens polled by Gallup trusted the judgement of those holding public office,[1] while a mere 19 per cent trusted their representatives in Congress.[2] Even more depressingly, a MORI poll of February

---

[1] <www.gallup.com/poll/164360/americans-approval-congress-september.aspx>; accessed 11 November 2013.

[2] <www.gallup.com/poll/164678/political-trust-american-people-new-low.aspx>; accessed 11 November 2013.

2013 found that 18 per cent of British citizens trust politicians to tell the truth, fewer even than trust estate agents (24 per cent), journalists (21 per cent), and bankers (21 per cent).[3] These are all lamentable figures for professions whose work requires public trust. The loss of trust in bankers has been especially acute. In 1983 nine out of ten people polled by NatCen Social Research thought that banks were well run; by 2013 that proportion was just one in five.[4]

The impression of a loss of trust in public institutions is, then, well founded. But what does it mean? Much of the reportage and resultant gossip seems to presuppose a previous golden age in which trust was widespread. But what kind of trust? Placed by whom in whom and for what purposes? Our casual observations, though not altogether misplaced, lack historical context, in fact lack any but the most rudimentary concept of what trust is and how it functions within different societies. This book explores what trust—and distrust—have meant in different societies in different periods of history, so that we can better understand what we mean when we talk today of a loss of trust.

It is important to make one thing clear at the outset: when we talk about trust, we are talking of our feelings about the future. These are often vague and indefinite, since in routine circumstances we operate on auto-pilot. Everyday life involves us all in webs of trust which we do not even notice. Not at least until they suddenly go wrong. Most days I travel around London by bus or Underground, assuming that I will not be blown up by a bomb. This assumption is so routine and unremarkable that it is scarcely worth dignifying with the word 'trust'. Except that on 7 July 2005 several bombs exploded on the Underground, and one on a bus in Tavistock Square, killing 52 people and wounding more than 700. Even a very routine form of trust suddenly seemed fragile. For several weeks the possibility of a repeat attempt was at the back of Londoners' minds, prompting distrust of anyone on public transport who looked unusual or was carrying heavy objects. Then gradually people's suspicions faded and normal insouciance resumed.

These are extreme circumstances, though. Let us take a more mundane example, one in which the way we routinely trust and distrust is influenced by social circumstances. In the 1990s a Russian tax inspector, incredulous at the high rate of tax collection in Sweden, asked the political scientist Bo Rothstein how on earth it was achieved. Rothstein answered that most Swedes paid their taxes because they believed (a) that everyone else does, and (b) that the revenue will be honestly spent on purposes beneficial to society. The Russian had to observe in reply that on the contrary Russians avoided paying taxes because they believed (a) that few of their fellow citizens paid in full, and (b) that their money would be misappropriated by corrupt politicians and businessmen. Rothstein calls this kind of situation a 'social trap'.[5] The only rational thing for an individual to do in those circumstances is to

---

[3] <www.ipsos-mori.com/researchpublications/researcharchive/3133/Politicians-trusted-less-than-estate-agents-bankers-and-journalists.aspx>; accessed 10 September 2013.

[4] NatCen Social Research survey, reported in *The Guardian*,10 September 2013, 13.

[5] Bo Rothstein, *Social Traps and the Problem of Trust*, Cambridge University Press, 2005, 2–4. I consider this situation further in Chapter 6.

distrust and to avoid paying tax as far as possible. But the individually rational generates the socially disastrous: state revenues fall short, hence schoolteachers and pensioners are paid very late or not at all. An individual deciding to trust and pay up would not improve the system; he or she would simply be a sucker. Social traps produce obstinately vicious circles of distrust, from which escape is extremely difficult.

Let us consider an example which illustrates several modes of trust simultaneously. For many people flying by air has become a routine activity. Which of us, before boarding an aircraft, checks every rivet, joint, and fuel duct in it? Or even the qualifications of the engineers responsible for maintaining and repairing those parts? Obviously we never do so. Yet our lives depend on the impeccable working order of every one of those parts, the skill and conscientiousness of the engineers and of the pilots. The fact is, we take them on trust because everyone else does so, and because planes very seldom crash. Besides, to do otherwise would require us to have both time and skills we don't possess. We don't 'decide' to board an aircraft: we just do it. We trust the pilot because he is well trained and has ample experience of flying, the engineers because they are qualified in aeronautics and metallurgy, the technicians because they know how to apply that knowledge to the repair and maintenance of aircraft, and the airline because it has a good safety record and a direct interest in keeping it up. Normally we do not reflect on these reassuring facts.

There is yet another form of trust involved in the 'decision' to board an aircraft. How do we know that planes seldom crash? Because the media—television, radio, newspapers—report the fact when they do, and that fortunately is not often. But what if we cannot trust the media? In the Soviet Union the media never reported plane crashes that involved the domestic airline Aeroflot. I recall that several of my acquaintances there would not fly on Aeroflot, as there were rumours that actually their planes crashed quite often. There was even a little ditty which did the rounds among sceptical potential customers:

> Quickly, cheaply, without to-do,
> Aeroflot will bury you.[6]

In flying, then, we are putting our trust in people, but not simply as individuals. We trust pilots and engineers as members of institutions which have certain procedures and draw on certain systems of knowledge. We rely on journalists who form part of honest and well-informed media organizations. We do something similar every day of our lives, without being aware of it. Only when a crisis occurs do we realize that we may have been misplacing our trust.

Time, place, and social context are crucial to the trust assumptions on which we base all our thoughts and actions. That is why we cannot dismiss those assumptions as trivial or irrelevant to our real lives. If we are to understand how any society functions we have to take account of them, even though they are difficult to

---

[6] *Bystro, deshevo, bez khlopot | Pokhoronit vas Aeroflot.* My thanks to David Christian for reminding me of this example of Russian oral culture, and for devising the snappy translation.

identify. They constitute the mental map with the aid of which individuals learn to navigate the social terrain in which they have to operate. I have chosen to grace these assumptions with the word 'trust': that word lies at the centre of a semantic chart (see Chapter 2, 'What is Trust?') which would include other words like confidence, faith, belief, reliance, and so on. Without them we would all be paralysed, unable to undertake any social action. As the German sociologist Niklas Luhmann has observed, 'A complete absence of trust would prevent [one] even getting up in the morning.'[7]

Routine, unthinking trust is, then, part of the texture of our everyday lives, whether we recognize it or not. We have to bear that in mind when examining our current 'crisis of trust', because some of the warnings about it are bogus. In her 2002 Reith Lectures, Onora O'Neill questioned whether today's levels of trust are really lower than in the past. We sometimes claim not to trust doctors, but, she pointed out, when unwell, the great majority of us nevertheless make straight for our doctors to get advice and help. 'Perhaps', she suggests, 'claims about a crisis of trust are really evidence of an unrealistic hankering after a world in which safety and compliance are total, and breaches of trust are totally eliminated.'[8] We continue also in practice to rely on banks, governments, politicians, police, journalists, and security services to give our lives a dependable framework within which we can live in our own way. We all need money and physical security. We all need public servants who will formulate policy and manage public risk. We all need an authority to detect and prevent crime. We all need reliable information on what is going on around us and practical ideas about how to rectify whatever goes wrong.

In short, we are all interdependent. We all rely on most other people doing their duty and acting ethically in order to lead anything like a normal life. Trust is a vital ingredient in this web of interdependence. If we cannot trust our public institutions to work properly, then the quality of social life deteriorates. As this book will illustrate, once generalized social trust declines to a certain point, then it plunges rapidly and damagingly. People reconfigure their trust at a lower level, placing it in the leader of their party, faction, religious or ethnic movement—and possibly in armed forces connected to those movements. Then we enter a Hobbesian world, in which social peace can only be preserved, if at all, by an overbearing authoritarian government. Many intelligent and honest Russians, especially of an older generation, feel that the recent instability and disorder in their own country justifies continuing authoritarian rule.

The West is still a long way from such a serious degradation of social trust, but the events of the last decade or so have moved us some distance along the road which leads there. The countries of the eurozone have compounded the problem through the defective design of their currency, followed by mistaken economic policies.[9] The EU's polling organization, Eurobarometer, showed in spring 2013 that trust in the Union had declined steeply since 2008 in Germany, France, Italy,

[7] Niklas Luhmann, *Trust and Power*, Chichester: John Wiley & Sons, 1979, 4.
[8] Onora O'Neill, *A Question of Trust*, Cambridge University Press, 2002, 11–12, 19.
[9] For the crucial importance of trust in money, see Chapter 4.

Spain, and Poland—all countries whose populations had previously supported the EU by considerable majorities.[10] None of us, even in apparently very stable societies, are immune from the regularities of trust, which I illustrate in the following pages. In the West today an inept response to a serious economic crisis is gradually depleting the capital of social trust built up in the past.

There was never, though, a golden age of trust. Only historical ignorance could lead us to assume there has been. Trust and distrust have been pervasive features of all human societies, but their nature and context changes along with social change. Our present crisis is genuine and serious, but so far it is poorly understood, because we know little about the historical background to contemporary configurations of trust, the ways in which we trust and distrust nowadays. They have been transformed in advanced western societies during the last half century, and this transformation underlies our unease. In what follows I will aim to place those recent changes in historical perspective, in order to help us become more aware of the ways in which we trust nowadays—as well as more attentive to whether what we trust is genuinely trustworthy.

Most writers on trust lack a historical background. Sociologists, anthropologists, and other social scientists have given a good deal of attention to trust, as I explain in Chapter 2, but their work usually lacks a historical dimension. For their part, historians themselves have scarcely broached the subject at all. This is strange, since the recently flourishing disciplines of cultural and linguistic history, and the history of feelings, are well adapted to studying trust, the mental maps which embody it, and their changes over time. Historians today are good at analysing identities, representations, discourses and narratives, but they mostly fall short of understanding what connects those perceptions with decisions and actions. This is where trust comes in. The problem, I think, is that, in the various 'cultural', 'linguistic', and 'affective' turns of recent decades historians have been excessively seduced by two theorists whose work has on the whole been fruitful in studying past societies, Clifford Geertz and Michel Foucault.

Geertz's attraction for historians is very understandable. His major contribution to social science was to free anthropology from the emphasis on observed *behaviour* and to insist that the *meanings* people themselves ascribed to their behaviour was just as worthy of study. Culture Geertz defines as 'socially established structures of meaning'.[11]

Where I believe Geertz is misleading or at least inadequate is in his conscious strategy of interpreting human behaviour in terms of texts. 'Doing ethnography', he writes, 'is like trying to read...a manuscript.'[12] In giving a 'thick description' of a Balinese cockfight, he describes its drama as a text, which he compares with *Macbeth*. In my view, while it may be a text, it is certainly more than that, since Geertz is describing the real behaviour of real people in a specific social setting. Analysing social

---

[10] *The Guardian*, 25 April 2013, 1. See further in Chapter 7.
[11] Clifford Geertz, 'Thick Description: Toward an Interpretive Theory of Culture', in C. Geertz (ed), *The Interpretation of Cultures*, London: Hutchinson, 1975, 5.
[12] Geertz, 'Thick Description', 10.

practices as a text may help us to interpret them, and to understand repeated actions, but it does not equip us to give an account of how real people take decisions and act in a specific social setting. To do that, we need the concept of trust or its semantic neighbours.

Foucault distorts historical study in another way, through an excessive emphasis on *power,* which he sees as being 'inscribed' into all our social relationships, all our discourses and practices. Yet his concept of power is frustratingly vague. It is 'intentional and non-subjective': that is, it operates through the intentional activity of collectives of people who are nevertheless unable to foresee or to determine the results of what they are doing. It is also multi-directional, 'operating from the top down and also from the bottom up'. It is 'exercised on the dominant as well as on the dominated; there is a process of self-formation or auto-colonisation involved'. As the bourgeoisie gained power during the seventeenth–nineteenth centuries it had to 'exercise strict controls primarily on its own members. The technologies of confession and the associated concern with life, sex and health were initially applied by the bourgeoisie to itself.' Even truth statements reveal not the truth—which anyway in an objective sense does not exist, in Foucault's view—but the nature of the power relationships in the society which produced the statement.[13]

There is something profoundly unsatisfactory about a concept of power which is so vague and all-embracing, which proceeds from no particular source or centre, and which is lacking in all subjectivity and direction. At times one feels that Foucault was deliberately not noticing what was under his nose: people's mutual sympathy, their lively and apparently ineradicable tendency to seek reciprocal relationships with one another. Many of his evasions and circumlocutions could be avoided if one postulates that much of what he explains through power would be better explained by an associated but independent human propensity: trust. We need to replace his 'genealogy of power' with a genealogy of trust.

All this is frustrating, since, as I have remarked, historians' growing skill at interpreting culture, language, and feelings equips them well to study the diverse forms trust and distrust assume in different societies. Doing so might also help us to recover a sense of wonder at the complex and on the whole—admittedly with glaring exceptions—effective institutions of trust and cooperation which characterize the modern world, some of them consciously designed but some of them spontaneously generated. The sociologist Paul Seabright reminds us that 'Where there are no institutional restraints on it, systematic killing of unrelated individuals is so common among human beings that, awful though it is, it cannot be described as exceptional, pathological or disturbed. . . . In the circumstances it is astonishing that systematic exchange among non-relatives should have evolved at all, let alone that it should have become the foundation of the fantastically complex social and economic life we know today.'[14] This situation presupposes a remarkable

---

[13] 'Les Mailles du pouvoir', in Michel Foucault, *Dits et écrits*, Paris: Gallimard, 1954–75, iv. 182–201.

[14] Paul Seabright, *The Company of Strangers: A Natural History of Economic Life*, Princeton University Press, 2004, 53.

development of routine trust between major actors in economic life.[15] The tools of cultural history are well adapted to explaining this development. We need to understand it better, because the forms trust has assumed in modern societies are actually in growing jeopardy, from threats to which we pay little attention.

One historian who has studied trust seriously, Ute Frevert, has performed very useful work by indicating how usage of the word 'trust' and its cognates in various European languages has changed over time. She shows in particular how the development of constitutional democracy and a market society has rendered many of our social contacts impersonal; in reaction, both politicians and commercial advertisers have persistently used the word 'trust' as an artificial, indeed fraudulent, way of suggesting personal warmth where none exists.[16] My aim in the present book is to take things further by considering not only the word, but the whole semantic field surrounding it, together with its social contexts, and the different ways in which different societies have endeavoured to create and sustain solidarity.

It is important to use the concept of trust systematically now, not only because of the widespread perception of a 'crisis of trust', but also because not studying trust explicitly and in historical context has led us into serious errors in recent decades. Western nations have been endeavouring to promote democracy and free markets in non-western countries. In doing so they have tended to overemphasize structures of *power* and *law*: good governance, free elections, constitutional guarantees, human rights, and the like. These are of course crucial, but advancing them without understanding how trust and distrust operate is likely to be ineffective or even pernicious. One misconception in particular has in recent decades bedevilled attempts to understand and generate social solidarity: the theory, deriving from a misreading of Adam Smith, that the free market is self-regulating, can provide against risk, and can offer a secure basis for economic development. During the 1990s I observed at first hand how Russian society was seriously damaged by the dogmatic pursuit of such an agenda.[17] There and elsewhere westerners have been recommending economic and political reforms which are as likely to undermine social trust as to promote it.

Not by chance, we are now also misunderstanding the crisis which has recently engulfed advanced western countries. I will look at some of the results of this misunderstanding in Chapter 6. The theory of the self-regulating free market has turned out to be dramatically wrong, but nearly all our politicians are still mesmerized by it. In Chapter 4 I offer an alternative explanation of how trust in money has evolved and how markets operate.

---

[15] See Chapter 4.

[16] Ute Frevert, 'Vertrauen – eine historische Spurensuche', in Frevert (ed), *Vertrauen: Historische Annäherungen*, Göttingen: Vandenhoeck & Ruprecht, 2003, 7–66; *Vertrauensfragen: Eine Obsession der Moderne*, Munich: C. H. Beck, 2013. I attempted an initial historical treatment of trust in 'Trust and Distrust: A Suitable Theme for Historians?', *Transactions of the Royal Historical Society*, 16 (2006), 95–116. Despite its title, the book by Kieron O'Hara, *Trust from Socrates to Spin*, Cambridge: Icon Books, 2004, is not really a study of how trust has functioned in past societies. It is an intelligent and discriminating analysis of how the word is used in late twentieth- and early twenty-first-century societies, drawing for some of its insights on thinkers of the past.

[17] See Chapter 6.

The study of trust helps, then, to explain both why many western attempts to introduce democracy in non-western countries during the 1990s and 2000s have failed, and also why we are coping badly with our own crisis.

The opening chapter of my book looks at a society which exemplified some of the highest levels of distrust seen in the modern era: the Soviet Union in the 1930s. It is an awful warning from history: a reminder of what can happen if we allow social trust to continue dwindling. Chapter 2 examines the ways in which social scientists have conceptualized trust. I suggest that their work, though sometimes useful, has proved inconclusive for lack of historical material. I hypothesize that trust is mediated through symbolic systems and the associated institutions, which change over time, usually gradually, sometimes abruptly. Chapter 3 then considers how trust has been deployed through one such symbolic system, religion and its institutions. Chapter 4 does the same for money and financial institutions. Chapter 6 examines how trust has been reconfiguring itself in recent decades both in religion and in finance, and how in both cases new forms of trust and distrust have been generated. Here I suggest that our growing trust in money—still very strong despite the financial crisis which began in 2007—affects all forms of trust in our society today, including religion. The other major focus of our trust today is the nation-state, even though our economy is increasingly global. Chapter 5 explains how the nation-state has gradually assumed this status, through absorbing many trust-generating symbols from earlier social formations. In Chapter 7 I suggest why that continues to be the case right up to the present.

Susan Reynolds, a leading scholar of the European middle ages, has taken trust seriously as a legitimate subject of historical study. All the same, she once wrote, 'I am not at all sure that a history of trust is possible.'[18] At times I have been tempted to share her view. But it has seemed important at least to try. Unless we can better understand the invisible bonds of trust which hold our societies together, and the way in which those bonds evolve and change, we are in serious danger of degrading them further. History offers too many examples of the disasters which could then overwhelm us.

What follows is not a comprehensive history: that would scarcely be possible. Instead, I have selected illustrative materials from quite a wide variety of epochs and countries—most of them European, since Europe is what I have spent most of my life studying. Their relevance is, though, I believe, universal. I have tried to offer enough empirical material to provide the basis for an informed debate about the real meaning of our current 'crisis of trust' and its historical origins. In the process I hope I will have prompted historians to use the concept of trust as a tool for understanding societies very different from our own.

---

[18] Susan Reynolds, 'Trust in Medieval Society and Politics', in *The Middle Ages without Feudalism: Essays in Criticism and Comparison on the Medieval West*, Farnham: Ashgate Variorum, 2012, xiii. 1.

1

Land of Maximum Distrust
The Soviet Union in the 1930s

One of the most remarkable and heart-rending documents to come out of Russian archives in the last twenty years is the letter Lenin's former comrade-in-arms Nikolai Bukharin wrote to Stalin from prison in December 1937.[1] It displays with maximum poignancy some of the agonizing dilemmas of trust and distrust which agitated Soviet leaders in the 1930s.

In March, as part of an 'anti-rightist' campaign, Bukharin had been expelled from the party and arrested. Under interrogation he began to confess to the accusations made against him, totally groundless though they were, of colluding with imperialist powers to bring about the invasion and dismemberment of the USSR. In December it was confirmed that he would go on trial for the 'crimes' of which he was accused. Having observed previous show trials, and knowing both the inner workings of the party and Stalin's own overbearing character, he could anticipate that he would be found guilty and probably executed. In that situation he wrote a desperate letter to Stalin, begging that the death penalty not be applied to him, that he be allowed to live and render further services to the Communist Party to which he had devoted his life.

He was not just begging for pardon, though. Much of the text is rambling, confidential, and intimate, as if addressed to a close personal friend. Bukharin heads the letter 'Personal' and 'Very secret', and specifically requests that no one should read it without Stalin's express permission. He asks to be allowed 'to write this letter without resorting to officialese [*ofitsial'shchina*], all the more so since I am writing this letter to you alone: the very fact of its existence or non-existence will remain entirely in your hands'. Throughout, Bukharin addresses Stalin with the intimate *ty*, and at one point uses Stalin's conspiratorial nickname, Koba—a reference to the pre-revolutionary underground where they were comrades together. He draws a crucial distinction between the public arena, before which he will not retract the false confessions he has made, and his private, personal relationship with Stalin, where he cannot bear the thought that Stalin actually believes in his 'crimes'. 'Believe me, my heart boils over when I think that you

[1] The English text of Bukharin's letter is in J. Arch Getty and Oleg Naumov (eds), *The Road to Terror: Stalin and the Self-Destruction of the Bolsheviks, 1932–1939*, New Haven: Yale University Press, 1999, 556–60. I have modified the translation in a few places, drawing on the Russian original in *Istochnik*, 1993, no. 0, 23–5.

might *believe* that I am guilty of these crimes and that in your heart of hearts you *yourself* think that I am really guilty of all these horrors.' Facing death at the hands of Stalin, Bukharin is still obsessed with the idea of restoring his former comrade's *personal* trust in him.

He recalls with remorse an incident when Stalin had called him a trusted friend, one incapable of intrigue; yet at that time Bukharin had already had a confidential conversation with another party leader, Lev Kamenev, in which they had agreed that Stalin's ruthless and cynical authoritarianism was damaging the party. Indeed Bukharin had referred to him as a 'Genghis Khan' whose 'line is ruinous for the whole revolution'.[2] This conversation was remarkable, since the two men belonged to opposite wings of the party, which distrusted each other profoundly. Kamenev was a member of what by then, with Bukharin's approval, had been stigmatized as the party's 'left deviation'; Bukharin himself belonged to the 'right opposition'. The Central Committee, controlled by Stalin, had condemned both.

They would both have liked to bring their criticisms before the party Central Committee, but they knew that such a step would be denounced as 'factionalism' under the 1921 resolution 'On Party Unity', which ironically they had both voted for. Their conversation led nowhere, except that Stalin learnt of it, and it intensified his distrust of both men. In his letter Bukharin actually beseeches Stalin's forgiveness for his disloyalty. 'God, what a child I was. What a fool! And now I'm paying for this with my honour and with my life. For *this* forgive me, Koba. I weep as I write. . . . Oh, Lord, if only there were some device which would make it possible for you to see my flayed and tormented soul! If only you could see how I am attached to you, body and soul, quite unlike Stetsky or Tal.'[3]

Throughout his letter, Bukharin continues to draw a sharp distinction between political and personal trust. He reiterates that the party must be unanimous and ruthless towards its enemies, and even potential enemies. In his letter he tries to imagine himself in Stalin's position, leader of a party carrying out 'universal-historical tasks'. He praises the idea of a general purge, which draws in not only the guilty, but also 'persons potentially under suspicion', and hence perhaps not guilty at all. He calls the purge 'great and bold', necessary because of 'the prewar situation' (which justifies distrust towards the outside world) and 'the transition to democracy' (which justifies distrust towards internal enemies). He can see a justification for his own approaching fate, since he too had taken part in factional struggles and undermined party unity. 'One has to react to the danger created by the fact that people inevitably talk about each other and in doing so arouse an *everlasting* distrust in each other. (I'm judging from my own experience. How I raged against Radek, who had smeared me, and then I myself did the same thing.) In this way [i.e. by a general purge], the leadership is bringing about a *full*

---

[2] Stephen Cohen, *Bukharin and the Bolshevik Revolution: A Political Biography, 1888–1938*, New York: Vintage Books, 1975, 290–1; Anna Larina (Bukharina), *Nezabyvaemoe*, Moscow: APN, 1989, 88–90.

[3] A reference to two officials of the party's press department, who had given evidence against Bukharin.

guarantee for itself.' In other words, he acknowledges that leading the party to success in a hostile world requires the maximum distrust, vigilance, and ruthlessness.

The letter displays, then, an incongruous mixture of emotions. On the one hand, Bukharin has no illusions about Stalin's cold-blooded vengefulness and therefore his own likely fate, which he accepts in the name of party unity. Yet on the other hand, he still wants to invoke their old comradeship, to put his trust in Stalin's friendship, and to re-establish his own reputation for trustworthiness. This is not just a tactical ploy, as one can see from Bukharin's undignified, confused, and inconsequential language; he describes strong personal feelings of fear in a way quite unsuited to a letter requesting pardon. 'Have pity on me! Surely you'll understand—knowing me as well as you do. Sometimes I look death openly in the face, just as I know very well that I am capable of brave deeds. At other times I, the same person, am so confused that nothing remains of me. So, if the verdict is death, let me have a cup of morphine, I *implore* you.'

What could have impelled Bukharin to write such an intimate, agonized, and ambivalent letter, and even to implore *Stalin's* forgiveness? In order to understand that, we have to examine the Communist leaders' previous experience, and also what kind of society they were creating, what its trust vectors were, and especially how those vectors impinged on the leaders themselves.

What we see in Bukharin's letter is a final desperate attempt to invoke lingering personal trust in circumstances justifying intense distrust. To understand his ambivalence, one has to place it in its specific social setting, and to go back to the 1917 revolution and even before. Before the revolution, the future Bolshevik leaders had been in the underground, enduring privation together, sustained by their shared belief in their own mission to carry out a revolution which would benefit the whole of humanity. They had suffered arrest and exile. With the triumph of the revolution, both Bukharin and Stalin had belonged to the party Central Committee, and had lived through the period of civil war and the subsequent establishment of one-party Communist rule, when it often seemed that the party could not succeed. They knew that they were surrounded by enemies and by popular indifference or hostility even while, as they saw it, they were trying to bring happiness to humanity. In spite of their disagreements, through these tumultuous events they forged a strong sense of mutual dependence and mutual trust, without which they could scarcely have persisted in their endeavour. Absolute trust in the party became a hallmark of Communists. This was as true of Bukharin as of all the others.

Yet this trust was always under pressure. The very intensity of the struggle bred its own enmities, even—or perhaps especially—within such a tightly knit band of leaders. The civil war had taught them that all opponents and even waverers must be treated as deadly enemies, to be attacked and destroyed. They were fighting for absolute good against absolute evil, and anyone who claimed to perceive intermediate shades of grey had to be spurned as an apostate. The messianic and apocalyptic narrative which underlay the spiritual life of Communists divided the world into 'comrades' and 'enemies'. 'He who is not with us is against us' became a commonplace. Such an outlook naturally generated intense trust and intense distrust. The 10th party congress in 1921 tried to prevent this process getting out of hand by passing a resolution 'On Party Unity', which forbade the formation of factions and made Central Committee decisions mandatory for all Communists.

All the same, so serious were the problems facing the party that, during the 1920s, different opinions continued to be aired, and factions continued to be formed around the party leaders expressing them. Each faction tried to assume absolute moral authority or, in the words of one scholar, 'to position itself as the one most conscious and therefore best capable of interpreting comrades' trustworthiness, commitment to the Revolution, and moral potential'.[4] That meant that disputes over the best strategy tended to polarize opinion, transforming intense trust into intense distrust. This tendency was deepened by the fact that, when transferred from one post to another, each leader would take with him his own trusted colleagues and subordinates, often civil war comrades. During the 1920s Stalin strengthened his own position by aiding and abetting such moves, at the same time using them to isolate and defeat rival leaders.[5] Both the 'Left Deviation' and the 'Right Opposition' were 'unmasked' and defeated at party congresses. Stalin, as the party's General Secretary, took the opportunity to expel Lev Trotsky, the leader of the Left, from the party, and had him expelled from the Soviet Union. Once Trotsky was in exile, Stalin then demonized him as an 'enemy', even the principal enemy, of the Soviet state.

In a one-party state these configurations of trust could not but shape the whole structure of society. Young people striving to make their way in this new world did their utmost to ensure that they were assigned to one of the categories of trusted rather than distrusted. In this respect the criteria used for admission to *rabfaks* (workers' faculties in universities)—instruments of upward social mobility par excellence—are illuminating. One had to be between 18 and 30 years of age, to have mastered reading, writing, basic arithmetic, and political literacy, to have experience of manual labour or to have served in the Red Army. Top priority was given to party and komsomol (Communist youth movement) members, then to workers and workers' children, then to poor peasants and their children. The art of getting on in life was to fill out in the approved manner a biographical questionnaire, emphasizing the trusted categories and omitting the distrusted ones. One learnt, in short, to 'speak Bolshevik'.[6] Local party leaders would examine the questionnaire. At that stage others' denunciations were encouraged, and applicants were then confronted with discrepancies in their statements.

[4] Igal Halfin, *Intimate Enemies: Demonizing the Opposition, 1918–1928*, University of Pittsburgh Press, 2007, 327.

[5] Gerald M. Easter, *Reconstructing the State: Personal Networks and Elite Identity in Soviet Russia*, Cambridge University Press, 2000, chapters 2–4.

[6] Stephen Kotkin, *Magnetic Mountain: Stalinism as a Civilization*, Berkeley and Los Angeles: University of California Press, 1995, chapter 5.

Sometimes an *ochnaia stavka* would be held, a personal confrontation with an applicant's accusers.[7]

The general social predisposition to distrust was intensified by policies the Bolsheviks promoted immediately after the revolution. The new Soviet state consciously set out to destroy everyday routines and stable reputations. It murdered the Tsar, the source of symbolic (and more than symbolic) authority in the old Russia, it undermined the church and weakened the family, it overturned property relationships and transformed the educational system. Thereby the institutional bulwarks of habitual trust were enfeebled or eliminated, making routine activities much more unpredictable. The civil war of 1917–21 intensified the process by creating new enmities, intensifying old ones, and rendering elementary everyday processes like gaining food, clothing, and shelter unpredictable. In September 1918 the writer Mikhail Prishvin noted in his diary 'I can feel even the best and cleverest people, scholars included, beginning to behave as if there were a mad dog in the courtyard outside.'[8] In this milieu everyone became fearful, and learnt to be more distrustful, a tendency which prepared the way for the grotesque levels of distrust prevalent in the 1930s.

Take for example the policy of compelling bourgeois and aristocratic householders to give up their 'excess living space' for the inhabitants of overcrowded housing. Princess Sofia Volkonskaya had to accept two new tenants in some of the rooms of her family's flat, people they had never met before and from a totally different social background. She later recalled, 'Nothing could be more irritating than the feeling of being, even at home, under the constant eye of the enemy. "Take care." "Shut the door." "Do not talk so loud; the Communists may hear you." Pin-pricks? Yes, of course. But in that nightmare life of ours every pin-prick took on the dimensions of a serious wound.'[9] Everyday life became a sphere of fear and distrust.

As they promoted rapid social change through coercion and violence in the industrialization and collectivization of the 1930s, Communists encountered the bitter enmity of many peasants and workers, some of whom swore that Stalin was the Antichrist. The precipitate collectivization of agriculture combined with de-kulakization[10] led to a sharp fall in agricultural production and in some regions actual famine. Kulaks were 'unmasked'; many of them were treated as unredeemable 'enemies', and deported to penal settlements in distant regions, where conditions were so harsh that some of them did not survive.[11] Some local party leaders,

---

[7] Igal Halfin, *From Darkness to Light: Class, consciousness and salvation in revolutionary Russia*, University of Pittsburgh Press, 2000, especially chapters 4–5.

[8] M. M. Prishvin, *Dnevniki, 1918–1919*, Moscow: Moskovskii Rabochii, 1994, 169.

[9] Sofia Volkonskaya, 'The Way of Bitterness', in Sheila Fitzpatrick and Yuri Slezkine (eds), *In the Shadow of Revolution: Life Stories of Russian Women from 1917 to the Second World War*, Princeton University Press, 2000, 156.

[10] The expropriation and often deportation of the more affluent peasants.

[11] Lynne Viola, *The Unknown Gulag: The Lost World of Stalin's Special Settlements*, Oxford University Press, 2007; Nicolas Werth, *Cannibal Island: Death in a Siberian Gulag*, trans. Steven Randall, Princeton University Press, 2007.

appalled at the deprivations they were being ordered to inflict on local populations, tried to block or at least slow down their implementation.

The haste of the first five-year plans, and the inexperience of most administrators and many workers, led to serious output shortfalls, and a spate of accidents, breakdowns, and explosions. Everybody's lives were in upheaval, with new and often dangerous experiences presenting themselves every day. Deprived of information and of ideas about how these difficulties might be tackled, the population was harassed and terrorized, often ready to accept the only explanation available to them: wrecking and sabotage by 'enemies'.

There were many other factors which heightened leading Communists' distrust during the early to mid-1930s, both of the outside world and of whole categories of people in their own society. The Japanese invasion of Manchuria in 1931 and the Nazi accession to power in Germany in 1933 greatly strengthened systematic enemies of Communism and brought them closer to the Soviet borders. Franco's seizure of power in Spain in 1936 created a new crisis for the Communist International (especially since followers of the reviled and exiled Trotsky were very strong there); Japan's invasion of China in 1937 deepened the threat it presented to the Soviet Union.

In this atmosphere of escalating external and internal tensions, the NKVD (security police) was dedicated to uncovering and rooting out enemies, real and imaginary; its mission was the exercise of total distrust, and its outlook pervaded the whole of social life. The NKVD itself resembled a secret society: its existence was known, but its membership, its activities, and its procedures were guarded by a wall of total secrecy. It had informers in every workplace and every communal apartment. As a result, everyone had to exercise great care in their social life, constantly assessing who might be an informer keen to betray unguarded remarks. Whom to trust and whom to distrust became a vital existential question for everyone. Many people went around with a small suitcase, packed with essentials; they feared they might have been 'betrayed', could be arrested without warning, and sent to the prisons and labour camps of the Gulag.[12] This was the 'Terror' which has justly given its name to an epoch of Soviet history: terror is the natural human response to a powerful and pervasive organization one strongly distrusts.

The effect of the poisonous atmosphere on the general population, especially on young people, who had never known another world, was to arouse in them a constant and pervasive paranoia. As a young worker later recalled, everything was attributed to enemies. 'At school they said: "Look how [the enemies] won't let us live under Communism—look how they blow up factories, derail trams, and kill people—all this is done by enemies of the people". They beat this into our heads so often that we stopped thinking for ourselves. We saw "enemies" everywhere.'[13]

[12] Getty and Naumov (eds), *The Road to Terror*, especially the introduction; Patrick Watier and Ivana Marková, 'Trust as a Psycho-Social Feeling: Socialization and Totalitarianism', in Ivana Marková (ed), *Trust and Democratic Transition in Post-Communist Europe*, Oxford University Press for the British Academy, 2004, 25–46.

[13] Orlando Figes, *The Whisperers: Private Life in Stalin's Russia*, London: Allen Lane, 2007, 274.

As a result the ordinary everyday exchange of thoughts, hopes, and feelings became virtually impossible. Human relationships were frozen by non-communication. Children grew up believing this was normal. One child whose father was arrested in 1936 later recalled, '"You'll get into trouble for your tongue". That's what people said to us children all the time. We went through life afraid to talk. Mama used to say that every other person was an informer. We were afraid of our neighbours, and especially of the police.' Another recalled, 'I knew subconsciously that I had to keep quiet, that I could not speak or say what I thought. For example, when we travelled in a crowded tram, I knew I had to remain silent, that I could not mention anything, not even things I saw out of the window.'[14]

Mikhail Prishvin, a writer by no means wholly opposed to Stalin, noted in his diary in October 1937: 'People have completely stopped trusting each other. They devote themselves to work and do not even whisper to one another. There is a huge mass of people raised up from poor social backgrounds who have nothing to whisper about: they just think "That's how it should be". Others isolate themselves to whisper, or study the art of silence. Yet others have simply learnt to keep quiet. . . . Gas masks are no use! What we need to protect ourselves against is psychological infection, the mask of gloom and silence.'[15]

The authorities' distrust reached its apogee in the notorious NKVD Order no 00447 of July 1937, which targeted a medley of 'socially dangerous elements'. They included former kulaks who had ended their exile sentence, former members of non-Communist parties or White movements, officials and elites of the old regime, returned émigrés, recidivist criminals, underground traders, sectarians, and church members who had been in custody. At a time when the danger of war was growing, it was felt that any of them might become the core of a treacherous internal opposition. Much later, in retirement, Viacheslav Molotov, Stalin's Prime Minister, remarked, 'Thanks to 1937 [the year of maximum "vigilance" and terror] we had no fifth column when the war came.'[16] The implementation of this order had top priority: NKVD officials were given targets and had to report every five days on their fulfilment. Given the hysteria and hypertrophied obsessions of the time, many tried to over-fulfil those targets.[17]

Stalin's personality was ideally suited to this situation. Cautious, flexible, observant, vigilant, vengeful, and ruthless, he was a virtuoso operator in a society of rampant distrust. By the mid-1930s his distrust had also become focused on the party apparatus itself, rather than on the leaders of former oppositions. Many provincial party leaders, as we have seen, had dug themselves in and gathered their

---

[14] Figes, *Whisperers*, 251–2, 254.

[15] M. M. Prishvin, *Dnevniki, 1936, 1937*, St Petersburg: Rostok, 2010, 762–3.

[16] *Sto sorok besed s Molotovym: iz dnevnika F. Chueva*, Moscow: Terra, 1991, 390. Molotov was of course wrong: tens of thousands of Soviet citizens fought on the German side during the Second World War. But his motive at the time is clear.

[17] Rolf Binner and Marc Junge, '"S etoi publikoi tseremonit'sia ne sleduet": Die Zielgruppen des Befehls no. 00447 und der grosse Terror aus der Sicht des Befehls', *Cahiers du monde russe*, 43 (2002), 1, 181–228.

comrades around them. They were now dedicated to conserving their power and enjoying the good things of life within the walled sanctuaries of plenty they had created for themselves amidst a society of scarcity. The genuine ideological conflict of the 1920s having passed, their paramount commitment was not to any particular party line, but to the defence of their power and privileges. Some of them tried to resist or at least delay the implementation of central commands which inflicted dreadful suffering on their population; others—'working towards' the regime— exceeded the arrest quotas laid before them. They also grossly exaggerated indus- trial output figures or requested central funding on the basis of promises which they then never fulfilled. In mid-1934 Stalin referred to provincial party secretaries as 'appanage princes', who delayed carrying out Moscow's orders and submitted false reports of the situation in their subordinate territories.[18]

In December 1934 Sergei Kirov, first secretary of the Leningrad party commit- tee, was assassinated. Whoever was ultimately responsible for the deed, it intensi- fied the leaders' suspicion that 'enemies', especially 'Trotskyists', had wormed their way deep into the party apparatus. In mid-1935 a 'verification of party cards' was ordered, and the NKVD was invited to participate in the process—the first time that the secret police had been allowed to interfere in internal party affairs. All the same, Stalin remained dissatisfied, suspicious that local party bosses were still protecting their own protégés, and that these included many secret 'enemies'.

At the Central Committee plenum of February–March 1937, Stalin declared that 'Agents of foreign states have been conducting their wrecking, diversionary and espionage work, with the active participation of Trotskyists, affecting to a greater or lesser extent all, or almost all, our economic, administrative and party organisa- tions. [They] have wormed their way not only into lower level organisations but into some responsible posts as well . . .' These agents' strength, according to Stalin, lay in the fact that they held party membership cards. 'The party card grants them political trust and opens access for them to all our institutions and organisations. . . . They have deceived our people, have abused that trust, have discreetly practised their wrecking and betrayed our state secrets to enemies of the Soviet Union.' Meanwhile, 'some comrades, both in the centre and locally, have not only failed to discern the true face of these wreckers, diversionists, spies and murderers, but have proved so careless, naive and benevolent as quite often to smooth the way for the promotion of these agents of foreign powers to responsible posts'. The only way to tackle this danger, he admon- ished, was never to forget that the Soviet Union was surrounded by hostile capitalist powers, and to exercise 'vigilance, real Bolshevik revolutionary vigilance'.[19]

Rampant distrust gripped the inner life of the party leadership. Former opposi- tionists, who had attempted serious discussion of political problems, were charac- terized as 'deviationists', then as opponents 'with terrorist intentions', and finally as 'enemies of the people'. This was the meat-grinder which dragged in Bukharin among its victims.

---

[18] Getty and Naumov, *The Road to Terror*, 205.
[19] 'Materialy fevral'sko-martovskogo plenuma TsK VKP(b) 1937 goda', *Voprosy istorii*, 1995, no. 3, 3–4, 8.

Stalin dramatized the narrative of conspiracy and betrayal in the show trials of 1936–8. He projected an image of himself together with a faceless Central Committee (faceless because many of its real members were being arrested and accused of incredible crimes) as staunch defenders of the heritage of Lenin, steering their courageous and undaunted path through throngs of double-dealers, traitors, and terrorists, all of them 'enemies' attempting to destroy the Soviet Union and restore capitalism.

Did Stalin actually believe the grotesque fantasies on account of which he murdered his 'enemies'? That is impossible to say. He and the Bolshevik leaders had created such an all-enveloping narrative of total trust and total distrust that they themselves had to follow it through to the bitter end, whether or not they believed it all. Even those who were convinced they themselves were innocent of the charges against them could not feel sure that those accused alongside them were equally blameless. They had no alternative narrative with which to explain what had gone wrong. In most cases it is impossible to say whether they denounced 'enemies' out of conviction or cynically to save their own skin and perhaps seek advancement. The key point is that universal distrust was now the *modus operandi* of the entire system—yet all the leading actors were under an inner compulsion to declare total trust in the party, because without that they were 'enemies' and in any case their lives were meaningless.[20]

All the Soviet leaders were in the grip of this paranoid vision. Perhaps the most sober of them was Ordzhonikidze who, as Commissar of Heavy Industry, did endeavour to protect his enterprise managers from false denunciations. When it came to former oppositionists, though, he was ferocious. On the Zinoviev–Kamenev[21] show trial he commented in a letter to Stalin, 'Shooting them wasn't enough. If it had been possible, they should have been shot at least ten times over.... They caused tremendous harm to the party. Now, knowing what they're made of, you don't know who's telling the truth and who's lying, who's a friend and who's a double-dealer. People don't know whether they can trust this or that former Trotskyist or Zinovievite.'[22]

Anyone who hesitated was doomed. In those circumstances Stalin was able to indulge his desire for untrammelled power and his ruthless drive to get rid of all possible 'enemies'. But the intense distrust took its toll of him too, if one is to believe Khrushchev, who asserts that towards the end of his life Stalin once said to him: 'I'm done for. I don't trust anyone. I don't even trust myself.'[23] He had reached the logical end-point of the process which had hoisted him to supreme power.

---

[20] Gabor Rittersporn, 'The Omnipresent Conspiracy: On Soviet Imagery of Politics and Social Relations in the 1930s', in J. Arch Getty and Roberta T. Manning (eds), *Stalinist Terror: New Perspectives*, Cambridge University Press, 1993, 99–115.

[21] Former leaders of the Left Opposition.

[22] Oleg Khlevniuk, *Master of the House: Stalin and his Inner Circle*, trans. Nora Seligman Favorov, New Haven: Yale University Press, 2009, 154.

[23] N. S. Khrushchev, *Vospominaniia: vremia, liudi, vlast'*, Moscow: Moskovskie Novosti, 1999, ii. 77.

A poignant example of the way in which officially inspired distrust could become contagious yet also coexist alongside total trust is the fate of Iuliia Piatnitskaia. She was the wife of a Comintern official, Osip Piatnitsky, who was arrested in July 1937. She had been attracted to him through his devotion to Marxist ideology. 'When I was very young, a mere girl, I knew that my love would be infinite and would exalt my beloved. Oh, I knew that I would seek only a person gripped by the ideal of serving mankind in science, in struggle or in art.'[24] Her husband, though in some ways a stiff and unbending person, had lived up to her expectations. He was so dedicated that he would try not to notice the petty intrigues going on around him. When she reproached him for this, he would reply, 'Remember I serve only the working class, not individual people.'[25] Iuliia herself always used to be proud of his devotion to his work and accepted willingly 'that he was the most modest and honest of people, that we [she and their children] came well down his list of priorities and that we received nothing from those in power except occasionally by accident'.[26]

Osip's arrest plunged Iuliia into a wholly new and terrifyingly unstable world. It meant first of all material deprivation. He had left her some loan certificates and savings entered in a savings book, enough to live on for two or three years, but the NKVD operatives searching their flat had simply stolen them. She lost her job and was evicted from their flat into a squalid communal apartment. Even worse was that friends and colleagues ignored her: 'Everyone knows that they robbed us of everything, that we have nothing to live on, nothing to eat, but no one will stir a finger. If we die, no one will take the slightest interest.'[27] She was often tempted to commit suicide, but decided to live on because her two teenage sons needed her.

The only way she could make sense of what had happened was to draw on the stock of images and narratives by which high party officials had always lived, and which were now being reiterated at full volume by Yezhov and Stalin. Osip, she concluded, had been surrounded by spies, counter-revolutionaries, or at best corrupt careerists who had not shared his ideals but betrayed them. She applauded Yezhov's drive to eliminate such enemies. Hearing that Bukharin and others were about to be executed, she imagined for them an even worse fate, being displayed to the public in a cage to die a lingering death. 'Let them see us struggling together for a happier life, let them see how we love our leaders, who do not betray us, how we are defeating fascism, while they are idle, fed like beasts, and not regarded as people.'[28] She even allowed the paranoid official narrative to poison her relationship with her younger son, Vovka. When he received a bad school report (the older son, Igor, had by this time been arrested), 'I reminded him that he was the son of an "enemy of the people", that he showed by his behaviour that he was the brother of an "enemy", and so on. Tears came to his eyes, and he said "Am I guilty that I am

---

[24] Iuliia Piatnitskaia, *Dnevnik zheny bol'shevika*, Benson, Vt.: Chalidze Press, 1987, 93.
[25] Piatnitskaia, *Dnevnik*, 33.   [26] Piatnitskaia, *Dnevnik*, 45.
[27] Piatnitskaia, *Dnevnik*, 38.   [28] Piatnitskaia, *Dnevnik*, 88.

the son and brother of enemies? I don't want you to be my mother, I want to go into an orphanage".'[29]

Piatnitskaia was still in the grip of a trust framework which had sustained her all her life, of messianic hopes derived from her youthful revolutionary upbringing, and of corresponding diabolic fears.

With the closing down of any public space for the circulation of information and ideas, or for the redress of grievances, quite a number of Soviet citizens responded by writing personal letters to authority figures, such as Stalin, Molotov (the Prime Minister), or the party newspaper *Pravda*. Total distrust is intolerable, and many of these letters display a kind of surrogate trust—either simulated, or 'hope against hope', or in some cases perhaps even genuine. These letters typically appealed to a leader to rectify some abuse or to help the writer in a difficult situation for which there seemed to be no other solution. Writers would often address the recipient as a trustworthy figure (*Tovarishch Zhdanov, chutkii, rodnoi*—which sounds mawkish in English: 'Comrade Zhdanov, sensitive, dearly beloved') and continue in terms like 'knowing your love and care for children'. They would lay out the trustworthy credentials of the writer ('decorated shock worker', 'mother of three children', 'I am a Communist since 1918 and lost my health—an arm—for the new life') and then expound a story of innocent suffering, sometimes identifying 'enemies' who had inflicted it, and conclude by asking for a personal intervention. In a significant minority of cases, some official remedial action did follow, so that such letters offered a stunted replacement for a public sphere.[30] In the absence of regular procedures for identifying abuses and sorting them out, the desire to trust someone in power is acute—and not always hopeless.

Eventually the disfunctionality of this situation presumably became obvious even to Stalin. Terror had removed key personnel from the administration, police, and armed forces, while those not arrested were often too terrified to take necessary decisions. Moreover, it had become difficult or impossible to hire replacement cadres with any confidence.[31] Even Stalin could not exercise power if the levers of that power were broken. In late 1938 he began to circulate instructions that denunciations were to be much more carefully examined before action was taken. In the later years of his rule, he kept terror as a weapon, but used it far more selectively.[32] By that time, in any case, Soviet ideology had begun to create its own narratives of stability, normality, and historical memory, as well as to codify and consolidate its own rituals, customs, and practices.[33]

---

[29] Piatnitskaia, *Dnevnik*, 75–6.

[30] Sheila Fitzpatrick, 'Supplicants and Citizens: Letter Writing in Soviet Russia in the 1930s', *Slavic Review*, 55/1 (spring 1996), 78–105; Alexey Tikhomirov, 'The Regime of Forced Trust: Making and Breaking Emotional Bonds between People and State in Soviet Russia', *Slavonic & East European Review*, 91/1 (2013), 78–118; Alexander Livshin, 'Bridging the Gap: Government–Society Dialogue via Letters', *Slavonic & East European Review*, 91/1 (2013), 57–77.

[31] Cynthia Hooper, 'Trust in Terror? The Search for a Foolproof Science of Soviet Personnel', *Slavonic & East European Review*, 55/1 (2013), 26–57.

[32] Khlevniuk, *Master of the House*, 199–201, 251.

[33] Geoffrey Hosking, *History of the Soviet Union*, 3rd edition, London: HarperCollins, 1992, chapter 8.

People in general put their trust in symbolic systems and the doctrines and institutions associated with them,[34] in this case the secular religion of Marxism and the party set up to fulfil its mission. The more all-embracing the religion, the more fervent the trust placed in it. In the course of dedicating themselves to the belief system, adherents of the party created strong ties of trust with their colleagues, reinforced by the struggles of revolution and civil war. Trust is highly contagious: the spectacle of others reposing total confidence in a belief system and prepared to sacrifice themselves for it draws others towards it. This was true not only in Russia. Western Communists, in a very different social setting, reproduced the intense trust/intense distrust paradigm. Of his time in the Italian Communist Party, Ignazio Silone wrote, 'I . . . had to adapt myself, for a number of years, to living like a foreigner in my own country. One had to change one's name, abandon every former link with family and friends, and live a false life to remove any suspicion of conspiratorial activity. The Party became family, school, church, barracks; the world that lay beyond it was to be destroyed and built anew. The psychological mechanism whereby each militant becomes progressively identified with the collective organisation is the same as that used in certain religious orders and military colleges, with almost identical results. Every sacrifice was welcomed as a personal contribution to the "price of collective redemption"; and it should be emphasised that the links which bound us to the Party grew steadily firmer, not in spite of the dangers and sacrifices involved, but because of them.'[35]

Trust creates rigid boundaries around itself, especially in conflict situations; across those boundaries virulent distrust is projected. When serious dilemmas arise within a system demanding total trust, they bring up the question of where those boundaries lie. If members of the group begin to express doubts, they can suddenly find themselves on the other side of a boundary—a boundary which in itself remains rigid and unforgiving. Distrust is just as contagious as trust: once it sets in, it takes hold in an abrupt and cumulative way which individual actors find it almost impossible to resist. Both trust and distrust develop their own dynamic, which can grip whole societies. The Soviet Union in the 1930s was one of the most extreme cases, but convulsions of total distrust can burst out in many circumstances. In the twentieth and early twenty-first centuries, there are abundant examples of terrorist movements, genocides, and ferally destructive wars which have resulted from the uncontrolled escalation of distrust into murderous fear and hatred.[36]

In later decades, the Soviet leaders themselves gradually learnt to rule without indiscriminate mass terror. After Stalin's death, his successors launched major campaigns to regain the trust of the people. They promised 'socialist legality', that is, a legal system not wholly dependent on the whims of political leaders. They released prisoners from the Gulag, eased censorship, and stepped up investment in

---

[34] See below, Chapter 2.

[35] Richard Crossman, *The God that Failed*, New York: Harper, 1949, 99.

[36] In Chapter 3, I examine an earlier example, the witch-hunting craze of the sixteenth and early seventeenth centuries.

material welfare: housing, education, public transport, and a functioning if never generous social security system. The population gained certain de facto rights which they could rely on.[37]

Total distrust eased somewhat. But generalized social distrust, once it gains a grip, does not disperse easily. Besides, although state terror diminished, it did not disappear entirely, and the security police (renamed the KGB) continued to maintain an army of informants reporting on what ordinary people were doing and thinking. The question of whom one could trust and whom one should distrust remained paramount in the lives of most Soviet citizens. Their reaction was to mask or dissemble feelings for most social purposes, to use a 'wooden language' in public places and to avoid unnecessary personal contacts—a milder version of the non-communication described by Prishvin.[38]

Many people also managed to improvise a small circle of friends and acquaintances, whom they learnt to trust by repeated contact and monitoring. Some would be trusted for certain purposes only, such as obtaining scarce consumer goods or mediating contact with influential officials. With others one felt able to speak freely. Some scientific and cultural institutions became tiny oases of free speech, where colleagues felt at ease with each other; others were riven by disputes between rival factions struggling for ideological hegemony or for preferential access to the good things of life. In all cases the radius of trust was limited: to an employer who dispensed favours effectively, to colleagues who would refrain from making a denunciation, to friends who would offer emotional support and perhaps help out materially. In the non-Russian republics, ethnic patron–client networks fulfilled some of the same functions. State and social institutions—the police, law courts, the media, even religious associations—could not usually be relied on to offer effective assistance in critical situations.[39] This phenomenon—the limited radius of trust and the inadequacy of official institutions—continues to characterize post-Soviet Russia. In Chapter 6 some of the implications will become clearer.

Many westerners, though, would consider Russia/the USSR as an exceptional country. Can we really learn important lessons for our own societies by studying it? I believe we can and should. First, however, we need to ponder the problems of using trust and distrust as concepts, and to appreciate how they can be deployed to help us gain a better understanding of the way societies function. To this I turn in Chapter 2.[40]

---

[37] Mark B. Smith, *Property of Communists: The Urban Housing Program from Stalin to Khrushchev*, DeKalb: Northern Illinois University Press, 2010, especially 12–19.

[38] Watier and Marková, 'Trust as a Psycho-Social Feeling', 25–46.

[39] I have examined these issues at greater length in my *History of the Soviet Union*, chapters 12–14. See also Geoffrey Hosking, 'Social Solidarity in Russia and the Soviet Union', in Marková (ed), *Trust*, 47–62.

[40] Chapter 2 is inevitably somewhat abstract in character; readers who are less interested in theoretical questions may wish to proceed straight to Chapter 3.

2

The Coconut Tree

The Ups and Downs of Trust

The history of the Soviet Union in the 1920s and 1930s suggests that, once unleashed, distrust can spread like a forest fire in dry, windy weather and imperil the very framework of society. The only way for rulers to hang on to power in such conditions is by the application of mass terror—which then, of course, escalates the distrust to epidemic proportions. But the Soviet Union is an extreme example. How is it relevant to us in advanced western nations? After all, we have democratic political systems and market economies which have evolved over centuries to restrain the exercise of power and prevent social breakdown.

So we like to think, and up to a point it is true. But I believe our society is more endangered than we usually think. We need therefore to be more conscious of the—usually not obvious—ways trust is routinely deployed in it. Stalin's terror is a warning of the consequences of not caring for the webs of trust which make our life comparatively safe. Configurations of trust are as important as those of power. Trust and distrust are part of the deep grammar of any society. The way in which we relate to each other, trust or distrust each other, determines much of our social behaviour. In order to take decisions and act in real life, we need trust in other people, in institutions, or simply in the future.

The workings of trust are, however, much less obvious and easy to identify than those of power. I pointed out in the Introduction that in flying with an airline we unthinkingly trust individuals, institutions, and systems of knowledge. Sometimes we trust unconsciously and distrust consciously. Only when a crisis occurs do we realize that we have been misplacing our trust. A person lets us down, an institution fails to perform as expected, a chance event disrupts our plans, a system of knowledge seems less reliable: for example, recent debates on climate change or genetic engineering illustrate how public distrust of science can be aroused. At that point we become aware that we have been trusting, and perhaps inappropriately. Distrust is much easier to identify than trust, and it can take hold with alarming speed. As an Indian policymaker has commented, 'Confidence grows at the rate a coconut tree grows, and it falls at the rate a coconut falls.'[1]

A dramatic example of distrust spreading rapidly as the result of a single disastrous event was the aftermath of the earthquake and nuclear meltdown at

---

[1] Montek Ahluwalia, at the Davos World Economic Forum, Davos, quoted in *The Guardian*, 2 February 2009, 28.

the Fukushima power plant in Japan in March 2011. First of all, on top of immediate death and destruction, hundreds of thousands of people had to evacuate their homes, many of them permanently. Confidence in everyday routines was abruptly supplanted by uncertainty about the future, compounded by concerns over whether radiation might have caused incurable disease and whether food grown anywhere near the nuclear station was safe to eat. Pregnant mothers were worried about the health of their unborn babies.

In normal circumstances, one relies on the advice of government and specialists in the relevant science. But it soon became evident that the Japanese government and Tokyo Electric, the plant's operator, were not coming clean about the extent or the full effects of the disaster. They made inconsistent statements, issued radiation readings which turned out to be incorrect, and raised safety limits arbitrarily in order to downplay the crisis. Emergency workers protested, 'They didn't tell us anything. Nobody mentioned a meltdown. We didn't get any critical accident training or instructions.' An expectant mother avoided eating fish, meat, or eggs, and complained, 'I don't trust anything they say. Tokyo Electric and the government have told us so many lies.' Depression and suicide were reportedly on the increase—both consequences of a sudden loss of trust in people and of confidence in the future. Some Japanese, though, rediscovered trust in unexpected places. One displaced university lecturer commented a year later, 'Since 11 March people haven't trusted scientists who receive funding from the government. They trust people who act without government funding and who work together with them.' A nation which traditionally trusted government implicitly refocused its trust on independent professional associations and voluntary groups.[2]

In the last three decades or so, social scientists have written a good deal about trust, but their work has been inconclusive, partly because the concept is genuinely difficult to pin down, but also I think for four other reasons. First, they tend to isolate trust from other concepts and try to produce a theory applicable to all societies.[3] I shall do the opposite: I shall treat trust in relation to other concepts (while not ignoring their distinct shades of meaning) and say a great deal about specific historical circumstance and social background. We take individual decisions about whom to trust, but because we are social beings those decisions are deeply influenced by the norms and expectations of the society in which we live. The social determinants of trust are crucial, and they are not always obvious.

Second, social scientists deal mainly with reflective and conscious trust, that is, cases where an individual has to make a conscious choice about whether to trust a particular individual or institution. I will argue that unreflective trust is at least as

---

[2] Geoff Brumfiel and Ichiko Fuyuno, 'Japan's Nuclear Crisis: Fukushima's Legacy of Fear', *Nature*, 483 (8 March 2012), 138–40; Simon Avenell, 'From Kobe to Tohoku: The Potential and the Peril of a Volunteer Infrastructure', in Jeff Kingston (ed), *Natural Disaster and Nuclear Crisis in Japan: Response and Recovery*, London: Routledge, 2012, 53–77.

[3] Kieron O'Hara, *Trust from Socrates to Spin*, Cambridge: Icon Books, 2004, 70.

important in shaping the way societies function. Indeed, precisely because it is unreflective it becomes part of the deep grammar underlying our beliefs and practices.

Third, most social scientists assume that trust is voluntary. Yet the primary trust situation—of the infant towards its parents—is certainly not voluntary. And in many social situations we have little choice but to trust. This is partly because to distrust everyone and everything is literally intolerable: we saw how in the Soviet Union, in the most unpromising environment, citizens would try desperately to trust the Communist Party and its leader. Even in democratic societies life is complex, and in most circumstances we have in practice to trust doctors, lawyers, financial advisers, and the government, even when we have inner reservations about them. Hence—in opposition to most social science theory—I shall use the term 'compulsory trust' or 'forced trust'.

Last, many, though not all, treat trust as a good in itself. They do not sufficiently emphasize the distinction between trust as such and trust in the trustworthy.[4] Misplaced trust is pernicious, leads to disillusionment and embitterment, then, if it persists, to cumulative distrust, and ultimately to social breakdown. It is a destructive, not a constructive, force. Though distrust should not normally be the default position, *some* monitoring of a trust relationship is essential. This is a delicate task, for obtrusive monitoring itself undermines trust. Onora O'Neill's 2002 Reith Lectures, which did much to bring trust into public awareness, especially emphasized and clarified this point.[5]

Historians have not entered this debate very much, partly because trust is difficult to discern in the texts of documents; it has to be teased out 'between the lines'. (Distrust is easier to study, in this sense.) They do, however, have two great advantages when approaching questions of trust. The first is that historians do not examine economies, political structures, or social welfare systems in isolation: they are interested in whole societies. Western economists working in the former Soviet bloc during the 1990s may have been well versed in economic theory, but they were not able to place their economic counsel in a wider context, to see that measures which promote growth in one society will stifle it in another, or even endanger the social fabric. An economy is part of a web of interrelationships which make up society as a whole. Historians are better placed than most social scientists to study the entirety of that web.

Furthermore, historians locate their studies in the flow of time. A social problem is not like a chess problem, where the previous moves needed to reach the position on the board are irrelevant to the solution. Societies are composed of people whose mentality and outlook have been constituted by their previous life experience and that of those around them. Their future actions will be strongly, perhaps

---

[4] See for example Niklas Luhmann, *Trust and Power*, trans. Howard Davis, John Raffan, and Kathryn Rooney, Chichester: Wiley, 1979; Marek Kohn, *Trust: Self-Interest and the Common Good*, Oxford University Press, 2008.

[5] Onora O'Neill, *A Question of Trust*, Cambridge University Press, 2002.

decisively, influenced by that experience. It is vital to know what their past was and to understand how they reacted to it.

The current fashion for cultural and linguistic history has provided us with many of the tools necessary to study trust, but it stops half way, before reaching the threshold of trust. It is overwhelmingly concerned with identities, narratives, discourses, and representations, and often treats social reality as a 'text'; it does not move on from interpreting what people think and imagine to understanding what motivates them to take decisions and act, which is a vital part of historical explanation. That extra step has to involve at least a measure of trust in individuals, in institutions, in systems of knowledge, and even just in fate.

Historians are in any case much more accustomed to studying power than trust. The two are closely—directly or inversely—linked; but the link is not usually specified. A recent (otherwise very good) book which fails to do this is Francis Fukuyama's *The Origins of Political Order*—an omission the more striking in that Fukuyama had previously written extensively about trust.[6] One of his main claims in *The Origins of Political Order* is that the evolution of the modern state has been a long and often unsuccessful struggle against kinship in its various forms: extended families, clans, tribes, which pursue their own narrow interests, often at the expense of the wider society. In order to explain why people should feel such deep allegiance to their kin in the first place he gives pride of place to religion, the worship of ancestors.[7] But Fukuyama's explanation takes us only part of the way. Why worship ancestors? Surely the paramount motive is the need for protection and solidarity, which is strengthened if one can celebrate it as deriving from a distant past—'great time', in the usage of Mircea Eliade. As the Russians say, 'One man on a battlefield is not a warrior.' To cope with the struggles and tribulations of life, everyone needs co-warriors for battle, mutual aid for the more routine problems of peacetime. The family is the most obvious source of such support, preferably the extended family, which means the clan, or more broadly still the tribe, simply because they are larger and more diverse. One can place more trust in them than in one's own resources. Blood relationship is not the driving imperative. As Fukuyama admits, tribes can arise even when there is no consanguinity. Criminals group together in 'brotherhoods', and the Mafia has its 'godfathers'. The motive force behind the creation and maintenance of tribes is the need for some kind of solidarity and mutual trust in a dangerous world.[8]

The great problem about kinship dominance is that tribes lack an overarching authority. When one of them kills a member of another tribe, or steals horses from it, there is no way of enforcing restitution except by vengeance; to which the other

---

[6] *The Origins of Political Order from Prehuman Times to the French Revolution*, London: Profile Books, 2011; *Trust: The Social Virtues and the Creation of Prosperity*, London: Penguin Books, 1996; *The Great Disruption: Human Nature and the Reconstitution of Social Order*, London: Profile Books, 1999.

[7] Fukuyama, *Origins*, 59–62.   [8] Fukuyama, *Origins*, 59.

tribe can only respond by reciprocal vengeance. Hence tribes tend to live with intermittent and spasmodic bouts of blood feuds against other tribes. This is exhausting and debilitating, and means coping with permanent insecurity. That is why, as Fukuyama explains, monarchs sometimes manage to outbid kin: they can offer justice and restitution in a more peaceful manner. The king's courts will, moreover, usually provide more objective justice than biased local courts dominated by self-seeking tribal chiefs and warlords.[9] The fundamental motive in both types of allegiance is trust. Who can more effectively protect you, provide justice and give you confidence in your future?

This process illustrates a central theme in this book: at a time of crisis, or when trust systems are obviously functioning poorly, it makes sense to try to enlarge the radius of trust. Instead of two negative-sum games (one side can only gain at the expense of the other), one seeks a higher-level positive-sum game (both sides gain together).

The same point applies to taxation. Increasingly from late medieval times monarchs needed to tax their subjects, often heavily, to raise the armies required to conduct modern warfare. They could tax more effectively if they did so at least with the appearance of fairness. Fukuyama points to 'a central lesson of tax policy, which is that extraction costs are inversely proportional to the perceived legitimacy of the authority doing the taxing'.[10] To reformulate his assertions as a question: can the monarch be trusted to levy taxes fairly and to spend them on genuine common concerns rather than on rewarding powerful cliques at court? Will the revenue be used for the benefit of the whole community, and not to support one clique or social class in its negative-sum gains at everyone else's expense? The failure to offer satisfactory answers to such questions and thus uphold legitimacy was, in Fukuyama's view, the major cause of the French Revolution.

In explaining why political development has been transformed for the better since the Industrial Revolution, Fukuyama asserts 'the key is the possibility of sustained economic growth'. He attributes this possibility to (i) strong government, combined with (ii) the rule of law, and (iii) the accountability of political leaders, which, as he says, 'produced a political and economic system so powerful that it came to be widely copied around the world'. This is on the whole valid, but there is a missing link. What he does not point out is the enormous expansion of credit (i.e. financial trust) which those three factors made possible, and without which sustained economic growth would not have taken place. In his account of what he calls the 'Glorious Revolution' in England in 1688–9 he mentions the accompanying financial revolution only in passing.[11] I shall show its significance in Chapter 4.

All this is not to deny the value of Fukuyama's book. It is a well-argued and skilfully presented account of the historical evolution of modern power

---

[9] Fukuyama, *Origins*, 69–71, 260. See Chapter 5, section on 'Law'.
[10] Fukuyama, *Origins*, 343.   [11] Fukuyama, *Origins*, 476, 479, 417–20.

structures. But we need to complement it with an account of the emergence of modern trust structures. This book starts that process.

WHAT IS TRUST?

One of the many difficulties involved in studying trust is that it is several phenomena at once. It is first of all a *feeling*. One feels safety and security in the sense that there is no threat, that one is free to act as one wishes. Distrust awakens feelings of uncertainty, suspicion, foreboding, and fear, the sense that one is constrained in one's actions, cannot do what one wishes, or may even be forced to act against one's will. Both these states relate to future actions and are in part socio-culturally determined, but they are also definitely personal feelings—although, in the case of trust, that feeling is often unconscious, not brought to the surface unless some unexpected event arouses an element of distrust.

Trust is also an *attitude*. It is a more or less lasting view held about some object, event, or person(s) in the outside world. It is a frame of mind, outlook, or perspective which influences one's behaviour or one's disposition to act or think in certain ways. The same is true of distrust. Attitudes are not unchangeable, but they are also not momentary, as feelings may be. Viewed as an attitude, it makes sense to ask questions about trust in opinion polls. These attitudes may or may not be consciously held, but they are more likely to form part of a person's character than feelings. The attitudes may well be shared by others, and in that way are part of the social fabric.

Trust is also a *relationship*, between oneself and another person, collective of persons, or institution. It is part of an ongoing interaction, and the other person's behaviour can modify the nature of that trust, even turn it into distrust. The actions of both parties can change the relationship. Here the social context is even more salient when we seek to illuminate the nature of trust.

All three aspects of the word 'trust', then—as feeling, attitude, and relationship—imply a social context, and they are all to do with behaviour and action or the potential for action. That is why trust and distrust have such possibilities as explanatory concepts in trying to understand the way societies operate. They are especially valuable for the historian, for attitudes and relationships change as society changes, that is, they are at least in part socially constructed. Recent research suggests that this is true even for feelings.[12]

---

[12] This is strongly argued by Ute Frevert in *Emotions in History—Lost and Found*, Budapest: Central European University Press, 2011. See also Claire Armon-Jones, 'The Thesis of Constructionism', in Rom Harré (ed), *The Social Construction of Emotions*, Oxford: Blackwell, 1986, 32–56; as an example, see Joanna Bourke, *Fear: A Cultural History*, London: Virago, 2005.

Trust is notoriously difficult to define, but the effort should be made, as a kind of anchor for a vital but slippery concept. I offer two complementary definitions:

1. Attachment to a person, collective of persons or institution, based on the well-founded but not certain expectation that he/she/they will act for my good.

2. The expectation, based on good but less than perfect evidence, that events will turn out in a way not harmful to me.

The two modes of trust are linked, since one can often provide against possible misfortune by combining with other people whom one trusts.

It will be evident immediately that trust overlaps with a good many other concepts, such as confidence, hope, faith, belief, expectation, reliance, and so on. They all concern the ways in which we relate to other people and to our own future in the course of taking decisions. We all have to deal with risk, and most of us seek security through persons, institutions, procedures, and methods we can trust, rely on, in which we have confidence or faith. These words have distinct shades of meaning, yet they all occupy the same semantic map.

Some sociologists posit a radical difference between trust and confidence.[13] For example, the need for 'trust', in Adam Seligman's view, arises in complex modern societies, where social roles are so diverse that we are regularly confronted with the unfamiliar, and have therefore consciously to assess our options for social action, without having all the required information to do so. In earlier eras, when social structures were simpler and encounters with the unfamiliar much less frequent, unreflective 'confidence' was sufficient.

This is not convincing. There was no doubt a general evolution of the kind Seligman describes (though there was plenty of role diversity in, say, ancient Greece or much of medieval Europe), but the very attempt to draw a rigid dividing line between the traditional and modern world betrays its own insufficiency. There were many different 'traditional' worlds. Besides, the transition of which Seligman speaks was gradual, and so, I would argue, is the distinction between trust and confidence. It makes sense to talk of confidence where trust is based on especially good knowledge or long and favourable experience. It is often more appropriate when applied to institutions rather than persons. But there is no sharp dividing line between the two terms. Indeed, in French and Spanish they are the same word: *la confiance, la confianza.*

I would locate the various words clustered around trust as follows, depending on the extent to which we have the knowledge we need to cope with contingencies, and on the extent to which we are free to do so.

[13] Adam B. Seligman, *The Problem of Trust*, Princeton University Press, 1987; Luhmann, *Trust and Power*; Russell Hardin, *Trust and Trustworthiness*, New York: Russell Sage, 2002.

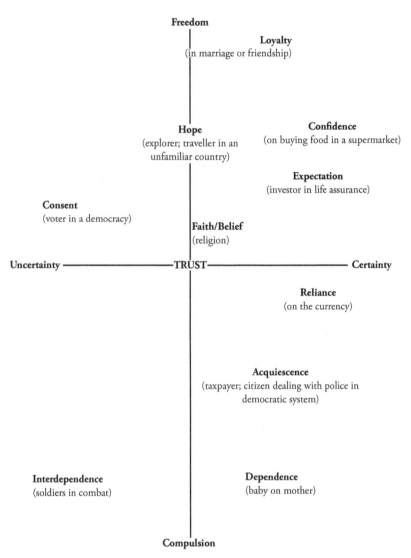

Trust: A Semantic Map

SOCIOLOGISTS ON TRUST

Sociologists may lack a historical awareness, but their work does point to some of the general features of trust common to different societies. Most of the classical sociologists did not specifically theorize the word trust, but it is often implicit in what they wrote. Max Weber, for example, launched his career with a study of British and German stock exchanges. The British ones, he noted, were private associations, rather like gentlemen's clubs, which guaranteed a tight, mutually trusting membership by charging a high subscription fee, requiring financial guarantees for new applicants as well as approval from existing members. German exchanges, by contrast, were run by chambers of commerce and membership was open to anyone with sufficient capital, whatever his social standing. The Hamburg exchange, where merchant guilds had venerable traditions, was relatively orderly, but the Berlin one, which lacked such traditions, tended to tolerate irresponsible speculative deals.[14] This was the first time he adumbrated a theme which was to become central to him: the connection between commerce and ethics. He later showed that the ethical systems of Protestants in Europe and Jains in India also promoted successful commerce.

In his main writings Weber classified social actions in four categories, each of which can be interpreted to illustrate one kind of trust:

- Goal-oriented—we trust those with whom we cooperate to achieve some shared aim, or those whom we believe to be competent in some particular activity.

- Value-oriented—we trust because we believe in someone's virtue, honour, or other shared value.

- Affectual—we trust those we like or love.

- Traditional—we trust those we have become accustomed to, or those whom habit inclines us to trust.[15]

Similarly, his classification of types of legitimate authority indicates types of trust:

- Traditional—we trust leaders and institutions to which we have become accustomed.

- Bureaucratic—we trust stable institutions which function according to proven competence and clearly defined rules.

- Charismatic—we trust leaders for their personal qualities, the 'grace' which we attribute to them.

Emile Durkheim is important because he attempted a moral account of trust. He was concerned with the way traditional forms of social solidarity had broken down, eroded by the conditions of urban, industrial society, with its increasingly diversified division of labour. Many individuals as a result were afflicted by 'anomie', a condition of living without values and hence feeling alienated from society. Unlike Comte, Spencer, and the utilitarians, he did not believe that individual rationality could produce social harmony. Every society, he asserted, was 'a moral society, and a state of order . . . among men cannot follow from any entirely material causes, from any blind mechanism. . . . It is a moral task.'[16]

---

[14] Reinhard Bendix, *Max Weber: An Intellectual Portrait*, London: Heinemann, 1960, 23–30. The text is in *Gesammelte Aufsätze zur Soziologie und Sozialpolitik*, Tübingen: Mohr, 1924, 256ff. Ironically, today one would have to reverse the comparison between British and German stock exchanges.

[15] See the analyses by Barbara Misztal, *Trust in Modern Societies: The Search for the Bases of Social Order*, Cambridge: Polity Press, 1996, 54–60, and by Ute Frevert in 'Vertrauen—eine historische Spurensuche', in Frevert (ed), *Vertrauen: historische Annäherungen*, Göttingen: Vandenhoeck & Ruprecht, 2003.

[16] Durkheim, *Professional Ethics and Civic Morals*, London: Routledge, 1957, 12, quoted in Barbara Misztal, *Trust in Modern Societies*, Cambridge: Polity Press, 1996, 43.

But how, according to Durkheim, was this moral task to be accomplished? It could no longer be done through the communal performance of inherited rituals, as in most past societies. It could only be done through an enlightened understanding of self-interest within the context of shared social values. For the fostering of this understanding and the maintenance of those values he assigned a paramount role to the state and to religion. The state was responsible for the institutional underpinning of socialization and the maintenance of law and order, since it stood at the apex of a multiplicity of social groups reflecting the interests of diverse individuals.[17] Religion was 'a symbolic rendering and affirmation of the reality and power of society'.[18] It dealt in 'beliefs and practices which unite into a single moral community called a church all those who adhere to them'.[19]

The weakness of Durkheim was that he did not appreciate that social groups may have not only diverse but mutually contradictory visions of the society in which they live. His sociology offers no grounds for resisting the claims of the state or of the dominant church, or for not participating in the collective secular (in his era usually nationalist) rituals which affirm the value of society. In this respect he was a true child of Rousseau. He viewed trust as being focused on society as a whole, and did not allow for the possibility of its being focused on smaller associations which did not share the interests or culture of the whole.

Among classical sociologists Georg Simmel offered the most explicit understanding of trust. Like Durkheim, he was concerned by the increasing complexity of modern society, and especially by the way in which each individual, standing at the intersection of diverse social roles, occupies a specific and unrepeatable location in society, so that traditional communal solidarity no longer works for him/her.

Simmel considered one of the dominant forms of social relationship to be economic, that is, exchange between people who know little or nothing of each other. In this he continued the tradition of Adam Smith. But his interpretation of the 'invisible hand' is quite different from Smith's. Simmel did not accept that smoothly functioning markets emerge automatically from individuals' rational and self-interested behaviour. He believed exchange would not be possible without humans' pre-existing tendency to trust one another. 'Without the general trust that people have in each other, society itself would disintegrate, for very few relationships are based entirely upon what is known with certainty about another person, and very few relationships would endure if trust were not as strong as, or stronger than, rational proof or personal observation.'[20]

Simmel's major sociological work, *The Philosophy of Money*, asserted that money existed to fix this predisposition to trust and make it economically effective, and thus to lubricate exchange. He explicitly compares trust in money with faith in God. 'Economic credit contains an element of this supra-theoretical belief, and so

---

[17] See Anthony Giddens (ed and trans.), *Emile Durkheim: Selected Writings*, Cambridge University Press, 1972, 192; and Durkheim, *Moral Education*, trans. Everett K. Wilson and Herman Schnurer, New York: Free Press, 1973, 80.

[18] Quoted in Gianfranco Poggi, *Durkheim*, Oxford University Press, 2000, 167.

[19] Quoted in Giddens, *Capitalism and Modern Social Theory*, Cambridge University Press, 1971, 107.

[20] Georg Simmel, *The Philosophy of Money*, London: Routledge, 1978, 178–9.

does the confidence that the community will assure the validity of the tokens for which we have exchanged the products of our labour.'[21] Money, like legitimate power—and often in partnership with it—enlarges the radius of trust. It enables us to trust a great variety of people about whom we know little or nothing. For that reason, as Simmel pointed out, it is especially useful to society's marginalized groups, who are otherwise distrusted: Armenians in Turkey, Parsees in India, Jews in much of Europe.[22]

We have already seen that Soviet society had its own distinctive forms of trust and distrust. Three modern Central European sociologists who began their lives under Soviet-style socialism were especially sensitive to the high levels of generalized social distrust it generated, and were hence concerned to specify conditions conducive to its opposite: generalized social trust. Ivana Marková, from Czechoslovakia, considers the basis of the social order in totalitarian societies to be 'the socialization of distrust', both because the security police holds everyone under a greater or lesser degree of observation, and because the regimentation of all public discourse deprives one of 'trust in words, in communication and in other people... Thinking becomes imprisoned in a codified semantics of words and deprived of any possibility of self-expression and personal identity.'[23] For that reason Marková lays great emphasis on the importance of dialogical exchange and on expressing authentic personal feeling as a crucial aspect of any society which fosters trusting relationships. In her view the symbolic systems of language and culture together with a free public media and institutions of learning and research are crucial in promoting social cohesion.

Unlike most sociologists, Barbara Misztal is fully aware of unreflective trust. She uses Weber's categories to delineate what she calls the 'habitus' of trust—which for her is 'a protective mechanism relying on everyday routines, stable reputations and tacit memories'.[24] It reduces social complexity, enabling us to function on 'auto-pilot' for much of our life, saving effort and attention for the unfamiliar; without any serious reflection we can trust our judgement and the people we interact with. She pays especial attention to the way in which both individuals and institutions build up a reputation for competence, virtue, probity, or honourable behaviour, which enables them to be trusted.[25]

Misztal shows how collective memory functions as a mechanism for reducing the complexity and restricting the uncertainty of our social environment, making interaction with those around us easier to interpret. The Soviet state, of course, created its own version of memory, embodied in Stalin's *Short Course in the History of the Communist Party of the Soviet Union*, which focused on the history of the class struggle and the Bolsheviks' leadership of workers and peasants in the revolution. This memory was bolstered by rituals and commemorative events, also intended to reinforce a new hierarchy and a new form of social solidarity. But this memory was monolithic

---

[21] Simmel, *Philosophy of Money*, 179.   [22] Simmel, *Philosophy of Money*, 221–5.
[23] Patrick Watier and Ivana Marková, 'Trust as a Psychosocial Feeling: Socialization and Totalitarianism', in Marková (ed), *Trust and Democratic Transition in Post-Communist Europe*, 25–46.
[24] Misztal, *Trust*, 102.   [25] Misztal, *Trust*, 120–39.

and uncontested; Misztal emphasizes that memory needs regular monitoring and correcting, otherwise it can too easily be manipulated by unscrupulous political leaders, a process which in the long run generates powerful distrust.[26]

However, Misztal's ideas for how political trust might be promoted in the modern global world are inconclusive. Another Polish sociologist, Piotr Sztompka, is more specific. He has identified four conditions for what he calls the 'culture of trust':

1. Normative coherence: the confluence of law, morality, and custom to provide a set of norms to enable people to engage confidently with each other, and within which trust is normally unreflective. The opposite is normative incoherence, or what Durkheim called anomie, within which distrust is much more likely to be the default option in social interaction.

2. Stability. The first condition will operate more effectively if it is long lasting, and changes only gradually and in a consistent direction. Under these conditions, in everyday interaction trust does not need to be calculated but can be exercised out of habit. In periods of fast social change one's expectations of other people's reactions become uncertain, and placing trust thus needs much more conscious calculation. Suspicion and distrust become much commoner.

3. Openness. It is important that the structure of society and government is as transparent as possible, that people have information about the way they function and how their components interact, and also access to comments and ideas about them. Where a lot of information is secret or too complicated to understand, trust is likely to be withheld, rumours, gossip, and conspiracy theories will abound, and people will be more prone to look for 'enemies'. Similarly, where the public exchange of ideas is restricted, they will still be exchanged privately, but without the verification and clarification made possible by open discussion, so that extreme, paranoid and violent theories can more easily take hold, promoting intense distrust. This is the soil in which terrorism—including state terrorism—can readily take root.

4. Accountability. When things go wrong, as happens even in high-trust societies, it is important that we should be able to identify who is responsible, hold them to account, and if possible obtain some redress for damage. This is a guarantee that power will not be routinely abused and obligations will normally be respected. It is an insurance policy against misfortune, which enables people to feel more secure and to adopt a more trustful orientation towards other people, institutions, and contingencies.[27]

---

[26] Misztal, *Trust*, 139–56; and see her book *Theories of Social Remembering*, Maidenhead: Open University Press, 2003.

[27] Piotr Sztompka, *Trust: A Sociological Theory*, Cambridge University Press, 1999, 122–5; Sztompka actually proposes five conditions, but in my view they resolve more coherently into the four I have outlined.

In recent sociological thinking there have been two predominant approaches to trust. One is derived from functionalism. The German sociologist Niklas Luhmann, for example, believes that trust is functional in dealing with the world's complexity. It is an attitude of epistemological parsimony. In normal life one is simply not able to assemble all the relevant information and assess all the risks involved in any particular course of action. 'The complexity of the future world is reduced by the act of trust. In trusting, one engages in action as though there were only certain possibilities in the future.' Without trust, everyday life would be impossible; indeed 'one would not even be able to get out of bed in the morning'.[28]

This is unduly reductionist. Luhmann's theory implies that trust is merely a convenience, and it says nothing about the influences which incline an individual to trust rather than distrust. It also ignores the question of whether trust is well placed. Is one trusting in things or persons that are trustworthy—or not? For Luhmann trust is mainly a way of simplifying decisions; morality or even common prudence do not come into his calculations.

This functional approach is often combined with a theory of rational choice. Perhaps its most prominent recent exponent is Russell Hardin. He sees trust as an extension or indirect manifestation of one's own self-interest, what he calls 'encapsulated interest'. 'I trust you because I think it is in your interest to take my interests seriously. . . . You value the continuation of our relationship, and you therefore have your own interest in taking my interests into account. That is, you encapsulate my interests in your own interests.'[29] This perception can be derived from three possible sources: (i) an ongoing relationship, providing previous experience; (ii) love or friendship; and (iii) reputation, that is, trustworthiness perceived through the eyes of others rather than from one's own previous experience.

The rational-choice approach to trust can be modelled in the Prisoner's Dilemma game: there are two players faced with choices which affect them both, yet who cannot communicate with each other except by their actions. In each round each player has the choice either to cooperate with the other or not to, that is to defect. If both cooperate, they receive a score of 3 each. If both defect, they receive a score of 1 each. But if one cooperates and the other defects, the cooperator receives 0 and the defector 5. The best strategy depends on the number of rounds. If there is only one round, the optimal strategy must be to defect; then one is certain of at least receiving 1 and has the hope of receiving 5. If there is an infinite number of rounds, then it turns out that, to maximize possible future returns, the best strategy is to cooperate on the first round and thereafter to do whatever the opponent does. So given infinite repetition, the game does indeed suggest that preliminary trust is best. If, however, the number of rounds is known, then the shadow of the last round—when defection is best—casts its shadow over all the previous rounds, and defection is the best choice then too.[30] In Dostoevsky's *The Brothers Karamazov* a lieutenant regularly runs up credit with a merchant, and just as regularly pays off his debt—that is, until he is posted elsewhere. On the

---

[28] Luhmann, *Trust and Power*, 3, 20.   [29] Hardin, *Trust and Trustworthiness*, 1.
[30] Robert Axelrod, *The Problem of Cooperation*, London: Penguin, 1990, 6–11.

last occasion, he disappears without paying and leaves the merchant out of pocket.[31]

This model does replicate quite well many real-life situations where one is dealing with a partner whose intentions are unknown and not easily ascertainable. In an arms race, for example, each nation expands its own armaments because it is uncertain of the intentions of possible enemies and therefore has to assume the worst. Those potential enemies then do exactly the same, for the same reason, making war more likely. This is the 'security dilemma', familiar to international relations theorists.[32]

Similarly, in an international economic depression, each country is faced with the question of whether or not to erect trade barriers against other countries. Such barriers would protect one's own industries, but at the cost of reducing the overall level of world trade, and thus in the long run probably undermining one's own industries too. In each case, when trust is missing, the individually rational decision generates the worst outcome for all. The best option, not allowed in the game's rules, would be for the two players to consult and find ways of turning a negative-sum game into a positive-sum game.

As it is, though, the Prisoner's Dilemma offers no secure rational grounds for making trust the default option. It is true, there are many real-life situations where it is anticipated that an exchange relationship will be frequently repeated, and most people in practice are prepared to treat them as infinite. As against that, many such relationships are one-off or at least short-lived, and then on the premises of the model trust is not the best option.

Like many social science models, the Prisoner's Dilemma does not offer direct prescriptions about how to behave in real life. What it does is to offer an abstract mock-up, so that we can better understand the distinctive characteristics of actual situations. Treating such mock-ups as real can create dangerous illusions. Regarding trust as purely interest-based and rational, and then creating mathematical models on this assumption—the predominant approach in recent economic theory—has severely impoverished our understanding of how human beings interact in the market, and is doing great damage to our social fabric, as I shall argue in Chapter 6.

An interesting example of rational choice theory incongruously (but deliberately) applied is the seventeenth-century French thinker Blaise Pascal's wager on the existence of God. His argument runs like this. There are two possibilities: either God exists or He does not. If He *does* exist, and you do *not* believe in Him, you risk a terrible fate after death; if you *do* believe in Him, you lose little or nothing in this life, but gain richly in the afterlife. If He does *not* exist, it does not matter much either way. So the rational choice is to believe in Him. Of course Pascal did not regard this argument as the fundamental motive for believing: he merely wanted to

---

[31] Quoted in Hardin, *Trust and Trustworthiness*, 1–3.

[32] Ken Booth and Nicholas J. Wheeler, *The Security Dilemma: Fear, Cooperation and Trust in World Politics*, Basingstoke: Palgrave Macmillan, 2008.

suggest to the non-believer that belief was not irrational. Once the step of deciding to believe was taken, Pascal believed that other more powerful motives would come into play—like those I outline in Chapter 3—and the believer's life would become richer and more fulfilling.

The main alternative to functionalism and rational choice is the normative account of trust, which gives pride of place to the individual's agency and moral sense. Martin Hollis, for example, argues that the individual is never a free-standing rational actor. 'We who construct the action are social beings before we are particular individuals and are plural before we are singular.' As individuals we are formed by social interactions, and therefore the justification for trust must lie within society rather than originate with the individual and his interests. Hollis considers what motivates car-drivers to give lifts to hitchhikers or donors to give blood. Neither action can be explained in Hardin's terms, since there is no obvious return (at least in those countries where blood donors are not paid) and no likelihood of a continuing relationship such as would justify an interest-based explanation. Both actions presuppose a broad conception of community and of mutuality.[33]

This is an existentialist and communitarian account of trust: human beings exercise trust because they would like others to trust them and accept that this entails being trustworthy oneself. By acting trustingly they also advance the cause of generalized social trust, which in Hollis's view could not otherwise be rationally grounded. They create reality as well as act within it, and in their own small way contribute to fashioning a society in which it is easier to exercise trust.[34]

Robert Frank makes a similar point in a different way. He asks why we tip a waiter or a taxi-driver in a distant city, when we are never likely to meet the recipient again. He argues that 'the motive is not to avoid the possibility of being caught, but to maintain and strengthen the disposition to behave honestly. My failure to tip in the distant city will make it difficult to sustain the emotions that motivate me to behave honestly on other occasions. *It is this change in my emotional make-up, not my failure to tip itself, that other people may apprehend.*'[35] This account lays the emphasis on the way individuals construct their own identity in relation to the community. They become trustworthy by cultivating and sustaining the internal disposition to behave honestly and to trust others to do likewise. They thus not only interpret reality but in a modest way also change it.

There is quite a good chance, moreover, that by trusting one will elicit a positive response from partners and interlocutors. Trust usually (not always, of course) generates trust in those who interact with us. Dr Johnson, a doughty proponent of sociability, declared: 'It is happier to be sometimes cheated than not to trust.'[36] In

---

[33] Martin Hollis, *Trust within Reason*, Cambridge University Press, 1998, quotation on p. 115.

[34] Most religions justify trust in this way, as I shall suggest in Chapter 3.

[35] Robert Frank, *Passions with Reason: The Strategic Role of the Emotions*, New York: Norton, 1988, 18–19; italics in the original.

[36] From *The Rambler*, no. 79, 18 December 1750, in *Oxford Dictionary of Quotations*, 6th edition, ed. Elizabeth Knowles, Oxford University Press, 2004, p. 425, no. 20.

the same spirit, the seventeenth-century French moralist La Rochefoucauld, not usually thought of as a particularly trusting person, nevertheless averred that 'It is more shameful to distrust one's friends than sometimes to be deceived by them.'[37] Distrust tends to provoke reciprocal distrust. Again in the words of La Rochefoucauld: 'Our distrust justifies others' deceit.'[38] It thus closes off both knowledge and options. As Diego Gambetta has commented, 'Trust begins with keeping oneself open to evidence, acting as if one trusted, at least until more stable beliefs can be established on the basis of further information.'[39] Besides, trust is a form of capital that is not depleted by use: on the contrary, it is self-reinforcing. Like skilfully invested financial capital, it often yields fruitful returns in our social life: hence the widely used term 'social capital' associated with it.[40]

There is a rational-choice method of reaching a similar point. It is articulated by Russell Hardin, 'If I generally distrust people, I will discover little about their actual trustworthiness because I will choose not to interact with them. It follows that I will have to make choices with less information to go on than other, more optimistic people have.'[41] The German theorist Guido Möllinger suggests taking an 'as-if' approach: in exercising an advance of trust, he argues, one is 'building on reason, routine and reflexivity, suspending irreducible social vulnerability and uncertainty *as if* they were favourably resolved, and maintaining thereby a state of favourable expectation towards the actions and intentions of more or less specific others'.[42]

Similarly, according to Niklas Luhmann, distrust leaves a social actor 'little energy to explore and adapt to his environment in an objective and unprejudiced manner, and hence allows him fewer opportunities for learning. Relatively, trust is the easier option, and for this reason there is a strong incentive to begin a relationship with trust.'[43] Here, back in the real world, we are a long way from the isolated and ahistorical actors of the Prisoner's Dilemma, and even rational choice theory has moral implications. Any satisfactory theory of trust must include a moral element. It cannot be deduced from rational choice alone.

We need, then, both rational-choice and moral conceptions of trust. Much trust, for example in the market-place, is instrumental and is based on self-interest and rational choice. But a theory of trust cannot be adequately based on it alone; indeed, such a theory is seriously deficient and likely to do damage. Without positing that human beings seek trusting interactions out of moral considerations, we will not understand the full potentiality of trust.

---

[37] La Rochefoucauld, *Maximes*, ed. F. C. Green, Cambridge University Press, 1946, no. 84.

[38] *Maximes*, no. 86.

[39] Diego Gambetta, 'Can we Trust Trust?', in Gambetta (ed), *Trust: Making and Breaking Cooperative Relations*, Oxford: Blackwell, 1988, 234.

[40] James S. Coleman, 'Social Capital in the Creation of Human Capital', *American Journal of Sociology*, 94 (1988), Supplement, S95–120.

[41] Hardin, *Trust and Trustworthiness*, 131.

[42] Guido Möllinger, *Trust: Reason, Routine, Reflexivity*, Amsterdam: Elsevier, 2006, 111.

[43] Luhmann, *Trust and Power*, 72. Möllinger, *Trust*, 111.

ANTHROPOLOGISTS AND TRUST

Anthropologists have introduced a crucial element to the study of trust: they link it with symbolic systems, notably myth, magic, religion, art, science, and the rules of economic and matrimonial exchange.

In dealing with another person and in facing the future one is dealing with unknowns. Another person is always partly unknown; when one has known another individual a long time, one knows him/her much better and may well as a result be more trusting, but there always remains an element of the unknown. Still more does that apply to situations in which decisions have to be consciously taken about the future. One is always to some extent dealing with the 'Other'; hence trust is about seeking security and avoiding unnecessary risk.

Trust and distrust are, then, alternative means of dealing with the unknown Other, that is, with persons or things outside our previous experience, uncontrollable and possibly dangerous. Obviously such encounters arouse anxiety. Usually human beings respond in one of two ways: either by extreme hostility to destroy the danger or by an exaggerated display of warmth and hospitality to arouse reciprocal feelings in the Other.

In his famous investigation of the Trobriand islanders, the anthropologist Bronislaw Malinowski showed how the inhabitants of a group of scattered Pacific islands dealt with this dilemma. He found that they had evolved a regular form of ritual exchange and gift-giving, known as the Kula. Parties from one island tribe, led by their chieftain, would regularly visit another island, bringing with them valuable objects as presents. They would expect to receive other valuable objects in return, and would assess the inter-tribal relationship according to what they received. This was not trade, since the valuables would soon be passed on in another exchange. In fact, it became customary for red shell necklaces called *soulava* to move clockwise round the archipelago, and for white shell bracelets called *mwali* to move anti-clockwise. Each exchange was accompanied by elaborate ceremony and the performance of various kinds of magic.

Mystified at first by this apparently pointless gift exchange, Malinowski came to the conclusion that the object of the Kula was to maintain peaceful inter-tribal relationships (in my terms, to broaden the radius of trust) in a situation where constant fighting would have spelt mutual destruction. 'The main attitude of a native to other, alien groups', he explained, 'is that of hostility and mistrust. The fact that to a native every stranger is an enemy is an ethnographic feature reported from all parts of the world. The Trobriander is not an exception in this respect, and beyond his own, narrow social horizon, a wall of suspicion, misunderstanding and latent enmity divides him from even near neighbours. The Kula breaks through it at definite geographical points, and by means of special customary transactions. But, like everything extraordinary and exceptional, this waiving of the general taboo on strangers must be justified and bridged over by magic.'[44]

---

[44] Bronislaw Malinowski, *Argonauts of the Western Pacific: An Account of Native Enterprise and Adventure in the Archipelagos of Melanesian New Guinea*, New York: Dutton, 1961 (first published 1922), 345.

It was normal to supplement inter-tribal relationships with personal ones. Malinowski found that the Kula bound some thousands of individuals into cross-tribal personal relationships, which underpinned the tribal ones. 'This partnership is a lifelong relationship, it implies various mutual duties and privileges, and constitutes a type of inter-tribal relationship on an enormous scale.' The overseas partner was 'a host, patron and ally in a land of danger and insecurity. . . . He also provides with food, gives presents, and his house, though never used to sleep in, is the place in which to foregather while in the village.' 'As to the economic mechanism of the transactions, this is based on a specific form of credit, which implies a high degree of mutual trust and commercial honour—and this refers also to the subsidiary, minor trade, which accompanies the Kula proper.'[45]

If the tacit terms of the Kula were not observed, the consequences could be very destructive. Malinowski heard a frequently told story about a tribe which generations ago had betrayed the tacit terms of the Kula. 'The natives of Gabu, receiving [representatives of a visiting tribe] at first with a show of interest, and pretending to enter into commercial relations, afterwards fell on them treacherously and slew the chief Toraya and all his companions. . . . [Afterwards] Tomakan, the slain chief's younger brother, went to the Koya of Gabu, and killed the headman of one of the villages, thus avenging his brother's death. He then composed a song and dance which is performed to this day in Kiriwina, and has indeed one of the finest melodies in the islands.'[46] Presumably this tale was frequently and ceremonially narrated because it served to remind listeners of the consequences of not observing the implicit accord symbolized in the Kula.

Malinowski's account of the Trobriand Islanders suggests that in an encounter of unknown peoples mutual trust is created by one side offering a gift, if possible a valuable one. To do so is to sacrifice something, and also to take a risk, since the gift may be rejected, but the consequences of not doing so are worse: distrust leading to chronic enmity and probably destructive fighting.

Claude Lévi-Strauss built on the insights of Malinowski in *The Elementary Structures of Kinship*, in which he suggested that reciprocity is a basic principle of all human societies. It was, he claimed, typically embodied in gifts, which were not commodities, but 'vehicles and instruments for realities of another order, such as power, influence, sympathy, status and emotion; and the skilful game of exchange . . . consists in a complex totality of conscious or unconscious manoeuvres in order to gain security and to guard oneself against risks brought about by alliances and by rivalries'.[47] He took the example of two strangers sitting opposite one another at the same table in a cheap restaurant. Social norms require that they sit in an uncommunicative silence—but such behaviour always conveys slight but palpable hostility: 'They feel both alone and together, compelled to the usual reserve between strangers, while their respective spatial positions, and their relationships to the objects and utensils of the meal suggest, and to a certain extent

---

[45] Malinowski, *Argonauts*, 85–6, 92.   [46] Malinowski, *Argonauts*, 291.
[47] Claude Lévi-Strauss, *The Elementary Structures of Kinship*, trans. James Harle Bell, London: Eyre & Spottiswoode, 1969, 54.

call for, intimacy.' So one of them makes a symbolic gesture, offering a glass of wine from his own carafe. That requires a response: 'Wine offered calls for wine returned, cordiality requires cordiality.... Further, the acceptance of this offer sanctions another offer, for conversation. In this way a whole range of trivial social ties are established by a series of alternating oscillations, in which offering gives one a right, and receiving makes one obligated, and always beyond what has been given or accepted.'[48] From this basic need for reciprocity Lévi-Strauss built his whole theory of marriage, kinship, and even the incest taboo. Exogamous marriage, in his view, was necessary to avoid 'the indefinite fission and segmentation which the practice of consanguineous marriages would bring about', turning families into 'closed systems or sealed monads' which would fragment society and generate repeated conflict.[49]

Taking reciprocity as a basic feature of any society, Lévi-Strauss proposed that it manifested itself through symbolic systems. 'Every culture can be considered as a combination of symbolic systems headed by language, matrimonial rules, economic relations, art, science and religion. All the systems seek to express certain aspects of physical reality and social reality, and even more, to express the links that those two types of reality have with each other and those that occur among the symbolic systems themselves.'[50]

The word 'symbol' derives from the Greek *symballein*, which means to 'throw together' or to 'join'. It refers to the custom of breaking a familiar object—a bone or a pot—into two, and giving half to two separate people. When the two meet, they can identify each other by checking if their two fragments fit together. In this way two members of the same sect or secret society could verify each other's credentials. A symbol thus acts as a bridge between the known and the unknown—potentially a creator of trust in the encounter with the Other.[51]

The etymological origin of the word gives us a clue to the power of symbols: they generate both meaning and relationship. They join together signifiers from disparate spheres of knowledge so that they gain new meaning by their combination. We can relate one symbol to another to gain new knowledge, and thus act in the real world with greater confidence. Symbols also have emotional power, whether or not one posits some kind of collective unconscious as the source of that power. They can stimulate us to strong feelings of attachment or abhorrence, trust or distrust. In their positive mode they are thus effective in bringing together individuals or groups who would otherwise have little in common, as in music, a shared ritual, or a festive meal. The symbol renders reality understandable and also enables human beings to act together to influence that reality. It is an indispensable component of culture, as Clifford Geertz has defined that term, as 'socially established structures of meaning' or 'A system of inherited conceptions expressed

[48] Lévi-Strauss, *Elementary Structures*, 59.   [49] Lévi-Strauss, *Elementary Structures*, 479.

[50] Claude Lévi-Strauss, *Introduction to Mauss*, trans. Felicity Baker, London: Routledge & Kegan Paul, 1987, 16.

[51] Anthony Stevens, *Ariadne's Clue: A Guide to the Symbols of Humankind*, London: Allen Lane, 1998, 12–13.

in symbolic forms by means of which men communicate, develop and perpetuate their knowledge about and attitude toward life'.[52]

That is why symbolic systems are so important. They enable us to trust both other human beings and also objects and events in the real world, at least in the sense that we can predict how they will behave. Through the symbolic systems of science and mathematics we are enabled to approach the external world with greater confidence. In myth, ritual, and magic, there may well be a placebo effect operating, but that is often successful too. The thinker who has done most to expound the importance of symbolic systems is Ernst Cassirer, who argued that man is a 'symbolic animal' and that he 'lives in a symbolic universe'.[53]

A symbolic system is also a filter which enables us to cope with a complex reality by deploying trust. In Luhmann's words, 'The personal and social arrangements in which one puts trust become *symbol complexes*, which are especially sensitive to disturbance and which, as it were, register every event in terms of the question of trust.'[54]

Trust is the indispensable foundation of human reciprocity and social interaction. We nourish trust in the natural and social orders through the operation of symbolic systems and the institutions which sustain them. Society is an intersubjective enterprise, in which we all participate by communicating meaning to one another and exercising an 'advance' of trust without knowing in every instance whether it will be reciprocated. We are enabled to do so by the existence of symbolic systems and institutions that have come down to us through centuries of history. The history of trust, I shall argue, is closely linked to the history of those institutions and symbolic systems. The main symbolic systems on which we rely to stabilize our social life are:

- Language, which enables the articulation of complex concepts and thoughts;
- Myth, which provides a narrative to explain the structure of the universe and the place of divine and natural forces and of human beings within it;
- Religion, which continues the work of myth, and also provides a number of resources for the maintenance of trust both in people and in contingencies (see Chapter 3);
- Science, which establishes a maximally non-subjective framework for understanding the natural world around us, and for that purpose draws extensively on the abstract symbolic system of mathematics;
- Law, which sustains a socially sanctioned framework within which personal and institutional relationships can be conducted, and when necessary enables conflicts to be settled in a non-violent way;

[52] Clifford Geertz, *The Interpretation of Cultures*, London: Hutchinson, 1975, 12, 89.

[53] Ernst Cassirer, *An Essay on Man*, New Haven: Yale University Press, 1962 (first published 1944), 25. Cassirer used the term 'symbolic forms', but I have preferred 'systems', as I wish to emphasize the articulation of their internal components and the possibility of generating new meanings by the rearrangement and reconnection of those components. See Ernst Cassirer, *The Philosophy of Symbolic Forms*, trans. Ralph Manheim, 3 vols, New Haven: Yale University Press, 1953–7; or for a brief introduction to his theory, *An Essay on Man*.

[54] Luhmann, *Trust and Power*, 28; italics in the original.

- Culture and the arts, which establish a subjective and evaluative framework for our perception of the world and of social relationships;
- Money, which enables us to exchange goods and services with people about whom we know nothing, and from whom we cannot expect the reciprocity of closer social interaction (see Chapter 4).

Most of these symbolic systems generate their own institutions. Religion, for example, gives birth to a church, or a priesthood, or to a corpus of learned men who claim special knowledge of the faith and its associated myths; it creates its own educational and charitable institutions, and the organizations necessary to sustain them. Science—in the broader sense of *Wissenschaft*, or learning—gives rise to schools, universities, and academies; in the ancient world and from the late middle ages onwards in Europe science and learning claimed to embody an autonomous field of value, independent of religion and political authority. Law has its courts, judges, and lawyers, with their own juridical codes, professional associations, training schools, and systems of learning, associated with both church and state, but claiming the right to judge both. Culture generates its own artefacts and also its own institutions: theatres, galleries, studios, concert halls, bands and orchestras, journals and publishing houses, professional associations and systems of training. Money is channelled through markets, through banks and their various devices for deposit, lending, and borrowing, and through state treasuries, with their taxation systems. These institutions all have their structures, routines, and accepted practices which enable people not closely acquainted with one another to 'read' with ease each other's words, gestures, and actions and hence to interact with confidence. They provide the 'habitus of trust'.[55]

In order to prevent this book expanding uncontrollably, I have chosen to focus mainly on only two of these symbolic systems, religion and money, with their accompanying institutions. I have selected them because they are both very important, yet seem so different from one another—though, as I shall suggest, they have some features in common. Moreover, they are both undergoing especially acute crises of trust right now. Then, in Chapters 5 and 7, I show how nation-states draw on these two and other symbolic systems as well for their appeal to our trust, which persists even though many contemporary institutions are global in scope.

TRUST, SOCIETY, AND THE INDIVIDUAL

Trust of some kind is involved in most decisions, including the decision to do nothing. Some of these decisions are easy—scarcely worth calling decisions—while others involve a lot of thought, assessment, and planning. In nearly all cases,

---

[55] The importance of symbolic systems for understanding trust is further outlined in my paper 'Trust and Symbolic Systems: Religion and Nationhood', in Ivana Marková and Alex Gillespie (eds), *Trust and Conflict: Representation, Culture and Dialogue*, London: Routledge, 2012, 17–36.

though, as we have seen, it is impossible to collate all the information and consider all the relevant arguments that one would need in order to take a wholly rational decision. In virtually all life situations, we have to be content with the information available to us, exercise our judgement as to the rest, and trust to that judgement to carry us through.

This is especially true for active people, such as entrepreneurs, pioneers, explorers, soldiers, who venture into unknown territory or go into battle. They have to press ahead without the assurance of success or even of survival. Their most remarkable feature, of course, is courage; but the doughtiest courage would fail if there were not the slightest hope of success, so that trust is an indispensable component of courage. One could object, of course, that trust is a kind of anaesthetic, that it impedes us from dealing with problems that could be realistically tackled. Sometimes that may be the case, but certainly not always, as Luhmann showed above.[56]

I believe that trust is the default position of most human beings. At the very least, we have a marked inbuilt tendency to trust unless confronted by cogent evidence that trust is unjustified. Once we think it unjustified, however, we respond with an equally strong and self-reinforcing tendency to distrust. In short, trust and distrust form one of the principal axes around which human social behaviour revolves, and they generate very powerful feelings. The boundaries shaped by trust form and are formed by the social context within which we all live, move and have our being.

The reason why trust is so fundamental to human beings is obvious from the life history of the individual. The psychologist Erik Erikson saw infant trust in the mother as the foundation of all human relationships and of the sense of well-being, of having a personal identity and of belonging to the world. 'Mothers create a sense of trust in their children by that kind of administration which in its quality combines sensitive care of the baby's individual needs and a firm sense of personal trustworthiness within the trusted framework of their culture's life style. This forms the basis in the child for a sense of identity which will later combine with a sense of being "all right", of being oneself, and of becoming what other people trust one will become.'[57]

We know that infants become strongly attached to their mothers at around the age of three to four months. Gradually thereafter they also become attached to a father or other family carer, to older siblings, then later still to playgroup organizers, teachers, and other outside carers. The stronger the relationship with the primary attachment figure, the more the infant is capable of forming secondary attachments to older persons, and then equal relationships with same-age playmates. If the primary attachment is for some reason weak, disrupted, or delayed, then those other attachments will also be slow to form or will remain weak. Moreover, if the infant experiences serious distress, it will regress towards the primary attachment to the exclusion of others. This suggests that a successful core trusting relationship is

---

[56] See above, 'Sociologists on Trust'.
[57] Erik H. Erikson, *Childhood and Society*, New York: Norton, 1993, 249.

crucial to all our later social interactions. During adolescence the primary attachment may weaken or even break off, but nearly all adolescents form strong relationships with alternative adult mentors and/or with colleagues of the same age.[58] In all these cases there is a very strong element of trust, and an equally strong negative reaction if trust is betrayed. One might of course argue that what is involved in the case of the infant is not really trust, but helpless dependence. However, helpless dependence is quite often the begetter of trust: the infant's situation falls well within the semantic map of trust which I set out above.[59]

Trust, then, plays a crucial role in the genesis of the personality, and therefore also in the development of the cognitive faculties. As we grow up, we make our first discoveries in life with the help of our parents. We take on trust what they tell us about the world and other people—to such an extent that in later life it is quite difficult to shake off the information, values, and feelings they have passed on to us, even when subsequent experience tells us they are misguided. In this way, trust makes an essential contribution to our cognitive equipment. It forms a constitutive part of the way in which we conceive the world. We later supplement what we have learnt from our parents through our contacts with siblings, partners, friends, colleagues, and people with whom we feel an affinity. Since we cannot learn everything by personal experience, we take on trust much of what they impart to us. At an even deeper level, their discourse, their ways of mentally constituting the world in which they live, becomes a usually unnoticed but firmly embedded part of our own world-picture. Learning to discriminate and not to trust everything learnt in this manner is one of life's most important, difficult, and sometimes painful processes.

In this way, trust is an indispensable part of socialization, of the way we learn about the society in which we live, and of how we learn to relate to each other and to face the future. It forms the underpinning of our decisions and actions. And because its specific forms vary with varying societies, trust needs to be studied in its specific social context. In tribal societies, city-states, feudal societies, land-bound empires, maritime empires, nation-states, and in the imperfectly globalized world, people trust and distrust others for reasons at least partly derived from the nature of the society as a whole.

Moreover, people find it easier to trust those who are like them or come from a similar background. This is Misztal's 'habitus of trust', an environment in which we can easily 'read' people's language, facial expressions, gestures, and behaviour, and hence function on 'auto-pilot' without making many conscious decisions. By contrast, interacting with people of different ethnic, religious, or social backgrounds requires more attention and alertness, and more considered decisions about whether to trust or distrust.

---

[58] John Bowlby, *Attachment and Loss*, i: *Attachment*, New York: Basic Books, 1969, 198–209, 307–9.

[59] See above, 'What is Trust?'.

TRUST AND INSTITUTIONS

The trust structures of any society are composed of 'trust networks', which arise where people peacefully interact regularly or work together to achieve some common purpose that requires mutual trust. They form nodal points in which trust is focused. They exist in every society and include extended families, village and parish communities, religious sects, municipalities, army units, guilds and professional associations, ethnic diasporas, educational institutions, scientific societies, credit networks, mutual aid associations, companies, and corporations.[60] These associations have developed at different periods of history, in different contexts, for different purposes and in different kinds of society. 'Trust structures' are then the wider social arrangements within which the networks are embedded—and with which some of them may well be at odds. In examining the networks, in each case, it is vital to understand the social setting in which they arise and function, for only thereby can one do justice to their practices and symbolic systems.

The great advantage of a trust network is that it tends to be durable, able to carry on complex activities without continual monitoring. Members are normally devoted to it unquestioningly and are willing to make sacrifices for it. Many trust networks offer some kind of mutual aid or social security for members going through a crisis. The most frequent matrix for a trust network is kinship, since here acquaintanceship is longest and the personal relationships are at their most intimate.

One crucial reservation about trust networks: they do not function harmoniously all the time. Everyone knows that members of the same family quite often quarrel, sometimes have deep differences of opinion, and occasionally break off relationships altogether. Nevertheless, it makes sense to regard families as miniature trust networks—whose role, for example, in the creation of economic enterprises has been crucial.[61] Most (though not quite all) families will prefer to settle conflicts internally rather than take them outside, 'wash dirty linen in public', and incur the risk of losing control of family affairs to external forces.

Here trust may imply little more than agreeing on a framework within which disputes can be peacefully settled so that mutually fruitful relationships may continue; but that itself is very significant. One reason that the Rothschilds were such a successful financial firm for most of the nineteenth century was that the family patriarch, Mayer Amschel, as he was getting old, dictated an agreement, which he stipulated should be signed by his three partners, his sons Carl, Amschel, and Salomon, and by any later partners. The document laid down that no partner was to engage in any independent business; it also specified the proportion of the profits each partner was to be entitled to, and how affairs should be dealt with on the death of any partner. One foundation of trust, then, may be to recognize the

---

[60] Charles Tilly, *Trust and Rule*, Cambridge University Press, 2005, 5–6.
[61] This is one of the main themes of Francis Fukuyama, *Trust: The Social Virtues and the Creation of Prosperity*, London: Penguin Books, 1996.

likelihood of difference and even conflict, and make provision to deal with it peacefully.[62]

Trust networks, even those in general harmony with society, tend to draw rigid boundaries around themselves, and to relate to outsiders with reserve sometimes amounting to distrust. The Rothschilds' agreement, for example, delineated the family firm very strictly. Even wives and children (unless sons became partners) were strictly excluded: they were denied access to any of the firm's accounts and correspondence. To reinforce the boundary, partners would write family letters in Hebrew, but business letters in English, French, or German, which most family members could not understand. When, after Mayer Amschel's death, his sons quarrelled, they nevertheless stuck to the firm's basic charter, and continued to do so in later crises.[63] Here the boundaries ran within even the family, marking out gender and age. As social norms change, such boundaries have to be reconsidered. Exclusions which are acceptable in some settings become intolerable in others, and arouse vehement distrust.

DIFFERENT MODES OF TRUST

Trust can be strong or weak; it can also be thick or thin. One might use the term 'strong trust', for relationships to which individuals commit valued resources—which may be the preservation of their health, beliefs, customs, home, and way of life, their profession or job, provision for their children or their own old age. That would include trusting the quality of education in a school or college, taking out a mortgage to buy a house, committing one's free time to voluntary work for a charity or religious movement, or placing savings in a pension scheme which may not bring any benefit for several decades but could prove a godsend in old age. In all these cases, decisions will normally be preceded by serious reflection and the weighing up of alternatives.

'Weak trust' would include more routine cooperative relationships in which decisions are routine, less is at stake or the risk is very slight. This would include trusting what we read in the newspaper, trusting that the food we buy in the supermarket is fit to eat, trusting that the money I earn today will have much the same value tomorrow, next month, and even next year. Sometimes, it is true, even in these relationships a malign outcome could have seriously damaging effects—the fish I buy in the shop could turn out to contain a toxic substance—but the risk is very slight and the transaction is routine, so for all normal purposes we ignore it. Here we can scarcely talk of 'decisions' at all.[64]

---

[62] This would be the view of the Polish sociologist Piotr Sztompka. See above, 'Sociologists on Trust'.

[63] Niall Ferguson, *The World's Banker: The History of the House of Rothschild*, London: Weidenfeld & Nicolson, 1998, i: 83–5, 283–6.

[64] This distinction was formulated by Tilly in his *Trust and Rule*.

There is no clear and unambiguous boundary between strong and weak trust, but rather a gradation, depending on the seriousness of the risk, the value of the resources committed, and whether the transaction is routine or deeply considered. Both forms of trust are, however, very important to the functioning of society.[65]

There is another distinction, between 'thick' and 'thin' trust, which cuts across that between 'strong' and 'weak' trust. 'Thick' trust rests on extensive knowledge, resulting from frequent or close contact with the person or institution one trusts, whereas 'thin' trust is based on slight knowledge, on infrequent or superficial contact. Four modes of trust can thus be delineated:

Strong thick trust	Strong thin trust
Weak thick trust	Weak thin trust

The upper left-hand and lower right-hand quadrants need little explanation. An example of strong thick trust might be getting married; of weak thin trust buying food in a supermarket. The lower left-hand quadrant is also easy to explain: one does not always need to risk major resources in a close or frequent relationship; one risks little in lending a close colleague the bus fare home. What is more surprising is that the upper right-hand quadrant, 'strong thin trust', also exists. Indeed, I will argue that it is ever more prevalent in our social life today, as a result of cumulative changes which have been taking place at least in the West for a very long time. One of the main reasons we often misrecognize trust today is that we have not been aware of the growing predominance of strong thin trust.

Russell Hardin would deny that thin trust is trust at all. In his view, 'Trust typically arises at the level of, and is grounded in, relatively small-scale interactions. It is not restricted to merely dyadic [one-to-one] relationships, but it cannot be grounded in interactions involving very large numbers of people.... Because most of us live in large-scale societies, we need devices other than trusting and trustworthiness to make many of our more or less cooperative activities go well.'[66] This is precisely the opposite of what Adam Seligman asserts.[67] It is such conceptual tangles which have persuaded me we need to treat trust as part of a broad semantic continuum.

In his recent book *The Better Angels of our Nature*, Steven Pinker argues that violence among human beings has been declining over recent centuries—admittedly with periodic sensational reverses. He attributes this gradual pacification to a number of developments. First, the modern state has become ever more powerful, curbing the aggressive rapacity of tribal or feudal warlords and imposing a monopoly of legitimate violence as well ensuring a more objective, less parochial administration of justice.[68] Second, social morals have evolved away from immediate gratification of desires and impulses, regardless of other people's feelings and

---

[65] Mark S. Granovetter, 'The Strength of Weak Ties', *American Journal of Sociology*, 78 (1973), 1360–80.

[66] Hardin, *Trust and Trustworthiness*, 199–200.   [67] See above, 'Sociologists on Trust'.

[68] Cf. Fukuyama, *Origins*, 69–71, 260.

of long-term consequences, towards a more reserved and calculating style of behaviour which takes into account other people's reactions and the long-term consequences of actions. Third, with the increase in both travel and dissemination of information, people have learnt both to understand other people's feelings and to appreciate that others' very different beliefs and practices are not necessarily signs of irredeemable evil. Fourth, the development of peaceful commerce has shown that acquiring goods, services, or land does not have to be at others' expense but can contribute to their well-being too; that life is not a series of negative-sum games, but can be turned into positive-sum games in which both sides can benefit from transactions. In the long run, this perception has impelled the globalization of our economies.[69]

In all these developments what has been happening has been a broadening of the radius of trust, upwards from local warlord to monarch; from confidence in the honour and courage of a superior to confidence in his social skills and capacity for realistic and judicious action; from narrow-minded insistence on one's own beliefs to acceptance and tolerance of others'; and from short-sighted and greedy acquisitiveness to participation in the mutual exchange of markets. One displaces risk upwards, seeking to place it on broader shoulders, to dissolve it within larger pools of resources or within institutions which ensure positive-sum games.

On the whole, this is a very positive development. One result, though, is that nowadays we know less well the larger entities with which we are dealing. Take the investment we make in a pension fund, often chosen by an employer or professional association: we entrust a large part of our lifetime savings to it, without knowing very much about it. The selection of a savings bank or insurance company might be more deliberate and more carefully assessed, but one is still likely to know little about its employees and to have little contact with them. Similarly, when we open our economies to competition from the entire world, we gain benefits but we are also taking on risks which we understand poorly or not at all, and are placing our fates in the hands of huge, globe-spanning financial institutions, whose ways are positively secretive.

The downside of enlarging the boundaries of trust, then, is that the resultant organizations are larger, more remote, and usually more impersonal. Lower-level trust structures are more personal and easier to understand. Hence we do not want to lose them altogether. In contacting a large, impersonal organization, one usually prefers to know an individual within it whom one can contact with any queries; or one pays a banker or investment adviser to place one's funds wisely. Trust in large and impersonal institutions is still best mediated by a personal trust relationship. Traders prefer to deal with the same interlocutor in the market or port. Most of us prefer to have a 'primary care doctor' or family practitioner to help us find our way through the national health care system. Similarly, when we have to deal with

---

[69] Steven Pinker, *The Better Angels of our Nature: The Decline of Violence in History and its Causes*, London: Allen Lane, 2011, chapters 2–4.

the social security system, we prefer to talk to the same person face to face each week, not a different person sheltered behind a glass screen.[70]

When we can, we still prefer to replace trust in institutions by trust in persons. But on the whole, forms of trust in the modern world tend to gravitate towards the 'strong thin' mode; it is a ubiquitous and crucial lubricator of the social mechanisms within which we all interact nowadays. This change has been very marked in recent decades, and it tends to give us the feeling that trust is declining, or that there is a 'crisis of trust'. There can be no doubt that our modes of trust have changed radically, and the implications for our social attitudes and feelings are far-reaching. Chapters 5–7 explore the implications of recent changes. First, though, let us look more closely at two very powerful trust-inducing symbolic systems, religion and money.

[70] Anthony Giddens, *The Consequences of Modernity*, Cambridge: Polity Press, 1991, 83–8.

3

Godly Homelands
Trust in Religion

Our Father, which art in Heaven,
Hallowed be thy name;
Thy kingdom come;
Thy will be done on earth as it is in Heaven.
Give us this day our daily bread,
And forgive us our trespasses,
As we forgive them that trespass against us.
And lead us not into temptation,
But deliver us from evil,
For thine is the kingdom, the power and the glory,
For ever and ever, Amen.

This prayer, offered by Jesus himself, is central to the ritual of all Christian churches. Most of it is aimed to fortify trust. The deity is addressed as a father, the head of our family and hence a familiar, strong, and trusted being. More than that, he is a father who is in heaven and thus able to control and direct events far beyond the family, hence can be trusted even more than an ordinary father. He is 'hallowed', because he exists in a higher realm of the sacred, in which human beings can have total confidence. 'Thy will be done' expresses acceptance and trust in whatever he has decided. The entreaties 'Give us this day our daily bread', 'deliver us from evil', and 'lead us not into temptation' look to God for help in dealing with everyday contingencies and their moral implications. 'Forgive us our trespasses, as we forgive them that trespass against us' evokes a moral order in which God's forgiveness inspires human beings to rebuild broken relationships and restore mutual trust. The prayer ends by projecting this harmony into a trustworthy future in which God's power and glory last for ever.

For Christians the Lord's Prayer is a focal point in a symbolic system which includes the Trinity, the life of Jesus, the crucifixion and resurrection. This system has its own internal rationality which governs the lives of committed believers, and influences the lives of all members of Christian societies. It is one of many religious symbolic systems which enable people to understand the world, to cope with it, to take decisions and act within it.

When it comes to generating trust, religion is the most all-embracing symbolic system. It has a number of trust-generating functions:

1. Epistemic: it offers us a secure knowledge of the world, in which we can place our faith.

2. Existential: it is identity-forming. It offers us a sense of ourselves, makes self-confidence possible, and hence provides a secure base from which we can trust others.

3. Salvific: it offers a way of salvation, not from all evil, but at least from radical contamination by evil, so that trust in ourselves and others is still possible.

4. Affective: trust is, among other things, an emotion, and religion offers it periodic nourishment, especially at times of difficulty or crisis.

5. Social/cultural: religion generates public institutions as frameworks within which people can readily interact trustingly.[1]

One might see generating trust as the most important function of religion. The former Archbishop of Canterbury, Rowan Williams, called his recent introduction to Christian belief *Tokens of Trust*. In his view belief is primarily an assertion not about existence, but rather about trust. Setting out the aim of his book, he declares that 'Christian belief is really about knowing who and what to trust. I shall be suggesting that Christianity asks you to trust the God it talks about before it asks you to sign up to a complete system. I hope it may become clear how, once you have taken the step of trust, the actual teaching, the doctrine, flows out of that.'[2]

In this vision of the Christian faith, Jesus occupies a paramount position because he is 'the one who makes God credible, trustworthy'. 'The trustworthiness of God as creator, his selfless attention to what is other than himself, is made concrete in Jesus.'[3] It follows that the church, at its best, is 'a community we can trust'. In its central ritual, holy communion, 'we are guaranteed the effects of Christ's death through receiving his life into our own—in the physical signs of bread and wine and in the faith and trust that goes with this action'.[4]

In different settings, we could say something similar about most religions. Their effect is to ensure the long-term cohesion of the community and to enable its members to face the future with confidence. They provide an interpretative context for trust both in people and in the future by invoking one or more deities, or a supreme principle, which are (a) benevolent, concerned with our fate; (b) strong, in a position to act effectively on our behalf; and (c) moral, concerned with creating harmony and mutual trust between people. The two vectors of trust, in people and in contingencies (fate, the future), thus converge on the deity or on an ultimate sacred principle which guides us. The myths associated with religion provide a narrative framework for trust, while ritual fortifies believers emotionally and strengthens their bonds with fellow believers.[5]

---

[1] I owe this account of religion's functions to a series of lectures by Professor Clemens Sedmak at the Alpbach European Forum, August 2009.

[2] Rowan Williams, *Tokens of Trust: An Introduction to Christian Belief*, Norwich: Canterbury Press, 2007, viii.

[3] Williams, *Tokens*, 65, 93.   [4] Williams, *Tokens*, 105, 115.

[5] Ernst Cassirer, *An Essay on Man*, New Haven: Yale University Press, 1962 (first published 1944), 90–107, provides an account of how myth evolves into religion.

In the individual human being religion probably has its origins in the very earliest interaction between parent and child. As we saw in Chapter 2, Erik Erikson saw the parent–child relationship as the foundation of all later trust/distrust relationships. He considered that religion fixed this trust and carried it over into adult life: 'The parental faith which supports the trust emerging in the newborn has throughout history sought its institutional safeguard (and, on occasion, found its greatest enemy) in organized religion.'[6] Erikson's parenthesis reminds us that the very feature which enables religions to generate trust also creates boundaries, across which equally powerful distrust is projected. This is, as we have seen, a general characteristic of trust. It certainly applies to organized religion.

According to Rowan Williams, belief in God often starts with trusting individual people, 'from a sense that we "believe in", we trust some kinds of people. We have confidence in the way they live; the way they live is a way I want to live . . . Faith has a lot to do with the simple fact that there are trustworthy lives to be seen, that we can see in some believing people a world we'd like to live in.'[7] This might be seen as a circular argument, but that is often true of religious statements: they are persuasive because they are self-reinforcing—for those who have found their way into the circle.

Most religions have authoritative personalities who play a special role in crystallizing the faith, giving it shape, and leading its community activities. On the whole believers will tend to look up to them and to trust them more than ordinary fellow human beings. There is a bewildering variety of such figures. Priests are experts in ritual, and often in the scriptures; they are also expected to exercise pastoral care. Rabbis are experts in the scriptures—more voluminous and diverse in Judaism—and also in the law. Mullahs or muftis are Islamic scholars and teachers, who advise on the correct conduct of religious life. Monks and nuns cultivate the spiritual life intensively, act as a spiritual resource for the community, and often also perform charitable tasks in education, in health care, or in offering hospitality to travellers and pilgrims. A guru acts as a spiritual guide and teacher to a group of disciples, often in a particular doctrine, technique of worship, or set of religious practices which he has developed himself or learnt from a previous guru.[8] All such figures, in their diverse ways, have to—and usually do—attract trust to exercise their functions effectively.

Few people—though there *are* a few, such as hermits and individual Hindu *sannyasins* (renouncers)—can conduct their religious life in solitude. Nearly all believers/worshippers need a community of some kind, with whom they can share their faith and feel a sense of mutual trust. Buddhism is probably the most world-renouncing religion, and the least dependent on social life, but even it has the *sangha*, the community of monks and nuns who pray, meditate, chant, and study,

---

[6] Eric H. Erikson, *Childhood and Society*, New York: Norton, 1993 (first published 1950), 250.

[7] Williams, *Tokens*, 21–2.

[8] Ninian Smart, *Dimensions of the Sacred: An Anatomy of the World's Beliefs*, London: HarperCollins, 1996, 215–35.

drawing closer to a higher world on behalf of the secular community around them.[9] Here mutual trust is involved: the monks depend on the community to feed and clothe them, and in return they provide spiritual guidance and often some pastoral or charitable care, such as conducting funerals. They act as a kind of treasury of spiritual merit and of trust on which the secular world can draw. As one of the Dialogues of the Buddha says, 'The Community of disciples . . . is worthy of offerings, worthy of hospitality, worthy of gifts, worthy of respect, the greatest field of merit for the world.'[10]

For religious communities ritual imparts an extra dimension to trust and exercises it in solidarity with other people.[11] In that way it deepens faith and strengthens the sense of community. But that sense of community usually requires an institutional setting—church, mosque, synagogue, shrine—to give it tangible and durable form. The institution then creates its own boundaries, which can become very rigid when believers are confronted with those of a different faith, or even a different variety of the same faith. Some of the world's most destructive conflicts have revolved around questions of religion. That is part of the paradox of trust.

To illustrate more closely religion's role in generating trust and distrust, it is time to consider some specific religions in their historical and social setting.

GREECE AND ROME

In the ancient world myth and ritual often served to reaffirm community and hierarchy in this world by drawing symbolic reinforcement from what was understood to be a higher sphere of existence, a world of gods and heroic forebears, a sacred world of higher truths and superior power, in which participants could place their trust even when the affairs of this world seemed unreliable and erratic.

In the ancient Greek city-states ceremonies were an affirmation and re-enactment of the two forms of trust—in fate and in other people—through the enactment of sacrifice. In the words of a leading student of Greek religion, ritual 'signals and creates situations of anxiety in order to overcome them. It leads from the primal fear of being abandoned to the establishment of solidarity and the reinforcement of status.'[12]

The archetypical ritual was the sacrifice of an animal to a god, followed by the communal eating of the roast meat. Hunting for food was accompanied by anxiety, as well as by the destruction of the killing, so that the sacrifice of the prey was a creative and collective means of overcoming anxiety and guilt. Furthermore, just as giving a gift strengthens social bonds, so making a sacrifice secured the

---

[9] Buddhism, at least in its Teravada form, has no gods, while its other forms regard them as real but not supreme beings.

[10] Keith Ward, *Religion and Community*, Oxford: Clarendon Press, 2000, 68.

[11] Smart, *Dimensions of the Sacred*, chapter 2.

[12] Walter Burkert, *Greek Religion*, trans. John Raffan, Cambridge, Mass.: Harvard University Press, 1985, 54–5.

community's relationship with its god. Participants would mark the occasion off from profane everyday life by washing, dressing in clean clothes, wearing garlands or other decorations, and going in procession, often to the accompaniment of music. After the solemn sacrifice, the parts of the animal not assigned to the god were roasted and consumed together by the participants, as a reaffirmation of their togetherness. At the same time, hierarchy was also reaffirmed: only the leading citizens were permitted to eat from the heart and liver. The right to participate in religious ceremonies was the paramount marker of a citizen's status.[13]

Gods were held to be powerful beings, whose aid could be invoked in dangerous situations. This might be a sea voyage: a new recruit in the Roman army wrote to his father in Egypt about a stormy crossing of the Mediterranean: 'I thank the lord Sarapis that when I was in danger at sea he straightway saved me.'[14] Romans also called on the gods to ensure the fertility of the crops or to cure an illness. Sick people would spend the night in a hall attached to the temple of Asklepios in Pergamum, in the expectation that the god would appear to them in their dreams, either to heal them forthwith or to prescribe a course of treatment.[15] In this way people could reawaken their confidence in the future and revive the spiritual strength to deal with the mishaps and hazards of life.

The layout of Roman cities reflected the close association of community and religious life. In Rome itself the forum where public business was transacted was usually in front of a temple where a god could be worshipped. When Julius Caesar built a new forum, he placed next to it the temple of Venus Genetrix, whom he claimed as an ancestor. Later Augustus built a larger forum beside the temple of Mars, whom he had invoked in his battles against Caesar's assassins and Mark Antony; around his forum were statues of past Roman heroes and in the centre one of Augustus himself.[16] In this way public business was directly linked to Rome's past and to the gods who had helped the city earlier and were trusted to do so again.

On a smaller scale, in family life, ritual was so arranged as to maintain links with ancestors. Funerals were staged with great solemnity and members of the family would visit the grave site thereafter on certain days and make libations or other offerings. In the home itself, Vesta, the goddess of the hearth, would receive an offering at mealtimes. On attaining manhood, boys would give up their childish toys and clothes to the Lares and Penates, the images of the household gods who guaranteed health, fertility, and prosperity; girls would do the same on getting married. The head of the household would normally preside on such occasions.[17] These practices linked everyday life and the cycle of birth, marriage, and death, with all their hazards, to a higher sphere where their due order would be guaranteed and their meaning would be given an extra dimension. Again, then, the cult heightened trust in fate and the mutual solidarity of family members past and present.

---

[13] Burkert, *Greek Religion*, 56–7.
[14] James B. Rives, *Religion in the Roman Empire*, Oxford: Blackwell, 2007, 93.
[15] Rives, *Religion*, 95–8.   [16] Rives, *Religion*, 110–12.   [17] Rives, *Religion*, 117–22.

TODAY'S MAJOR RELIGIONS

Trust and faith are paramount issues, though variously interpreted, in all religions. Historically speaking, the major religions of today arose in what some historians call the 'axial age', but I will not use that term here, since the relevant period is simply too long: it lasted for more than a millennium—from the sixth century BCE to the seventh century CE. Those religions grew out of social and cultural changes which took place in different periods in different civilizations: they included the creation of more complex political systems in the form of empires or city-states, the creation of written languages and elite literacy, and the emergence of complex and extended market relationships involving money and credit.[18] All of these changes required the evolution of new forms of trust, extended to unfamiliar people and to initially strange, even alien institutions.

Karl Jaspers called four historic figures the 'paradigmatic individuals': Confucius, Buddha, Socrates, and Jesus.[19] I would add Moses and Muhammad.

- What characterized all these individuals is that they operated in a period of crisis, but were able to stand back from that crisis, look more deeply at the roots of human feelings and actions, and reassess their own and others' behaviour.

- They all tended to speak in enigmas or parables, as a device to jolt us out of routine thinking habits and to suggest ways of riding above our superficial thoughts and desires. They all emphasized the importance of striving to empathize with other people, to understand their feelings and their suffering, to feel sympathy and offer compassion. That is, they gave priority to cultivating the qualities which make trust possible.

- They all preached a universal morality of virtue, compassion, self-restraint, and reciprocity, in variants of the idea 'Do as you would be done by'; as in the Ten Commandments or the Sermon on the Mount. That is, they valued the qualities which make us trustworthy.

- None of the six wrote down their ideas, though they all lived in societies where elite literacy was fairly well established: they preferred to communicate by word of mouth.[20] They emphasized the personal rather than the theoretical. Perhaps because of that they each created a collective of devoted followers or companions, who exercised and exemplified forms of mutual trust. Those followers were so impressed by the experience that they later compiled texts

[18] Robert N. Bellah, 'What is "Axial" about the Axial Age?', *Archives européennes de sociologie*, 46 (2005), 69–89.

[19] Karl Jaspers, *The Great Philosophers*, i: *The Foundations: The Paradigmatic Individuals*, trans. Ralph Manheim, London: Rupert Hart-Davis, 1962.

[20] Moses dictated the tablets of the Commandments. Muhammad is supposed to have transcribed the words of God in the Koran, though recent scholars throw doubt on this. Hence they may be partial exceptions.

based on what they had heard from their leader, or what had been passed down to them.

- They confronted suffering and especially death directly—the only future event which is a certainty, and which causes all human beings great anxiety, because we can have no secure knowledge of what follows. Jesus and Socrates did so by accepting a death they could have avoided. They believed that overcoming the fear of death and suffering is a question of our relationship to the world, the radical questioning of our routine knowledge of it, and a radical reordering of our relationships with other people.[21]

- They all sensed the nearness of God or of some higher reality, some higher principle governing the universe in general and human society in particular; their aim was to plug human beings into the enabling energy network generated by that higher reality, and thus to facilitate the exercise of trust.

- Directly or indirectly all of them except Socrates founded religions which are still very widespread centuries, even millennia, later. (And one might argue that Socrates, by cultivating systematic scepticism, laid the foundations for science, one of the other great symbolic systems that enable us to exercise trust, especially in relation to contingencies and the natural world.[22])

The texts which have grown out of the heritage of those founders contain much that concerns trust—in other people, in contingencies and in a deity or ultimate principle. Writing of the 'religions of the book', Judaism, Christianity, and Islam, the theologian Hans Küng asserts that belief in God 'is not irrational . . . but a highly reasonable trust. . . . For Jews and Christians, as for Muslims, faith is an unconditional entrusting and reliance of the whole person on God . . . an act of knowing, willing and feeling. It is an attitude—simple or very complicated—which is personal, lived out and trusting.'[23]

THE JEWISH–CHRISTIAN TRADITION

The Jewish–Christian tradition, from which the Lord's Prayer comes, abounds in texts expressing trust. In the Psalms they are sometimes placed in a military context. 'The Lord is my rock, and my fortress, and my deliverer; my God, my strength, in whom I trust; my buckler and the horn of my salvation, and my high tower. I will call upon the Lord, who is worthy to be praised: so shall I be saved from mine enemies' (Psalm 18: 2–3, Authorized Version).

---

[21] This probably does not apply to Confucius, who was focused almost entirely on this world.
[22] Science has partly taken over what Malinowski considered the other major function of religion, gaining mastery over the forces of nature. (Bronislaw Malinowski, *The Foundation of Faith and Morals*, London: Oxford University Press, 1936, 29–30.)
[23] Hans Küng, *Islam: Past, Present and Future*, trans. John Bowden, Oxford: One World, 2007, 89–90.

In the Jewish scriptures the Hebrew word translated as 'trust' (the root *bth*) has the more limited sense of 'feeling secure'. Isaiah added to it the concept of security through the relationship with God, which was one of mutual trust and faithfulness. In this sense, it found expression for the Israelites through their nation and its covenant with God; when this faith seemed to falter or be diverted, the prophets tried to renew it, but still as a decision of the nation rather than of the individual.[24]

In the Christian scriptures Jesus's sayings often use the word 'believe' in a sense very close to 'trust'. Belief, he teaches, overcomes death. 'Verily, verily, I say unto you, he that believeth on me shall have everlasting life.' Such belief, he suggests, is possible only in a universe created by a loving God: 'For God so loved the world that he gave his only begotten Son, that whosoever believeth in him should not perish, but have everlasting life' (John 6: 47; 3: 16).

In the epistles of Paul faith and trust are at the centre of the message: they are what enable human beings to overcome the greatest fear of all, that of death. 'But we had the sentence of death in ourselves, that we should not trust in ourselves, but in God which raiseth the dead: Who delivered us from so great a death, and doth deliver: in whom we trust that he will yet deliver us' (2 Corinthians 1: 9–10). As can be seen from these quotations from the Judeo-Christian tradition (at least as they are translated in the Authorized Version of the Bible), in the religious context, the word 'trust' stands very close to two other concepts, 'faith' and 'belief'. All three words imply placing one's confidence in a being or a principle whose existence is not absolutely certain—otherwise one would use the word 'knowledge'. There are shades of difference between the three words, but they exist in the same semantic field and overlap with one another.

In classical Greek *pistis* meant faith in the sense of individual trust in things which make us safe (for example weapons or a fortress) or in human beings, for example confidence in or reliance on someone to whom one is bound by an oath or covenant. It was not used for faith in a deity, but might denote an attitude to an oracle. In Hellenistic times, however, usage broadened: *pistis* was used, for example by Plotinus, to denote belief in entities that could not be perceived, and hence in God, in divine providence, and in the immortality of the soul.[25] This is also the sense in which it is used in the New Testament, especially by Paul, for whom it became the predominant designation of the relationship of human beings to God and to Jesus resurrected. 'Now faith is the assurance of things hoped for, the conviction of things not seen' (Hebrews 11: 1). *Pistis* now became an existential individual decision. In Bultmann's words, it implied 'acceptance of the Christian kerygma and consequently of the saving faith which recognises and appropriates God's work of salvation brought about by Christ', and it combined 'elements of obedience, trust, hope and loyalty'.[26]

---

[24] Rudolf Bultmann and Arthur Weiser, *Faith (Bible Key Words)*, trans. Dorothea Barton, London: Adam & Charles Black, 1961, 19–22, 44–5.

[25] Bultmann, *Faith*, 39–42.   [26] Bultmann, *Faith*, 68–9.

ISLAM

Muhammad's revelation, as recorded in the Koran, was also concerned with broadening and securing the basis of mutual trust. In the land of the Beduin Arabs—camel-borne desert nomads—inter-tribal warfare was endemic, fuelled by a tribal morality of birth hierarchy, pride, honour, and righting wrongs by means of vengeance. Each tribe had its own chief, its own assembly, and its own gods, intended to generate and sustain mutual trust within the tribe. Their feuding impeded the growing trade which passed through and enriched the Arab world, since trade depends on a wider basis for mutual trust.

Muhammad came from the Quraysh tribe, guardians of the Kaaba in Mecca, where shrines of all the tribal gods were kept. He was himself a merchant, hence anxious to find ways of overcoming tribal divisions. He preached a morality which transcended that of the tribes and rendered vengeance unnecessary, a morality of submission, not to tribal gods, but to the supreme God whom Arabs call Allah. Muhammad rejected as idolatrous the ritual sacrifices which were part of the tribal religions. Allah's moral law demanded humility, generosity, self-restraint, compassion, forgiveness, and recognition of equal humanity in all human beings (including men and women, free people and slaves). Loyalty to the tribe was replaced by the individual's relationship to God, who keeps account of his or her deeds and will in the end pronounce judgement over him or her. Islam also aimed at ethical commerce: it attributed great importance to observing contracts punctiliously. Feuding was strictly forbidden: disputes were to be brought before Islamic judges and settled according to Islamic law.[27]

Muhammad was rejected by most of the Quraysh tribe, since his message threatened to render their guardianship of the tribal shrines superfluous. The people of Medina, however, heard his message and invited him to come to their town, to settle destructive disputes between their two principal tribes. Muhammad succeeded in doing that, and thereby gained many converts to Islam. His first success, then, was to broaden the radius of trust within one city, which then became a base for further proselytization.[28]

According to the Koran, God is one and unique. There are no other gods but him, and trust in him must therefore be total: 'Allah—there is no god but Him. In

---

[27] Küng, *Islam*,153–7; Marshall S. G. Hodgson, *The Venture of Islam: Conscience and History in a World Civilization*, University of Chicago Press, 1974, vol. i, book 1, chapter 2.

[28] Hodgson, *Venture*, vol. i, book 1, chapter 2; Hugh Kennedy, *The Prophet and the Age of the Caliphates: The Islamic Near East from the Sixth to the Eleventh Century*, London: Longman, 1986, 158–82. This, at least, is the standard version, found in long accepted Muslim and Arabic sources. In recent decades, however, scholars have pointed out that those sources mostly date from a century or more after Muhammad's life, and that very little of what they tell us is corroborated by contemporary non-Arabic sources. See, for example, Patricia Crone and Michael Cook, *Hagarism: The Making of the Islamic World*, Cambridge University Press, 1977. Kennedy, *Prophet*, 352–63, argues cogently for the traditional account. Whichever approach one accepts, the rapid broadening of solidarity among Arab tribes is undoubted, and Muhammad's message and his leadership explain much of it.

Allah let the faithful put their trust.'[29] The Koran reveals the truth concerning him, and therefore supersedes all previous theological dispute: 'This Koran declares to the Israelites most of that concerning which they disagree. It is a guide and a blessing to true believers. Your Lord will rightly judge them. He is the Mighty One, the All-Knowing. Therefore put your trust in Allah, for the undoubted truth is on your side.'[30]

His attributes include justice, generosity, compassion, and mercy. He is omnipotent and omniscient, and his universe is perfect. 'Allah ... is the sovereign Lord, the Holy One, the Giver of Peace, the Keeper of Faith; The Guardian, the Mighty One, the All-powerful, the Most High!'[31] Moreover, each chapter of the Koran begins with the words 'In the Name of Allah, the Compassionate, the Merciful'. The Muslim faces the future with confidence because of his faith in these attributes. That faith requires him to practise submission (Islam) to God, learn to master the evil in his own nature, and conform to the moral principles and law of Islam. To help him, he is or becomes part of the community of the faithful: 'The true believers, both men and women, are friends to each other. They enjoin what is just and forbid what is evil.'[32]

Preserving the integrity of this community and spreading the faith are both vital. For that purpose *jihad* is prescribed: zeal in the faith, both as struggle against one's own evil nature, and as physical struggle against enemies of the faith, who might be non-Muslim tyrannical rulers or non-Muslim neighbours who by definition belonged to the 'realm of chaos'. 'The wrongdoers are patrons to each other; but the righteous have Allah Himself for their patron.' 'Be they men or women, the hypocrites are all alike. They enjoin what is evil, forbid what is just, and tighten their purse strings ... Allah has promised the hypocrites, both men and women, and the unbelievers, the fire of Hell. They shall abide in it for ever: a sufficient recompense. The curse of Allah is upon them; theirs shall be a lasting torment.'[33] Believers should reject them utterly, indeed make war against them: 'Believers, do not make friends with those who are enemies of Mine and yours.' 'Prophet, make war on the unbelievers and hypocrites, and deal rigorously with them.'[34]

Muhammad's message was in principle to apply to all humanity. In practice, especially during its early centuries, it was borne by Arab armies, and its spread by conquest was seen as not only legitimate, but obligatory. Because Islam was from the outset associated with extensive territorial conquest and hence empire, major splits and heresies cropped up much sooner even than in Christianity. Within thirty years of Muhammad's death (632) Islam was split between the 'party of Ali', or Shi'ites, who believed that only the Prophet's direct descendants could qualify for the office of *imam* (leader of the community), and the Sunnis, who held

---

[29] *The Koran*, trans. with notes by N. J. Dawood, London: Penguin Books, 4th edition, 1974, 90 (Arabic chapter and verse 64: 13).

[30] *Koran*, 87 (27: 75).   [31] *Koran*, 270–1 (59: 23).   [32] *Koran*, 328 (9: 71).

[33] *Koran*, 131 (45: 19), 327 (9: 67–8); for the history of the concept, see Michael Bonner, *Jihad in Islamic History: Doctrines and Practice*, Princeton University Press, 2006.

[34] *Koran*, 266 (60: 1); 328 (9: 73).

that the succession should be determined by the community of believers.[35] That division still exists and still promotes violent conflict. Moreover, the spread of peace by means of war has remained a paradox and a problem, as we shall see below under 'Peace of God' and 'The Crusades'. The paradox and problem are present in all universalist religions, but are especially pronounced in Islam.[36] It is the very human problem of the community learning to put total trust in its own members, and doing so by distrusting all outsiders.

CHINA

The teaching of Confucius was especially concerned with the way human beings behave and act in a social and political setting. He considered the cardinal virtue to be *zhen*, which has been variously translated as benevolence, love, altruism, kindness, charity, compassion, or magnanimity. Its root meaning is 'humaneness', and its pictogram consists of the elements 'human being + two', which implies that it denotes a righteous way for a human being to deal with the 'other'. When asked about it, Confucius replied, 'When you are away from home, behave as if receiving an important guest.' This implies reverence and courtesy combined with consideration. He adds 'Do not do to others what you would not like yourself.' The last sentence presents again, at least in a negative form, the Golden Rule which serves as a basis for trust between human beings, including those who do not know each other. This aspect of *zhen* is rendered by the word *shu*, which can be translated as 'reciprocity'.[37]

Between the above two sentences of Confucius' I have omitted one, which is equally important, but leads into another dimension of his thought: 'Employ the people as if you were officiating at a great sacrifice.' More than any other of the great religious leaders, Confucius was a political thinker, concerned to create in society the conditions which would facilitate mutual trust, harmony, and peace. His ideal was a just ruler, bearing the Mandate of Heaven and motivated by *zhen*. Such a ruler was capable of permeating the whole society with *zhen*: 'If there existed a true king, after a generation *zhen* would certainly prevail.'[38]

When asked what was needful for good government, he replied, 'Sufficient food, sufficient weapons, and the confidence of the people.' When asked which could if necessary be dispensed with, he replied, 'Weapons'. Then '"Suppose you were forced to dispense with one of the two which were left, which would you forgo?" The Master said "Food. For from of old death has been the lot of all men, but a people that no longer trusts its rulers is lost indeed."'[39] The paramount task of rulers, then, in Confucius' opinion was to keep the trust of the population.

---

[35] Küng, *Islam*, 186–7.   [36] Hodgson, *Venture*, i, book 1, 186.
[37] Raymond Dawson, *Confucius*, Oxford University Press, 1981, 37–41; the quotation is from the *Analects*, 12.2, trans. Arthur Waley, London: Allen & Unwin, 1938.
[38] *Analects*, 13.12, as translated by Dawson, *Confucius*, 41.   [39] *Analects*, 12.7.

Machiavelli, incidentally, radically disagreed. A prince should if possible, he asserted, be both loved and feared, but if both were not possible, then he should choose to be feared rather than loved. 'Love is held together by a chain of obligation which, since men are wretched creatures, is broken on every occasion in which their own interests are concerned; but fear is sustained by a dread of punishment which will never abandon you.'[40]

Machiavelli wanted to eliminate religion from politics and establish a separate morality for the latter, an approach opposite to that of Confucius, who believed political order and social harmony went along with harmony in the universe as a whole. Maintaining correct ritual was essential to preserving order both in the polity and in the universe. Hsün Tzu, a later follower of Confucius, declared that 'Through rites Heaven and Earth join in the harmony, the sun and moon shine, the four seasons proceed in order, the stars and constellations march, the rivers flow and all things flourish, men's likes and dislikes are regulated and their joys and hates made appropriate.'[41] To assist in this process, ritual was usually accompanied by dance, mime, singing to music, which was not only inherently enjoyable, but also ordered time and sound in such a way as to attach human beings to the cosmic order, the Tao.

Li, the word for ritual, originally meant sacrifice to gods or spirits, but later came to be used in purely secular ceremonial settings. It continued, however, to be associated with the idea of reciprocal service or gifts. So there is here an element of reciprocity and also one of stable and traditional behaviour, both of which are important, as we have seen, for generating trust. Ritual was perhaps especially indispensable in a society like China's whose laws were made by human beings rather than dictated by a supernatural power, if codes of behaviour were to be well known, repeated, and reliable. It was not just a matter of actions and words, but also of appropriate internalized attitudes, without which ritual would become mere vapid habit; those attitudes could then be carried over into family and social life, as well as contribute to political stability. 'To subdue oneself and return to ritual is humane. If for one day a ruler could subdue himself and return to ritual, then all under Heaven would respond to the *zhen* in him.'[42]

Chün-tsu, the term for a gentleman, originally meant 'son of a ruler' and so carried a connotation of high social status. Yet Confucius also applied it to any man of good morals, regardless of status. 'He should take loyalty and good faith as his first principles, and have no friends who are not up to his own standard. If he commits a fault, he should not shrink from mending his ways.'[43] The mark of such a gentleman is that he is someone who can be trusted. Confucius did not believe this was true of merchants, whom he consigned to the lowest rank of his social hierarchy, on the grounds that they pursued profit and material welfare.

Not everyone in China agreed with Confucius. The Legalists, like Machiavelli, thought that what mattered in the state was laws and obedience to them, motivated

---

[40] Niccolò Machiavelli, *The Prince*, Oxford University Press, 1984, 56.
[41] Dawson, *Confucius*, 31–2.   [42] *Analects*, 12.1, as translated by Dawson, *Confucius*, 30.
[43] *Analects*, 1.8, as translated by Dawson, *Confucius*, 54–5.

by fear of punishment—the opposite to Confucius' priority of cultivating moral identity and behaviour. Followers of Confucius rejected these contentions on the grounds that (i) laws could never provide for all possible contingencies, so that it was better to leave judgement to persons of superior moral insight; (ii) laws operated through fear of punishment and not through improving moral character. In the event, the Chinese Empire could not be ruled without law and its enforcement, but on the other hand, law itself took on a certain Confucian moral colouring.[44] Law and ritual, it seemed, were necessary complements to each other if generalized social trust was to be cultivated.

CHRISTENDOM

Religions are not just symbolic systems: they usually form their own institutions, to ensure the transmission of those systems, and to secure the stability and normative coherence within which trust can be fostered. Much of the history of all religions, then, concerns their struggles to reach agreement about the way those institutions should be created and organized. This was true above all of the monotheist and would-be universalist religions, especially when connected with empire, since for political reasons they had to aim at unanimity on matters of ritual, doctrine, and institution.

Sure enough, Diarmaid MacCulloch calls the relevant chapter of his *A History of Christianity* 'Boundaries defined', and further describes the process as 'a series of exclusions and narrowing of options'.[45] It is a story of putting together a regular structure for the church, and of defining the beliefs and practices which had to be accepted by anyone who wanted to participate in the church's defining ritual, the eucharist. The eucharist was intended to be an intense experience and to imbue congregation members with a stronger sense of mutual trust and of being joined spiritually and physically with the triune deity. But attaining that sense of spiritual union entailed imposing firm limits on what Christians could profess and what they could do.[46]

Some of these boundary markers are already apparent in the epistles of Paul, the earliest Christian documents. Christians had to define their religion as distinct from the Jewish one, from which they were becoming more and more aloof but with which they nevertheless wished to maintain scriptural ties. They also had to demarcate themselves from the Roman official cult, which hovered in the background to their lives and sporadically persecuted them. They set up their individual congregations, centred on a building modelled on the Jewish synagogue, but named after the Greek *ecclesia*, which had previously symbolized the collective

[44] Dawson, *Confucius*, 72–3; Michael Loewe, *The Pride that was China*, London: Sidgwick & Jackson, 1990, 153–5.

[45] Diarmaid MacCulloch, *A History of Christianity*, London: Allen Lane, 2009, chapter 4.

[46] Charles Freeman, *A New History of Early Christianity*, New Haven: Yale University Press, 2009, especially chapters 12–14.

identity of the Greek city-state. In a sense what they were doing was radicalizing and spiritualizing the Greek and Roman concept of citizenship—membership of the civic community provided protection and a sense of togetherness, both essential to mutual confidence. To stabilize and service their congregations they created a threefold ministry of bishop, priest, and deacon, with a programme of training and initiation to validate each. Preserving these institutions as a focus of trust in a generally hostile world became an absolute priority for Christian believers.[47]

Christian congregations in the Roman Empire attracted outsiders and held their loyalty by other features as well. One was that they systematically looked after their poor, sick, and old people: that was one of the purposes of having well-defined and durable structures. They also ensured that all their members had a decent burial—a cardinal concern for poorer people and those without relatives.[48] 'Martyrs' offered a quite different confirmation of the faith: the word means 'witness'. The public suffering and humiliation of those who refused to sacrifice to the Roman gods offered the strongest possible demonstration of how powerful their faith was—something to steel the loyalty of Christians and attract the admiration of non-Christians, as well as perhaps to awaken their revulsion at the Roman authorities who imposed such harsh penalties. At any rate, the relics of martyrs became sacred objects, and the stories of their lives sacred texts—symbolic affirmations of the identity, solidarity, and mutual trust of Christians.[49]

When Christianity became the official religion of the Roman Empire, the institutional problems in some ways got worse. The concept of a man being God (not just a god) provided the strongest possible link between the human and divine and thus tended to fortify the self-confidence of human beings. But on the other hand, it was not obvious what it meant. The complex idea inevitably created doctrinal tangles, especially unacceptable in a religious organization which set such store by unanimity.[50] What is remarkable is not that the church went through so many doctrinal splits and quarrels, but that its members attributed such importance to settling them, come what may. It seemed supremely important to them to create an institution in which ritual, symbolism, and doctrine were unanimously agreed, so that believers could place absolute trust in them.

BYZANTIUM AND RUSSIA

Christianity could be effective in steeling the courage of the faithful at times of crisis and providing a focus to fortify the community's confidence in the future. This was exemplified in seventh-century Constantinople: in 626 combined forces of Avar, Slav, and Persian troops besieged the city by land and sea, destroying its aqueduct to deprive it of water. The Emperor Herakleios and the

---

[47] MacCulloch, *History*, chapter 4. [48] MacCulloch, *History*, 160.
[49] Gillian Clark, *Christianity and Roman Society*, Cambridge University Press, 2004, chapter 3.
[50] Freeman, *New History*, chapters 22–4.

main army were far away, fighting the Persians on another frontier. At this desperate juncture, the Patriarch led a huge procession, consisting of most of the city's population, round the walls, bearing icons of Christ and singing hymns calling on the Mother of God for help. When the Avars attacked the walls, defenders reported seeing a woman leading the defence; they identified her as the Virgin Mary. The name Theotokoupolis, city of the Mother of God, already sometimes applied to Constantinople, gained new significance and fortified citizens' trust in their divine protector.

Mary's protection was later also credited with saving the city during the Arab attacks of 717–18 and that of the Rus warriors in 860. Visions were reported in the city's Blacharnae church, in which the dome opened up and Mary descended to pray at the altar for protection of the people. When she had finished, she spread her veil over the church. An icon was placed in the church to commemorate this vision of the Protective Veil, and on 1 October every year an all-night vigil was held to celebrate it. For similar reasons chapels or shrines with holy images would be built in fortifications, or at bridges and watermills, to provide security against attack, to ensure a safe journey, or a continuing supply of water.[51]

Similarly, in Rus in 1395, when the army of the Chingisid warlord Timur threatened Moscow, Metropolitan Kiprian (who had been ordained in Constantinople) brought the miracle-working icon *Mother of God of Vladimir* to the city to 'save the land of Rus'. When Timur desisted from pressing his offensive, it was widely rumoured that the Mother of God had appeared to him in a dream, commanding him to retreat. The icon was credited with this miracle, and a great reception (*sretenie*) was held for it in Moscow, before it was placed in the Cathedral of the Dormition in the Kremlin.[52] The site of the reception ceremony was marked by a monastery (*sretenskii monastyr'*), and the event celebrated annually on 26 August. The icon was later brought out on at least two other occasions, in 1480 and 1521, when Moscow was threatened by Tatar armies.[53] The most famous church in Moscow, usually known as St Basil's, is actually called the Pokrov church, that is the church of the Protective Veil, and it contains an icon of the veil of Constantinople, intended to strengthen the confidence of Muscovites that God was on their side and would protect them.[54]

These were occasional mass public displays of trust directed through religious symbols which offered protection and confidence at times of particular crisis. By contrast, private religious observance was routine, to rekindle confidence despite the recurrent uncertainties and crises of individual and family life. The seventh-century

---

[51] Judith Herrin, *Byzantium: The Surprising Life of a Medieval Empire*, London: Allen Lane, 2007, 15–16; Sharon E. J. Gerstel and Alice-Mary Talbot, 'The Culture of Lay Piety in Medieval Byzantium, 1054–1453', in Michael Angold (ed), *The Cambridge History of Christianity*, v: *Eastern Christianity*, Cambridge University Press, 2006, 81–3.

[52] *Polnoe sobranie russkikh letopisei*, 11 (1965), 58–61, quoted in Robert O. Crummey, *The Formation of Muscovy, 1304–1613*, London: Longman, 1987, 64.

[53] Lindsey Hughes, 'Art and Liturgy in Russia: Rublev and his Successors', in Angold (ed), *Cambridge History*, 286–7.

[54] Robin Milner-Gulland, *The Russians*, Oxford: Blackwell, 1997, 212–17.

priest Eustathios of Thrace told in a sermon the story of a man who commissioned an icon of St Michael Archangel. When he felt he was about to die, he took his wife's hand and placed it on the icon, on the archangel's hand, and said: 'Oh Archangel Michael . . . behold, in thy hands I place my wife Euphemia as a deposit, so that thou mayst watch over her.' After his death Euphemia kept a lamp lit before the icon and prayed before it three times a day, entreating Michael to help her and protect her from the Devil. After her own death, her mourners had the icon placed over her face as a pledge of continuing protection.[55]

In such ways icons were used to bolster faith and promote trust in superior powers at times of crisis and grief. They probably originated in the Roman *lares*. (Indeed the iconoclasts who were powerful in the eighth and ninth centuries regarded the veneration of icons as pagan idolatry.) Icons were believed to connect the believer with the holy person depicted on them, so that prayers would reach them and their protection and intercession could be entreated. Icons might hang in the ordinary home or in chapels, churches, and shrines, which would then be visited by believers anxious to be saved from some impending misfortune (death or disease) or seeking help in some important enterprise (giving birth or setting up a business).[56]

Both in Byzantium and later in Russia, there were strong traditions of the public veneration of wonder-working icons as an aid to confidence amid life's difficulties. These might appear in a dream, or in a vision seen by a believer in a wood or field, or by a river bank. In nineteenth-century Russia, for example, a merchant's wife who had been chronically ill for some ten years dreamt that she should pray before a certain icon of the Mother of God. When she did so, she heard Mary's voice urging her to have the icon painted. When she had accomplished that task, she suddenly felt much better. She reported the miracle to the parish priest and donated the icon to the church, so that other people could benefit from its wonder-working powers. The ending of the story illustrates the tension between individual and institutional trust: the church authorities remained sceptical about the alleged miracle, removed the icon, demoted the priest, and transferred him elsewhere.[57] Symbols can easily provoke intense personal trust which may conflict with trust in the institution that claims the function of validating them and thus setting the boundaries of belief. Once validated, such icons could be the proud possessions of a parish, become part of the congregation's history and attract pilgrims, or be carried in procession to other churches. Believers would have their own small copies made, which they could carry around with them to ward off misfortune. These icons, then, helped to give believers a sense of togetherness with other believers, of trust in God and confidence in the future.[58]

---

[55] Herrin, *Byzantium*, 98.   [56] Gerstel and Talbot, 'Culture of Lay Piety', 88–9.

[57] Vera Shevzov, 'Miracle-Working Icons, Laity and Authority in the Russian Orthodox Church, 1861–1917', *Russian Review*, 58 (1999), 26–48.

[58] Chris Chulos, 'Russian Piety and Culture from Peter the Great to 1917', in Angold (ed), *Cambridge History*, 348–70.

MEDIEVAL WESTERN CHRISTIANITY

According to the sociologist Adam Seligman, 'risk' is a concept that did not enter our mental repertoire till the seventeenth century. The *Oxford English Dictionary* confirms this. All the same, the medieval European world contained in abundance what we would call risks. Indeed they were more obvious. Famine, disease, fires, brigandage, and petty (or even not so petty) warfare were far more familiar to medieval (and earlier) people than they are to us today, at least in the developed world. Modern science and medicine, modern police forces, and modern economies, on the whole, work to shield us from many risks, and offer remedies when the worst occurs. Medieval people were more vulnerable. As Boccaccio wrote of the appearance of the Black Death in Florence in 1433, 'All human wisdom was unable to avert the onset of the terrible disease. The city had been cleansed and sick folk kept outside the walls . . . But nonetheless, towards the beginning of spring, the first appalling symptoms of the plague began to appear . . . [setting] at naught the skill of the physicians and the virtues of their science.'[59]

Trust was crucial, then, in the middle ages at least as much as in the modern world. Some medieval thinkers were well aware of this, and wrote of the import- ance of *fides* or *fidelitas*, which might be translated as 'trust' and 'trustworthiness' respectively. They deemed it essential for any kind of social life. Archbishop Baldwin of Canterbury (died 1190) wrote in his *Liber de commendatione fidei* that *fides* was necessary between husband and wife, friend and friend, master and vassal, emperor and knight, since without it there could be no stable household, city, or realm. He saw the Christian faith as a guarantor of this stability, and set *fides* in a conceptual framework whose key terms were *dilectio* (love) and *pax* (peace).[60] Thomas Aquinas equated *fides* with enduring trust in another person and loyalty to him or her, without which normal life was impossible to a human being as *animal sociale*.[61] Simon of Tournai (died 1201) asserted that *fides* was important for our understanding of the world. He placed it between *scientia* (knowledge) and *opinio* (opinion): it was the apprehension of what was *probably* true. Since human cognition is inherently obscured by sin, we have to act on probabilities, which *fides* enables us to do.[62] Within a completely different world view (Simon was mainly concerned with salvation), his outlook is close to that of Luhmann in the late twentieth century.

Medieval people were not immobile, as historians of the modern world some- times seem to assume. Traders moved about, especially long-distance ones, and so did pilgrims, as well as anyone engaged in warfare. Even those who were relatively

---

[59] From the introduction to the *Decameron*, quoted in Jonathan Sumption, *Pilgrimage: An Image of Medieval Religion*, London: Faber & Faber, 1975, 73.

[60] Petra Schulte, 'Einleitung', in Petra Schulte, Marco Mostert, and Irene van Rouswoude (eds), *Strategies of Writing: Studies on Text and Trust in the Middle Ages*, Turnhout: Brepols, 2008, 2–4.

[61] Schulte, 'Einleitung', 4–5.

[62] J. Wirth, 'La Naissance du concept de croyance (11–17 siècles)', *Bibliothèque d'Humanisme et Renaissance*, 45 (1983), 16–18.

fixed depended on various forms of patronage and protection, on the reliability of money, on the validity of charters defining their status, and on the loyalty of family, neighbours, and friends, none of which could be taken for granted at all times. Far from it. The semantic field surrounding the concepts of trust, faith, and loyalty was, then, at least as crucial in the middle ages as it is now. At that time, though, the concepts and practices of trust were configured in very different ways from those to which we have become accustomed. They were channelled far more through religious belief and religious institutions. Admittedly, most of what we know about the belief system of medieval people originates with the literate, who were not typical, so on that subject it is difficult to generalize. But it is clear that the institutions of the Christian church were crucial in giving people what sense of security they managed to achieve.

First of all there was the parish, which mobilized trust and underpinned mutual solidarity in a variety of forms. When it worked well, the parish arranged care for the poor, the sick, widows, and orphans. The church building provided villagers with a sanctuary in case of armed attack, a cemetery to keep them in touch with their deceased forebears, and a focus for community life, while the church's teaching inculcated an ideology which condemned selfish behaviour and indiscriminate violence. In some places the decision to build a church was the first communal event, and in many places its existence was taken as proof of the existence of an effective community, to be recognized at law and for some purposes dealt with as a single unit. The church bell would be tolled to call village meetings, which would usually be held inside the church building. Upkeep of the church and the remuneration of a priest imposed obligations that had to be collective.

The parish also delineated the moral community and joined it to a higher world, of angels, saints, and the triune God, through regular mass and communal prayers, and at least once a year through confession and the eucharist. Through baptism a child would be admitted to this community. The priest could bar a parishioner from the eucharist if he or she was unreconciled with a neighbour, and for persistent violators of the peace the church had the ultimate penalty of excommunication, which was a terrible punishment, since it excluded a person not only from the liturgy, but in practice from the community as well.[63]

The church also asserted its influence over what might be called the basic unit of trust, the family, by taking charge of marriage, defining it as a sacrament, and providing a structured set of rituals to indicate that it had taken place. From 1215 canon law required that banns had to be read in the parish church. Then, after a suitable interval, the vital stage of marriage, the wedding ceremony, would usually also take place in the parish church, with the exchange of promises and rings held in front of witnesses and blessed by the priest. Religious symbolism was endowing marriage with ever greater significance, as a microcosmic counterpart to celestial harmony. Sermons increasingly compared the marriage of man and woman to the

---

[63] Joseph H. Lynch, *The Medieval Church: A Brief History*, London: Longman, 1992, 126–9; Léopold Génicot, *Rural Communities in the Medieval West*, Baltimore: Johns Hopkins Press, 1990, 91, 105–7, chapter 4.

union of Christ and his church; they emphasized that Christ himself had blessed the wedding at Cana, and had spoken of man and wife as 'one flesh'. In this vision marriage was both a physical and a spiritual union of one man and one woman, not fully valid until consummated; it was freely chosen by the couple, and it was indissoluble. This interpretation of marriage became widely accepted in society as well as inside the church, even when it ran counter to male concupiscence or to kinship inheritance strategies—a striking example of the power of trust-generating symbolic systems when they are sponsored by an authoritative institution and embodied in social practice.[64]

Monasteries also played a strategic role in facilitating and maintaining medieval trust structures. They acted as forums for the exchange of both spiritual and physical goods. They cleared forests and cultivated land, growing produce for their own and charitable purposes. In return for this they received the protection of secular lords—who unlike them did have armed men at their command—and numerous gifts and endowments, including land and serfs.

By modelling a cosmos presided over by a benevolent God, monasteries helped people to feel confidence in themselves and their communities, and also to face stoically and even with optimism whatever fate held in store for them. Monasteries played humanity's part in ensuring God's grace by conducting the liturgy according to approved patterns in a daily and yearly cycle, offering to God what hard-working parishioners had not the time or resources to offer and thus guaranteeing His continued benevolence. They prayed for the souls of both the living and the dead, and according to some conceptions they accumulated beneficial stores of God's grace for distribution to those less able to earn it for themselves. They preserved the relics of saints, who interceded for the living in a higher realm, and also artefacts of culture and learning, both religious and secular. They offered shelter and food to pilgrims and travellers. They provided a refuge for those unable to look after themselves: crippled veteran soldiers, lepers, orphans, the destitute, sick, old, and infirm. Some elderly people would enter monasteries as they would today an old people's home; they made gifts as they did so, in approximate exchange for the services they hoped to receive and for prayers to be said for them in the afterlife. In that way they could face old age, death, and whatever lay beyond it with greater confidence.[65]

In general, monasteries were both the beneficiaries and the benefactors of a physical and spiritual 'gift economy'. One might see them as distributors of trust, rather as banks are distributors of money (which is actually trust in a different guise). When they functioned well, they enabled people to trust in the divine and in other members of society; they also provided reassurance, indeed a form of social insurance, in the face of possible future disasters.[66]

---

[64] Christopher N. L. Brooke, *The Medieval Idea of Marriage*, Oxford University Press, 1989; David d'Avray, *Medieval Marriage: Symbolism and Society*, Oxford University Press, 2005.

[65] Gerstel and Talbot, 'Culture of Lay Piety', 97–9; C. H. Lawrence, *Medieval Monasticism: Forms of Religious Life in Western Europe in the Middle Ages*, 2nd edition, London: Longman, 1989.

[66] Joseph H. Lynch, *The Medieval Church: A Brief History*, London: Longman, 1992, 129–32 and chapter 13; Giles Constable, 'Religious Communities, 1024–1215', in *New Cambridge Medieval*

In the search for security God was remote and for most people awesome. They needed less-forbidding figures who could intercede for them and in whom they could place their trust. That role was played by the saints and by the Virgin Mary, who combined two otherwise incompatible female virtues, virginity and mother-hood. Saints were people who had aroused admiration and reverence by their holy way of life. Those who had witnessed their deeds continued to look to them for help after their death, and tales of their achievements spread far and wide, especially if they had performed miracles, which suggested an especially close relationship with the divine power governing the world.

The tomb or relics of a saint acted like a magnet for suffering people, offering them at least a simulacrum of direct contact with him or her. Sick people would come with illnesses which had not responded to medical treatment. They trusted saints to do better than physicians, since it was widely believed that illness had spiritual causes, that it represented an *incursio diaboli*, an invasion of the body by the devil. Sufferers would drink water or wine in which the relic of a saint had been dipped. At Canterbury cathedral, for example, a cistern contained water in which blood scraped from the floor after Thomas à Becket's murder was reportedly diluted; the monks of Christ Church priory would prepare phials of this distasteful liquid to be imbibed by the sick.[67]

The road from London to Canterbury, celebrated by Chaucer, regularly had bands of pilgrims making for the tomb of St Thomas. It was usual to walk, since the physical effort involved was a first stage in the penance which restored spiritual and bodily health. As they approached Canterbury pilgrims would per-haps fast and make confession. When they reached the tomb they would remove their shoes, kneel, and pray, then present an offering, perhaps a candle or perhaps money. Some of them then lay down to wait for a miraculous cure, sleeping in the cathedral and begging for food. Others would attend a mass and then leave for home, expecting to be healed on the way or even after arrival.[68] They were partici-pating in a demanding ritual supposed to plug them into cosmic networks of trust.

Stories of miracles attracted intense interest, since they implied benevolent divine intervention in the affairs of this world. When miracles were rumoured at the monastery of St Trond, near Liège, it was overwhelmed by pilgrims, who 'filled the roads for half a mile around. Across the fields and meadows came such a crowd of pilgrims, being nobles, freemen and peasants of both sexes, that they had to be put up in tents, which made them look like a besieging army.... And offerings beyond belief piled up on the altar. Herds of animals were offered every day.... Linen, wax, bread, and cheese arrived, and above all purses full of money.' People of all social origins were seeking a reassurance which they could not find in their

History (henceforth *NCMH*), vol. iv, part 1, 335–67; Ilana Friedrich Silber, *Virtuosity, Charisma and Social Order: A Comparative Sociological Study of Monasticism in Theravada Buddhism and Medieval Catholicism*, Cambridge University Press, 1995, 145–56.

[67] Sumption, *Pilgrimage*, 73–84.

[68] Ronald C. Finucane, *Miracles and Pilgrims: Popular Beliefs in Medieval England*, London: Dent, 1977, 47–9.

everyday lives, and they were prepared to offer valuable physical gifts in return for spiritual comfort and renewal.[69]

Perhaps inevitably, therefore, the management of shrines and saints' relics lost some of its contact with the supernatural and became a mundane business activity. Churches and monasteries associated with particular shrines would disseminate material glorifying their protégé, compiling collections of miracle stories and asking pilgrims to hand them round back at home. Such was the hunger for guarantors of trust in something in the midst of an unstable and often threatening world that there was intense competition between different sites, fuelled by the occasional 'discovery' of a new relic. Wealthier ones would decorate their tombs and reliquaries with gold and precious stones. The tomb of St Thomas, for example, was said to be 'entirely covered with plates of pure gold. But the gold is scarcely visible beneath a profusion of gems, including sapphires, diamonds, rubies and emeralds...Exquisite designs have been carved all over it and immense gems worked delicately into the patterns.' This extravagance was partly public relations, but also perhaps a kind of insurance policy, physical capital stored up against the possibility of disasters.[70]

THE PEACE OF GOD

The way in which trust structures can also generate distrust is illustrated by the initially impeccably non-violent initiative of the 'Peace of God'. During the tenth and eleventh centuries, the breakdown of monarchical authority in Western Europe seems to have been at its most grave. Local warlords would conduct their feuds with little restraint, and in the course of them would attack merchants and steal their goods or lay waste the farms of their opponents. Women everywhere were vulnerable, as were clergymen, churches, and monasteries, since their buildings sometimes contained valuable objects. The greatest hope for the creation of peace and generalized social trust lay with the church, since it had at least the symbolic means of restraining malefactors and when necessary disgracing them or even expelling them both from the community and from the hope of God's grace. For that reason it was usually bishops who took the initiative in gathering local lords and commoners and demanding of them that they take an oath of peace.

The Peace of God originated in the south and centre of France, where monarchical authority was probably weakest. In 975 Bishop Wido of Le Puy convened the knights and peasant elders of his diocese in a large field and demanded from them an oath of mutual peace, respect for church property, and for the property and lives of the *pauperes*—that is, the poor and those who had renounced wealth for God's sake, such as monks and nuns.[71] Over the following decades, especially in

[69] Sumption, *Pilgrimage*, 160–1.   [70] Sumption, *Pilgrimage*, 152–6; quotation on p. 155.
[71] Hartmut Hoffmann, *Gottesfriede und Treuga Dei*, Stuttgart: Anton Hiersemann, 1964 (*Schriften der Monumenta Germaniae Historica*, no 20), 16–18.

France, Flanders, and Catalonia, a number of bishops undertook similar initiatives, usually with the support of the king's local officials, convening 'peace assemblies', great meetings of the local populace in a large hall or even the open air. Those present would take oaths before saints' images or relics not to molest the unarmed, such as clergy, pilgrims, peasants, merchants, women, and children. In some cases crowds would enthusiastically proclaim 'Pax! Pax!'

Here is an example from such a gathering, held in Charroux, in Aquitaine, in 989. 'Fortified by the synodal acts of our predecessors, in the name of our lord and saviour Jesus Christ, in the calends of June: I, Gombaud, archbishop of Second Aquitaine, and all my co-bishops of the province have gathered in the residence formerly known as Charroux. We are here, bishops and also clergy and many people of both sexes, to implore divine goodness. For we have seen in our dwelling places pestilential customs multiplying, in the absence of a Council, which has long not been held. Let divine grace root out harmful plants and plant healthy ones. Thus, assembled here in the name of God, we have decided as follows.' There follows a list of anathemas, on those who violate churches, who rob the poor, who steal farm animals, who attack or kidnap clergymen.[72]

A later variant was the Truce of God, initially introduced in Catalonia in 1027, which forbade *all* violence against anyone on Sundays, fast days, and certain saints' days—a prohibition which had a tendency to expand, so that in some versions only eighty days in the year were left on which fighting was in theory permitted.[73] Yves of Chartres, for example, ordained that 'priests, monks, clerks, pilgrims and merchants coming and going, and also peasants with their plough animals, seeds and sheep, should always be in safety. And We ordain that the truce should be strictly observed by everybody from sunset on Wednesday until sunrise on Monday, and from Advent till the eighth day of Epiphany.'[74]

The church's attempt to institutionalize generalized social trust in this way was sometimes fortified by elaborate ceremonial symbolism. In 994 in Limoges, where there was a plague, which many saw as God's punishment for the city's sins, citizens fasted for three days, then carried the remains of St Martial, their saint, up to a nearby hill; there they all concluded a *pactum pacis*, promising to refrain from violence and the oppression of the poor, under pain of exclusion from the church.[75] In such rituals of solidarity we may see the model for later urban communes and sworn assemblies of citizens, such as the *Eidgenossenschaften* of Switzerland. They also offered a model for later proclamations of *Landfriede* by princes and bishops in Germany. Some Catalan assemblies were broadly representative 'gatherings of the land', and may have supplied the model for the later Cortes,

[72] Dominique Barthélemy, *L'An Mil et la Paix de Dieu: la France chrétienne et féodale*, Paris: Fayard, 1999, 284–5.

[73] Hoffmann, *Gottesfriede*, 70–6, 84–5, 94–8; H. E. J. Cowdrey, 'The Peace and the Truce of God in the eleventh century', *Past and Present*, vol. 46 (1970), 42–67.

[74] Aryeh Grabois, 'De la trêve de Dieu a la paix du roi: étude sur les transformations du mouvement de la paix au XII siècle', in Pierre Gallais and Yves-Jean Riou (eds), *Mélanges offerts a René Crozet*, Poitiers: Société d'Études Mediévales, 1966, 586.

[75] Hoffmann, *Gottesfriede*, 27–9.

the Spanish parliament. In fact, in Catalonia by the late twelfth century the Peace had become almost an institutional order, with mass public oaths to proclaim it, armies to enforce it, and taxation to finance the armies and to compensate victims of violence.[76]

These collective peace oaths necessarily involved a paradox: to be effective, they had sometimes to be enforced by violence. For this purpose 'peace militias' would be formed. In Bourges in 1031, for example, Archbishop Aino presided over a peace council which decreed that all young men of 15 or over (presumably not including serfs or clergy) were to swear to defend the church and for this purpose to join a militia financed from church taxes. Such militias might themselves become involved in local feuds; indeed this actually happened to Aino's troops, who were inexperienced and poorly armed, and were defeated in a pitched battle with the well-trained knights of a local lord.[77]

Despite such setbacks, the peace movement was evidently popular and in many cases effective. It regularized the idea that the church might legitimately have recourse to arms where its cause was just. Popes sanctioned the *reconquista* campaign in Spain, in the interests of establishing peace by overcoming infidels. These moves helped to prepare the way for Gregory VII's radical reforms which aimed to establish the church as a parallel and alternative form of sovereignty superior to that of monarchs.[78] In the long run, however, monarchs proved more effective at enforcing peace, as we shall see in Chapter 5.

THE CRUSADES

Perhaps the Popes' most daring attempt to generate peace within Christendom involved redirecting the aggressiveness of knights outwards by extolling the spiritual value of what became known as 'crusading'. Urban II made his appeal to them at the Council of Clermont in November 1095. Referring to the Peace of God and its imperfect fulfilment, he declared: 'Although, O sons of God, you have promised more firmly than ever to keep the peace among yourselves and to preserve the rights of the church, there remains still an important work for you to do ... For your brethren who live in the east are in urgent need of your help, and you must hasten to give them the aid which has often been promised them.' If knights channelled their fighting capacities into the struggle to regain the Holy Land from its Muslim rulers, to liberate the church, and rescue fellow Christians there from pagan oppression, they would be ensured full remission of their sins. Then, Urban promised, they would become spiritual pilgrims, engaged in the 'Way of the Holy Sepulchre'. He promised all who took up arms and went to reconquer the

---

[76] Thomas N. Bisson, 'The Organized Peace in Southern France and Catalonia, ca. 1140–ca. 1233', *American Historical Review*, 82 (1977), 297, 309–11.

[77] Hoffmann, *Gottesfriede*, 104–7.

[78] Ernst-Dieter Hehl, 'War, Peace and the Christian Order', in *NCMH*, iv: *c.1024–c.1198*, part 1, Cambridge University Press, 2004, 191–8; H. E. J. Cowdrey, 'The Peace and the Truce'.

holy places 'immediate remission of their sins'. He referred to them as *milites Sancti Petri* or *fideles Sancti Petri*. 'Let those who have been accustomed to wage unjust private warfare against the faithful now go against the infidels and end with victory this war which should have been begun long ago! Let those who have long been robbers now become knights . . . Let those who have been serving as mercenaries for small pay now obtain the eternal reward . . . Set out on this journey and you will obtain the remission of your sins and be sure of the incorruptible glory of the kingdom of heaven.'[79]

There was a lively response, from civilians as well as armed men. Most were seeking personal salvation in the way Urban suggested. But the very act of encouraging them to go to war brought more militant and aggressive motives into play, exemplifying the rigid boundaries which Christianity, and especially Roman Christianity, was creating to mark itself off from all religious Others. Not only Muslims, but also Jews became the objects of intense and growing hatred. All down the Rhineland crusaders carried out pogroms against synagogues and Jewish quarters, massacring Jews who refused to convert. Forcible conversion was contrary to canon law, but senior clergy were unable to compel the crusaders to observe the ban, such was their animosity against Jews as well as Muslims, as enemies of the faith. They are reported as saying, 'It is unjust for those who took up arms against rebels against Christ to allow enemies of Christ to live in their own land.'[80] The crusading ideal made existing boundaries of trust more rigid and reinforced them with intense hatred.

Later crusaders even directed their aggression against Eastern Christians. In 1204, when in their opinion the Byzantine Emperor Alexius IV had failed to fulfil a promise to help them, the crusaders decided to attack Constantinople. After taking the city they looted and vandalized all the holy sites there; they seem to have concentrated on the symbols which attracted most reverence, and either desecrated them or seized them as booty. An early thirteenth-century Greek historian wrote: 'How shall I begin to tell of the deeds wrought by these nefarious men! Alas, the images, which ought to have been adored, were trodden under foot. Alas, the relics of the holy martyrs were thrown into unclean places! Then was seen what one shudders to see, namely the divine body and blood of Christ was spilled upon the ground or thrown about.'[81]

How did crusaders keep up their morale during the long unsettling journey to the Holy Land, when they faced hunger, thirst, exhaustion, both cold and heat, as well as sporadic attacks by Muslim armed detachments? Of this the existent sources

---

[79] There are no verbatim accounts of what Urban said, but several subsequent accounts exist, drawing on the memories of those who were there. See H. E. J. Cowdrey, 'Pope Urban II's Preaching of the First Crusade', *History*, 55 (1970), 177–88. The above text is taken from that of the priest Fulcher of Chartres, who was either present at the council or knew well someone who had been: S. J. Allen and Emily Amt (eds), *The Crusades: A Reader*, Toronto: Broadview Press, 2000, 39–40; Hoffmann, *Gottesfriede*, 249–50.

[80] Jonathan Riley-Smith, *The First Crusade and the Idea of Crusading*, 2nd edition, London: Continuum, 2009, 50–7.

[81] Nikitas Cloniates, in Allen and Amt (eds), *The Crusades*, 234.

tell us little: most accounts are retrospective and present a narrative of heroism, martyrdom, and suffering endured in the name of Christ. Evidently, though, their confidence that God was on their side was maintained by the church's symbolic resources. It devised a liturgy for blessing them before their departure. They would first prostrate themselves before the altar and make confession. Then they repeated psalms beseeching God's protection: 'Unto thee, O Lord, will I lift up my soul. My God, I have put my trust in thee. Let me not be confounded, neither let mine enemies triumph over me . . . Whoso dwelleth under the defence of the most high shall abide under the shadow of the Almighty. I will say unto the Lord, thou art my hope and my stronghold; my God, in him will I trust.' Then they would don a cloak embroidered with a cross, as a 'most invincible strength to thy servant against the wickedest temptation of the ancient enemy'.[82]

During the long journey and the campaigns crusaders would renew this symbolic source of confidence through repeated semi-liturgical practices: beginning each new stage of the march barefoot, or fasting before a major battle. Before the decisive engagement in Jerusalem in June 1099 they walked barefoot and in procession, carrying crosses around the city and visiting the holy places outside the walls.[83] The crusaders' battle-cry was *Deos hoc vult* (God wills this). At the battle of Dorylaeum (1097) the crusaders strengthened their own resolve by repeating, 'Stand fast together, trusting in Christ and the Victory of the Holy Cross!' After the battle their leader Bohemond of Taranto wrote a hymn of thanks for his troops to sing, based on Moses' hymn of gratitude after the Egyptians' destruction in the Red Sea. 'Thy right hand, O Lord, hath slain the enemy and in the multitude of thy glory thou hast put down our adversaries . . . You, O Lord, were with us, as a strong warrior. In your mercy you were leader and protector of the people thou hast redeemed.'[84] Some of the leaders carried relics with them to bolster confidence, and on one occasion the reputed discovery of the lance which had pierced Jesus's side on the cross was said to have restored faltering morale. Such symbolic links with divine providence heightened the crusaders' confidence, especially in times of great danger.

MUSLIM RESPONSE TO THE CRUSADES

Muslim response to the crusades was at first fragmented and limited. Since the tenth century Islam had been divided into two rival Caliphates: the Sunni Abbasid and the Shi'ite Fatimid. The former ruled Iran, Iraq, and part of Syria-Palestine, while the latter ruled Egypt, North Africa, and other parts of Syria-Palestine. Both claimed the heritage of the Prophet and thus religious and political authority over

---

[82] Allen and Amt (eds), *The Crusades: A Reader*, 193, 196.

[83] Jonathan Riley-Smith, *The Crusades, Christianity and Islam*, New York: Columbia University Press, 2008, 34.

[84] Thomas Asbridge, *The Crusades: The War for the Holy Land*, London: Simon & Schuster, 2010, 58, 73; Riley-Smith, *First Crusade*, 99, 140.

all Muslims. In the eleventh century the Turkic warrior-clan of the Seljuqs had seized power in Baghdad, but continued to rule in the name of the Abbasid Caliphate. Under their system the ruling dynasty distributed territories among their sons, so that when the crusaders arrived, the Seljuq realm was highly fragmented by family rivalries. Damascus and Aleppo, for example, continually strove to expand their territories at each other's expense. These kinship rivalries supplemented the religious disagreements with the Fatimids to render Muslims incapable of presenting any kind of united front. Some of their leaders actually sought alliance with the Franks rather than try to expel them.[85]

It took several decades before the various Muslim factions could reunite and act together in order to drive the crusaders out of the Holy Land. When they did so, it was because they were inspired by the ideal of *jihad*. The word, as we have seen, means effort, striving, or zeal on behalf of God, and it can assume either a spiritual or a directly military form.[86] The Syrian jurist al-Sulami in his *Book of Jihad* described the crusaders' bloody conquest of Jerusalem in 1099 as God's punishment of Muslims for neglecting their religious duties, especially *jihad*. For him the key was in the 'greater [spiritual] *jihad*': through repentance and through combating their own baser impulses, the Muslims might rebuild their strength and, with it, their political leadership, with the aim of conducting *jihad* as holy war against the Franks.[87]

While the Muslim world was so disunited, however, it was impossible to attempt the reconquest of Jerusalem. Eventually the religious writings impelled some political leaders to drop their rivalries and reunite to expel the Christians. First Nur ad-Din, then the more famous Salah al-Din (Saladin) espoused this cause and mobilized it both to extend their own symbolic political power, then to gather and inspire armies to reconquer Frankish-held territory, including ultimately Jerusalem. Historians debate which aim, the political or the religious, was more important to them, but it seems that the political ambition was a necessary precondition of success in *jihad*, not only in order to unite Muslim forces, but also to attract their confidence by the reputation of success in battle.

Sent to Egypt by Nur ad-Din, Saladin used his personal charisma and his success as a military commander to have himself appointed as vizier by the Fatimid Caliph. He then led the Egyptian army against the Zengid dynasty ruling Syria which had originally sponsored him. After conquering Aleppo in 1183 he proclaimed: 'Now that all the Muslim regions are placed under our jurisdiction or under that of our subordinates, we must, in return for that favour from Heaven direct our resolve, use all our powers, against the accursed Franks. We must fight them for the cause of God. With their blood we will efface the stain with which they have covered the Holy Land.'[88] He was combining the charisma derived from

---

[85] Anne-Marie Eddé, *Saladin*, trans. Jane Mary Todd, Belknap Press of Harvard University Press, 2011, chapter 1.

[86] See above, 'Islam'.

[87] Michael Bonner, *Jihad in Islamic History*, Princeton University Press, 2006, 139.

[88] Eddé, *Saladin*, 171.

successful warfare with the symbolism of *jihad* to gain the trust of those Muslims who had not yet committed themselves.

In this spirit, Saladin's propagandists spread the image of him as a man chosen by God to lead the Muslims to victory over the Franks. They emphasized his pious conduct and his strict observance of religious duties and ceremonies. They also used astrological signs and dream interpretations to prophesy victory for him.[89] Their message inspired others to join him, with the result that eventually he had sufficient forces to accomplish his promise. In July 1187 he defeated a large crusader army at the battle of Hattin, and followed his victory up by retaking Jerusalem a few months later.

The Muslim response to the crusaders illustrates how societies apparently fatally riven by internal conflicts can moderate them, even perceive their relative insignificance, in the face of a serious external threat, and then with strong leadership and evocative religious symbolism rediscover at least sufficient mutual trust for solidarity against the enemy. We shall see something similar later in the reaction of the sixteenth-century Dutch cities and provinces to the threat from Spain.[90]

The crusades teach us another lesson too. It is very striking that the original Christian impulse originated in a movement for the preservation of peace. In conducting a holy war for the recovery of the holy places, Christians were declaring their intention to create peace by violently eliminating what they saw as the sources of conflict, and to overcome the adherents of a religion which had itself made holy war an ideal. Two militant monotheisms were at grips with one another, each in the name of universal peace. Such are the paradoxes of trust.

Moreover, the motif of uniting for battle to eliminate disturbers of the peace still has resonance today, nearly 900 years later. In the days following the Al-Qaeda attack on the World Trade Center on 11 September 2001, US President George W. Bush proclaimed a 'crusade', a 'war on terrorism'. He later apologized for the use of the word 'crusade', realizing that it was gratuitously provocative to Muslims everywhere, but he insisted that the war itself 'will not end until every terrorist group of global reach has been found, stopped and defeated'. He was seeking to create peace by means of war.[91]

In like style, when NATO invaded Afghanistan in pursuit of the 'war on terror', Osama bin Laden, leader of Al-Qaeda, responded: 'The battle is between Muslims—the people of Islam—and the global Crusaders . . . The One God who sustained us with one of His helping hands and stabilised us to defeat the Soviet Empire is capable of sustaining us again and allowing us to defeat America in the same land.' In a direct echo of Saladin, he appealed: 'The *umma* is asked to unite itself in the face of the Crusaders' campaign, the strongest, most powerful and most ferocious campaign to fall on the Islamic *umma*. . . . Richard the Lionheart, Barbarossa from Germany and Louis from France—the case is similar today, when they all

---

[89] C. Hillenbrand, *The Crusades*, Edinburgh University Press, 175–7.
[90] See Chapter 4, 'Banking'.
[91] Bob Woodward, *Bush at War*, New York: Simon & Schuster, 2002, 45, 67.

immediately went forward the day Bush lifted the cross.'[92] Such is the enduring power of religious divisions: they continue to arouse intense distrust, grim solidarity, and a fascination with history.

WITCH-HUNTING

The power of religious symbols to generate distrust was dramatically and grotesquely revealed in the spasms of witch-hunting which swept across parts of Europe in the sixteenth and seventeenth centuries. The Reformation had transformed the symbolism of the Christian faith more than any event since the time of Constantine. Protestant reformers not only put their trust in the Word, but also condemned and then eliminated many of the rituals and sacred objects in which ordinary believers had placed their trust for centuries. A routine example of this traditional trust was making the sign of the cross before leaving home or embarking on any decisive or risky action. People would wear amulets to protect them against evil spirits; they would pray before images of saints, perhaps their own personal saint, or one connected with their occupation or with their parish, to fend off disaster or request a boon.[93] Or they would carry the sacrament round the fields in procession before spring sowing; in parts of Germany a cross would be carried at the head of the procession and the opening passage of each of the Gospels would be read at the four corners of a field to invoke divine protection against drought, flood, plague, and damage to crops or animals—the most likely misfortunes in a risk-prone agricultural cycle.[94] After the Council of Trent (1545–1563) Catholic reformers, though less radical than Protestant ones, also tried to eradicate practices which might be considered superstitious.

These reforms were the work of educated elites, and proved baffling or even threatening to ordinary believers, especially the illiterate. Deprived of many of their accustomed safeguards against danger and risk, they were less able to face the future with confidence, especially in relation to the fertility of animals, the crop-cycle, human procreation, marriage, and family life—all areas which in any society are subject to fortuitous and unpredictable eventualities. These anxieties contributed to a new and virulent form of distrust: witch-hunting.

In the middle ages it had been common for people to accuse certain individuals of being an evil influence on the community, of using black magic or casting the 'evil eye' to cause disease, impotence, infertility, or damage to animals or crops. Such accusations had usually remained individual and specific. During the late fifteenth century, however, a new, more comprehensive, and intellectually

---

[92] Quoted in Riley-Smith, *Crusades, Christianity and Islam*, 75–6.

[93] Keith Thomas, *Religion and the Decline of Magic*, London: Weidenfeld & Nicolson, 1971, 27–31; Eamon Duffy, *The Stripping of the Altars: Traditional Religion in England, c.1400–c.1580*, New Haven: Yale University Press, 1982, 268–97.

[94] R. W. Scribner, 'Ritual and Popular Religion in Catholic Germany at the Time of the Reformation', in his *Popular Culture and Popular Movements in Reformation Germany*, London: Hambledon Press, 1987, 20.

articulated vision of evil began to take shape. Some theologians asserted that certain people in the midst of the community, usually female, were not just inflicting casual misfortunes, but had actually concluded a pact with the devil and become accomplices in a great conspiracy designed to destroy godly society. Against the moral framework propounded by both Catholic and Protestant reformers, which envisaged human fertility and human love as contained within a strict and stable framework, the witch-hunters evoked a counter-world in which human affections were systematically abused, fertility destroyed, and families destabilized and fragmented. A treatise, called the *Malleus Maleficarum* (The Hammer of Witches), appeared in 1486 and was many times reprinted in the following century. It described the witches' pact with the devil, how they received his mark on their bodies, and then dedicated themselves to his work of destroying families, killing children, poisoning animals, and casting a blight on crops.[95]

The 'witches' thus accused were usually but not invariably older women, who in normal times were seen as the prime bearers of trust and community cohesion, but for that very reason were now suspected of being sowers of distrust and destroyers of community. They were said to intervene in human life at its most vulnerable stage, during pregnancy, childbirth, the lying-in, and the subsequent care of small infants, when trust in God and in other human beings is most pressingly needed. Witches were charged with causing the sickness and death of babies by poisoning them instead of feeding them. Midwives were especially vulnerable to being accused of witchcraft, if anything went wrong with a newborn child. So too were neighbours who had called during that period, or relatives who had helped. Ursula Götz, an elderly woman from Obermarchtal, a village near the Danube in south-west Germany, was suspected of being a witch in 1623, when her 3-year-old great-niece and her housemaid both died. Under interrogation, and threatened with torture, she confessed that she had met the devil years before in the form of a farm servant dressed in many-coloured clothes. She had found him attractive, he had seduced her, and then she had signed a pact with him that made her the devil's own. He had given her a salve which she had rubbed on her great-niece; she had also used it to cause sickness and death to sheep, cows, and horses as well as other human beings. In addition, under the devil's instruction she had sucked the blood from young children to replenish her supply of salve. She was found guilty, beheaded, and her body was thrown to the flames.[96]

A great many confessions followed this general pattern. How could this be so, since witches were not present at other witches' interrogations? Almost certainly, under torture or threatened with it, each witch would tell her interrogators what they most wanted or expected to hear. In 1598, for example, the court records of Lorraine report that Françatte Camont was 'racked severely, but would confess nothing, insisting she was a good Christian. Either later the same day or

[95] Brian P. Levack, *The Witch-Hunt in Early Modern Europe*, 2nd edition, London: Longman, 1995, chapter 2.
[96] Lyndal Roper, *Witch Craze: Terror and Fantasy in Baroque Germany*, New Haven: Yale University Press, 2004, 1–3, 127–32, 159.

subsequently she was tortured again, being racked "very severely", and finally asked to be released, saying she had been seduced by Persin [a common French name for the Devil] the previous year.' He gave her a powder, which 'she tried out on her cat, which died. Then she killed a series of animals, in revenge for minor offences in most cases. She had made the servant of Jacquot Rolbel's widow lame by sprinkling powder on his foot after he stole some of her oats at the mill.' There follows an inventory of malicious minor offences. Then at the end: '27 June 1598: Interrogation. She now said she was not a witch and had only confessed this because of torture, but was content for them to put her to death nevertheless. On the suggestion that Persin must have visited her in prison to persuade her to say this, she then agreed that the confession had been true. 7 July 1598: Sentence carried out.'[97]

The portrayal of an inverted—and perverted—world fulfilled roughly the same function as carnival, though of course it was far less entertaining. It reaffirmed the values of the godly world and reinforced trust in it by the vivid depiction of its opposite. It made sense only in the context of a universal church (or, now, three would-be universal churches: Catholic, Lutheran, and Calvinist) endeavouring to create a totally godly society and evidently not succeeding; it dramatized the contradiction by portraying the obverse, the construction of a totally ungodly society. At a time when it was feared that the final great battle between God and Antichrist might be at hand, it seemed crucial to some authorities both spiritual and secular to redraw boundaries much more emphatically, and to shore up the norms of the orderly society by reminding everyone of the dangers facing it.[98]

Witch-hunting was commonest in the Holy Roman Empire, Switzerland, Germany, and the borderlands of France—all countries and regions which were going through a complex, volatile, and highly contested religious evolution in the sixteenth and early seventeenth centuries. It was especially common in regions where there was a large religious minority, or which were close to the border with another state of different religious affiliation.[99] The campaigns tended to be especially vicious where traditional village or manorial courts were giving way to magistrates' courts, but were not yet fully integrated into royal court systems. Poorly trained magistrates were more likely to accept the narrative of diabolical conspiracy than royal or high-level judges, who had more detachment and were less likely to sanction the unregulated use of torture in the investigation. Inquisition courts were also less gullible in the face of witchcraft accusations, since they had more meticulous methods for assessing evidence.[100] All of this suggests that in periods of abrupt social and cultural change, when institutions are raw and unpractised, trust is unusually difficult to stabilize, and therefore distrust can become rampant.

---

[97] Brian P. Levack (ed), *The Witchcraft Sourcebook*, New York: Routledge, 2004, 183–4.
[98] Stuart Clark, 'Inversion, Misrule and the Meaning of Witchcraft', *Past & Present*, 87 (1980), 98–127.
[99] Levack, *Witch-Hunt*, 114–20.   [100] Levack, *Witch-Hunt*, chapter 3.

CONCLUSION

What do these illustrations, drawn from different time periods and global areas, tell us about trust? First of all, that religion is a very powerful symbolic mediator of trust. It fixes and strengthens the primal trust, posited in different contexts by Georg Simmel and Erik Erikson, which serves as a basis for all social life. At its most effective, religion offers people identity, knowledge of the universe and a place within it, a path to salvation, an emotional solace and reassurance, and a mutually supportive and trusting community. It has repeatedly served as a means for broadening the radius of trust, rising above the rivalries of tribes, cities, and even kingdoms. It brought together different peoples of the Roman Empire in a broad congregation in which a considerable degree of mutual trust was possible, with the solidarity and emotional confidence necessary to face daunting dangers. In the seventh century it overcame the conflicts which had divided the tribes of Arabia and generated among them mutual trust sufficient to undertake daring and extremely risky military campaigns. It provided much of the symbolic cement which held huge empires together for hundreds of years. In the late eleventh century crusaders from very diverse social and ethnic backgrounds cooperated with each other and through use of religious symbols generated sufficient optimism and confidence in the future to overcome seemingly insurmountable obstacles and achieve their goal of conquering Jerusalem. Muslims were able to respond effectively only when under Saladin they had overcome their own conflicts among themselves and created enough mutual trust to act determinedly together.

Yet those very examples indicate the ambivalence of religion's achievement. Religion poses the most crucial dilemmas of trust. It is a powerful generator of both trust and distrust. In the process of enlarging boundaries of trust it creates new and very tough boundaries of distrust: the virulent distrust between Christians and Jews, between Christianity and Islam, between Catholics and Protestants—distrust which can be overcome, if at all, only by a long, exhausting process of mutual accommodation when there seems to be no alternative.[101] This continues to be the paradox of religion today, as we shall see in Chapter 5.

---

[101] Benjamin J. Kaplan, *Divided by Faith: Religious Conflict and the Practice of Toleration in Early Modern Europe*, Cambridge, Mass.: Belknap Press, 2007.

4

Money

Creator and Destroyer of Trust

Genoa, January 19, 1308: In the name of the Lord, amen. Percivalle Grillo, son of Andreolo; Daniele Grillo; Meliano Grillo; Benedetto Contardo and Nicola Contardo, brothers, sons of the late Luchetto Contardo; Manuele Bonifacio; Antonio Grillo, son of Andreolo, acknowledge to each other that they have formed and made a *societas* for the purpose of maintaining a bank in the city of Genoa and of engaging in commerce and business in Genoa and throughout other [and] different parts of the world, according to what shall seem [proper] and shall be the pleasure of the partners themselves, to continue, God willing, for the next two succeeding years. This *societas* they acknowledge to be of £9,450 Genoese, in which sum they acknowledge to each other that each of them has or has deposited as below, viz: said Percivalle, £3,500; said Daniele, £2,000; said Meliano, £1,000; the aforesaid Benedetto Contardo and Nicola, his brother, £2,000; said Manuele Bonifacio, £450; and said Antonio Grillo, £500. This capital they acknowledge to be received in the hands of said Percivalle in money, in credits, in exchange to be received in France, and in a vein of iron in Elba. And the aforesaid partners have waived the exception and legal right by which they could speak against or oppose the aforesaid. And said Percivalle is to use this money in business and commerce in Genoa in said bank which he maintains, in the buying and selling of wares, and in exchange both in France and throughout other [and] different parts of the world, by sea and by land, personally and through his factors and messengers, according as God may dispose better for him, up to the time limit mentioned above, at the risk and fortune of the [partners]. And he has promised said partners of his to act in good faith [and] efficiently for the increase and preservation of said *societas*. And the aforesaid partners promised each other to guard and to preserve the goods and wares and money which may come into the hands of any one of them from the aforesaid *societas*, and not to defraud one another in anything. The profit which God may grant in the aforesaid *societas* shall be allocated to each of them pro rata to his capital. And they have promised each other in good faith to come to the accounting of the capital and profit of said *societas* at the end of the time limit; and each of them is to deduct his capital and to divide among them the profit pro rata to the capital of each one. The aforesaid *societas* and each and all of the above [conditions] the aforesaid partners promised each other, etc. Firm, etc., and for it, etc. And said Benedetto acknowledges that he is more than twenty-four years old, and said Nicola acknowledges that he is more than nineteen years old, and said Antonio acknowledges that he is more than nineteen years old. And they swore by the sacred Gospels of God, putting their hands on the scriptures, to undertake and to observe [everything] as above stated and not to do anything or to act contrary in any way by reason of their being minors or by any other cause. And they made the aforesaid [agreement] with the counsel of the witnesses written below, whom for this [purpose] they call their relatives, neighbours and counsellors. Done in Genoa in the Church of Santa Maria delle Vigne, in the year of the Nativity of the Lord 1308, fifth indiction, January 19, about nones. Witnesses: Arnaldo of Spigno, dealer in poultry; Manfredo; and Pagano of Moneglia, dealer in poultry.[1]

Here we have a document drawn up in 1308 by businessmen about to undertake together quite a risky venture, the establishment of a bank in Genoa to finance trade between that city, France, and elsewhere. They needed some way of cementing their mutual trust, and by the fourteenth century written agreements of this kind offered a widely accepted way of doing so. Two families formed the principal shareholders, the Grillos and the Contardos, joined by Manuel Bonifacio, who might or might not have been related by marriage. Even though they were closely related and presumably knew each other well, the signatories found it useful to create a precise record of the capital they had each contributed—some of it already involved in trade and mining—to set down their agreement and to bind themselves to it.

They also agreed to review the arrangements at the end of two years, and at that time to distribute the profits in proportion to the capital contributed. They were placing their personal honour and moral reputation at stake. In this case they call their association a *societas*, which gave it a generic structure, by that time well understood in commercial practice. They entrusted their combined capital to Percivalle, the largest investor, who was evidently to run the business. He for his part pledged his 'good faith', while they all undertook not to defraud each other. To provide a trustworthy foundation for their agreement, they signed it in front of witnesses, and they conducted the whole process in a church, swearing on the Gospel. The document itself invokes God several times, beseeching his help and acknowledging that ultimately all fortune, good or bad, comes from him.

Trading is one of the most ancient human activities. From the earliest recorded times, people have been moved by what Adam Smith in *The Wealth of Nations* called 'the propensity to truck, barter and exchange one thing for another'. In mutual commerce, he asserted, two individuals motivated by self-interest meet, and the outcome is mutually beneficial. 'Whoever offers to another a bargain of any kind proposes to do this: "Give me that which I want and you shall have that which you want."'[2]

---

[1] Renée Doehaerd, *Les Relations commerciales entre Gênes, la Belgique et l'Outremont d'après les archives notariales génoises aux xiii et xiv siècles,* Brussels: Institut Historique de Belge de Rome, 1941, iii. 966–8.

[2] Adam Smith, *An Inquiry into the Nature and Causes of the Wealth of Nations,* Oxford: Clarendon Press, 1976, i. 25–6.

Trade is necessary to sustain any way of life beyond the extremely primitive and localized. Human beings have traded even more continuously than they have made war. Consider, for example, Herodotus' description of the Carthaginians' trade with the tribes of West Africa:

There is a country in Libya, and a nation, beyond the Pillars of Hercules, which they are wont to visit, where they no sooner arrive but forthwith they unload their wares, and, having disposed of them after an orderly fashion along the beach, leave them, and, returning aboard their ships, raise a great smoke. The natives, when they see the smoke, come down to the shore, and, laying out to view so much gold as they think the worth of the wares, withdraw to a distance. The Carthaginians upon this come ashore and look. If they think the gold enough, they take it and go their way; but if it does not seem to them sufficient, they go aboard ship once more, and wait patiently. Then the others approach and add to their gold, till the Carthaginians are content. Neither party deals unfairly by the other: for the Carthaginians themselves never touch the gold till it comes up to the worth of their goods, nor do the natives ever carry off the goods till the gold is taken away.[3]

We cannot tell how common such practices were, but they suggest that the two parties involved had such a strong interest in trading with each other that they acted with considerable self-restraint and mutual trust, even when they had little evidence of each other's reliability. They did, however, have one intermediate token of trust, independent of either party: gold. Since gold is attractive, rare, and not liable to corrosion, it has often functioned as a catalyst of mutual trust.[4]

Trade on any scale has to be a joint venture. Above the level of the market stall or small shop, it is not something that a single person can conduct. The trader with any ambition needs partners or at least agents. But then the question arises: how can one trust the partners or agents? Mutual interest supplies some reassurance: after all, a business in which the partners constantly quarrel or deceive each other is unlikely to prosper. Restraint and trustworthiness bring their own reward. In the face of all the inherent risks of trade, though, one needs some more dependable guarantee of solidarity. For that reason many businesses are family affairs: families are not by any means always harmonious, but they have an interest in sticking together, and their members are likely to know from experience just how far they can trust each other.[5]

Outside the family, though, how was one to trust business partners? The commonest device was a legally registered partnership agreement, of which the document above is an example. That document then enabled the law, if necessary, to intervene to uphold the agreement. The relationship between law and trust is a complex one. In personal relationships, recourse to law is usually a sign of lack of trust, but here the relationship is explicitly commercial as well as personal. The

---

[3] Quoted in Richard Miles, *Carthage must be Destroyed: The Rise and Fall of an Ancient Civilization*, London: Allen Lane, 2010, 86.

[4] See below, 'Money'.

[5] This is the main theme of Francis Fukuyama, *Trust: The Social Virtues and the Creation of Prosperity*, London: Penguin Books, 1996.

signatories presumably knew each other well, but still thought it advisable to draw up a written agreement. Even close relatives might have reasons not to trust one another fully, and in commerce the risks were greater than in normal family interaction.[6] After all, trade, especially long-distance trade, has always been extremely risky. Robbers, soldiers of fortune, and wars of all kinds could destroy goods in transit, or indeed their owners. The weather was unpredictable, especially for sea voyages. Epidemics could quite suddenly cut a swathe through one's expected customers. Information was patchy, and conditions could change abruptly during the protracted journeys of merchants and their agents.[7]

A precise legal document created a tangible element of certainty in this turmoil. It bolstered mutual trust by providing reassurance that, in the unknown contingencies of the future, the signatories would have more to rely on than their memories and their mutual goodwill; they would have a precise record which they could quote to each other, and even lay before a law court, should that become necessary.

We can see such a motive operating in the very beginning of recorded history. Indeed the oldest human documents we possess record trading deals, that is, human beings already devising ways to combine their economic efforts in trustworthy forms.[8] As early as the late fourth millennium in Uruk in southern Mesopotamia the central institution was the temple, where goods were brought in, exchanged, and reallocated under the supervision of the local god. Already, then, trade was considered a priority occupation, worthy of divine protection and meticulous human documentation. The law code of Hammurabi (1792–1750 BCE) in ancient Babylon already took business partnerships for granted and stipulated: 'If a man gives silver to another man for investment in a partnership venture, before the god they shall equally divide the profit or loss.'[9] The ultimate guarantor of commercial honesty was a deity, who could impose supernatural sanctions for untrustworthy behaviour.

Documentation for the ancient world is most abundant (or least sparse) for the neo-Babylonian empire in southern Mesopotamia (626–539 BCE). The record suggests that business ventures on such principles were common, enunciated in what were known as *harranu* contracts. Typically a wealthy partner provided the capital, while an on-the-spot junior did most of the work, and might eventually be able to pay off his senior.[10]

---

[6] See the Rothschilds' written agreement, Chapter 2, 'Trust and Institutions', 45–6.

[7] Peter Mathias, 'Risk, Credit and Kinship in Early Modern Enterprise', in John J. McCusker and Kenneth Morgan (eds), *The Early Modern Atlantic Economy*, Cambridge University Press, 2000, 15–35.

[8] Marc van de Mieroop, *A History of the Ancient Near East, circa 3000–323 BC*, Oxford: Blackwell, 2007, 24, 28–9.

[9] Cornelia Wunsch, 'Neo-Babylonian Entrepreneurs', in David S. Landes, Joel Mokyr, and William J. Baumol (eds), *The Invention of Enterprise: Entrepreneurship from Ancient Mesopotamia to Modern Times*, Princeton University Press, 2010, 52.

[10] Wunsch, 'Neo-Babylonian Entrepreneurs', 51–2.

There is a widespread fallacy abroad in political and economic history that entrepreneurs are naturally independent of the state.[11] This is not true now and probably never has been. On the contrary, because their business is risky, most entrepreneurs endeavour to maintain confidence in their own future by seeking alliances with the powers that be, as a guarantee of support in hard times. Research shows how in Babylon the Egibi family, successful businessmen for whom abundant documentation survives, started out as junior partners in *harranu* arrangements, building relationships with royal officials and provincial governors, providing food, clothing, and services for palaces, temples, and administrative buildings. They acted as intermediaries between primary producers and the ruling elite, among their functions being tax-farming, an intermediary operation essential to the survival of a political system of any size or complexity.[12]

In later centuries in the Middle East, both Jews and Muslims further developed ways of combining with one another to achieve economic objectives. The nineteenth-century discovery of a huge collection of documents from the eleventh to thirteenth centuries in the Cairo *geniza* (storehouse, repository) has enabled historians to reconstruct many of these associations. Some were simple partnerships; others went under the name of *qirad* in Hebrew and *mudaraba* in Arabic, indicating 'mutual participation in an enterprise'.[13] The quantity of surviving documents suggests that the operation of these associations was normally meticulously recorded. Details laid down included the number and status of the contracting parties, the contribution each was to make, the rights and duties each was to have, the share of profit and responsibility for loss that each would bear, arrangements for regularly rendering account, and provisions for ending the association. In some contracts there was a specific proviso that each partner was expected 'to exert himself for the common good, to shun cheating and negligence, to act as a pious person and a gentleman [*sic* in translation], and not to put his own interests above those of his associates'.[14] Clearly such contracts were intended to boost mutual confidence.

In a common type of *qirad* or *mudaraba*, a sedentary investor would lend goods and/or money to a travelling agent, who might add some assets of his own. The agent would then use the capital on a voyage and, if everything went well, return with either a profit in money or more valuable wares to sell. The yield from the total transaction would then be divided between the two in a ratio agreed beforehand; often, the relevant agreement would be drawn up before a notary, who would advise on suitable legal terminology.[15]

---

[11] See for example Joyce Appleby, *The Relentless Revolution: A History of Capitalism*, New York: Norton, 2010.

[12] Wunsch, 'Neo-Babylonian Entrepreneurs', 40–61.

[13] S. D. Goitein, *A Mediterranean Society: The Jewish Communities of the Arab World as Portrayed in the Documents of the Cairo Geniza*, i: *Economic Foundations*, Berkeley and Los Angeles: University of California Press, 1967, 170–1.

[14] Goitein, *Mediterranean Society*, i. 172.

[15] J. H. Pryor, 'The Origins of the *Commenda* Contract', *Speculum*, 52 (1977), 6–7; Abraham L. Udovitch, *Partnership and Profit in Medieval Islam*, Princeton University Press, 1970, 170–6.

In such transactions very delicate issues of trust were involved, both in persons and in fate. Two parties were assessing risks and deciding how to share them. The investor was risking his capital, which might have taken years to amass; the agent was risking life and limb, perhaps his own ship, and was investing his time and labour. They could only assess these risks and reach a fair agreement on how to distribute them by using legal forms which were familiar and whose advantages and limitations were well understood.[16]

In certain circumstances, though, among people who knew each other very well and depended on each other's total reliability, written contracts could be dispensed with. Study of Maghreb trade in the same *geniza* document collection indicates that Jewish merchants there knew each other so well and encountered each other so often that they made their agreements simply by word of mouth before their own colleagues acting as witnesses. After all, notaries were expensive, and a merchant whose reputation was degraded by the breach of an agreement would have difficulty in carrying on business in future. For the same reason much business was conducted on credit rather than through immediate payment.[17] Here we are dealing with an unusually closely knit community of Jews whose forefathers had emigrated from Baghdad in the tenth century, when instability in the Abbasid Caliphate threatened their lives. Since its members usually formed both sides of any transaction, their word could indeed be their bond. Such was not the case for Percivalle Grillo, in the document quoted at the head of this chapter: he traded with a variety of ethnic groups across Europe.

The existence of the 'silk road', the trade routes stretching across thousands of miles of mountains and deserts between the Middle East and China, testifies to the extraordinary human capacity to accept risk as the necessary cost of trading and making a profit. The agents who did the actual travelling, selling, and buying were often part of a *mudaraba*-type contract, with their store of goods and their expenses provided by a sedentary investor; indeed it is difficult to see how traders could have coped with the huge risks without such associations. The routes taken depended on the political circumstances prevalent at the time (and they might change during the journey, adding to the risk). The unification of Central Asia under the Mongols improved conditions for a century or so (mid-twelfth to mid-thirteenth century): they provided routes with periodic way stations and caravanserais, where food and water could be obtained, as well as a modicum of protection against robbers and bandits. In return, of course, they levied substantial transit duties.[18] Recent research suggests that much of this trade was in fact quite localized and was connected with the contracting of military supplies between China and the city-states or oasis kingdoms of Central Asia. If traders relied on close relations with political authorities and kept their

[16] Pryor, 'Origins', 22–35; R. de Roover, 'The Organization of Trade', in *The Cambridge Economic History of Europe*, vol. iii, Cambridge University Press, 1963, 49–53. Udovitch, *Partnership*, 170–6.

[17] Avner Greif, *Institutions and the Path to the Modern Economy: Lessons from Medieval Trade*, Cambridge University Press, 2006.

[18] Janet L. Abu-Lughod, *Before European Hegemony: The World System, AD 1250–1350*, New York: Oxford University Press, 1989, 175–8.

journeys relatively short, then the risks may have been smaller than previous historians thought.[19]

In general, sea routes were safer, provided there were strong states ruling over the main port cities and able to provide some security against pirates. From the mid-seventh century the Umayyads, then the Abbasids, ruled over much of the coastline along the route, while at the far end the Tang dynasty ruled a united empire.[20]

Assessing and mitigating risk is at the heart of trade. From the Jewish and Muslim models mentioned above, medieval Italians like the Grillos and Contardos developed the *commenda*, in which an investor, a *commendator*, provided the capital for an agent, the *tractator*, to conduct trade, usually travelling abroad.[21] Another way of spreading risk was for several merchants to club together to hire or buy a ship and cargo, each contributing shares of both and each sharing the potential profits proportionately. In this way no single merchant had to commit so much capital as to be ruined if the voyage failed. Again, precise and well-understood legal forms were desirable for an agreement to be sustainable.[22]

Mutual trust became easier to maintain if such associations were formed for more than one voyage, or better still permanently. Partners shared the profits, but also bore liability for debts, up to the full extent of their personal as well as business assets. This was the origin of the *compania*, a name which suggests the sociability of breaking bread together; the term seems to have been used interchangeably with *societas*.[23] Most such associations began as family firms, whose members were long familiar with each other. As their businesses grew, they might later take on outside partners, while preserving control within a family nucleus and continuing to bear the family name as their badge.

MONEY

In the agreements fixing such arrangements much of the content is expressed in terms of money. We tend to take money for granted, and indeed in one form or another it has existed from very early periods of trade, as Herodotus showed in his account of trade between Carthage and Africa. The Grillos and Contardos expressed their respective shares in the form of Pounds or Libras. But we need to look more closely at money and understand why it is so important to us.

Money has several functions indispensable to all but the crudest forms of exchange. It is a store of value, interchangeable across innumerable varieties of goods and services, and preserving that value over time. For that reason, it is also a stable unit of account and a flexible means of payment. Consider what happens nowadays when you hire a car. You show your driving licence, make a down payment, probably with a plastic credit card. That payment includes third party

[19] Valerie Hansen, *The Silk Road: A New History*, Oxford University Press, 2012.
[20] Abu-Lughod, *Before*, 197–209.   [21] Pryor, 'Origins'; de Roover, 'Organization'.
[22] De Roover, 'Organization', 58–9.
[23] Robert Sabatino Lopez, *The Trade of Medieval Europe*, Oxford University Press, 1952, 185.

insurance and probably a sizeable deposit in case you damage the car seriously, or it is stolen. You mark a diagram indicating existing damage marks on the bodywork, and then you drive away. The hire firm entrusts you with a vehicle worth many multiples of your deposit and capable of killing someone if you misuse it. At the same time you trust them to have serviced the car properly so that it will not malfunction—since if it does, you yourself might well be killed or seriously injured. Yet you and the hire firm know very little about each other. This is merely a routine example of the strong thin trust[24] which lubricates today's complex economy.

Such mutual trust is very common in everyday life, so common in fact that we scarcely notice it. What makes it possible is money. One can imagine a life without money; indeed, for some socialists that was an ideal. It is possible to exchange goods and services either through barter or through reciprocal gifts. So cumbersome is barter, though, that from the time of the very earliest records societies were devising objects that could be used as a generally applicable standard of value and to enable more diverse forms of exchange.

All societies beyond the very primitive have, then, felt the need to create symbols they could trust as means of exchange and as stable indicators of value, since exchange, sale, or purchase all involve some risk. The Ashmolean Museum in Oxford has a permanent exhibition of the different types of money which have been used over the centuries. It includes shells, bangles, stones, rolls of cloth, various metals, and paper—objects which appear to have nothing in common except that, as the exhibition leaflet states, 'they all work as money because people place trust in them when they are used in transactions'. In Homeric ancient Greece cattle fulfilled this role; our word 'pecuniary' is derived from the Latin 'pecus', cattle. But cattle come in bulky, rather high-value units. It was handier to use something smaller, more portable, and more flexible. Cowrie shells were popular in many societies, being light, not too easy to find, and valuable in themselves since they could be worn as ornaments. The Chinese pictogram for money still contains the root image of the cowrie. Other objects have served the same purpose: arrowheads, spears, rings, wheels.[25]

In this respect metal coins had considerable advantages, once they began to be used. They were in themselves valuable, since gold, silver, and copper were found in limited supply and had first to be mined and refined. They could be manufactured in different weights to denote different values, and they could be carried in the hand, pouch, or pocket. They could also be stamped so that they bore the symbol of somebody or something widely trusted in the community. The first coins to be regularly used, those of the ancient Greek city of Lydia, bore the image of a lion's head, the city's emblem; similarly, Corinthian coins had a winged horse, Athenian ones an owl. Roman republican coins bore the image of Juno (goddess of the mint) or of mythological heroes; in imperial Rome the head of the emperor

[24] See Chapter 2, 'Different Modes of Trust'.

[25] E. Victor Morgan, *A History of Money*, Harmondsworth: Penguin Books, 1965, 11–12; Bin Yang, 'The Rise and Fall of Cowrie Shells: The Asian Story', *Journal of World History*, 22 (2011), no. 1, 1–25.

validated them. In the Abbasid Caliphate coins bore the motto 'There is no god but God', while the modern US dollar declares 'In God we trust'.[26]

There is one area, however, where money has no power: the afterlife. In Bruges art museum two paintings by Jan Provoost hang side by side. One of them shows a miserly merchant on his deathbed pointing to the healthy balance in his ledger and desperately trying to pass a promissory note across to the next painting, the afterworld, where a grinning skeleton refuses to accept it and preaches a little sermon on the limitations of finance. A reverend gentleman in the background appears to corroborate the skeleton's sentiments. Provoost's painting points to a salient and disturbing feature of money: its meagre content as a symbolic system, disconnected from eternal values. I shall return to this theme.

However that may be, using money is far more flexible and convenient than barter or gift, at least in this life. That is because it is a symbol both of trust and of power. A recent history of finance calls it both 'trust inscribed' and 'portable power'.[27] The trust is primary, though: money enables us to exchange goods and services with people we have never met before, may well never meet again, and have no other grounds for trusting. The power of money is derivative: money mediates power because in most times and places people trust it. If they do not trust it, as in a period of hyper-inflation, then it has little power.

No one thought about money more deeply than the German sociologist Georg Simmel, whose book *The Philosophy of Money*, published in 1907, remains the most serious study of its social implications. As we saw above,[28] he believed that money depended on pre-existing general social trust, fixed that trust, and made it economically effective.

In doing so, it offers alluring prospects to all who can acquire it. Jorge Luis Borges called a coin 'a panoply of possible futures'. For the deprived and unfree, even a small amount can be liberating: Fedor Dostoevsky observed in his Siberian convict camp that 'Money is minted freedom, hence for a man deprived of freedom, it is ten times more valuable.'[29]

Note, though, that such trust depends partly on confidence in the authority which issues the money and in the general stability of the social order. As Simmel observed, 'The feeling of personal security that the possession of money gives is perhaps the most concentrated and pointed form and manifestation of confidence in the socio-political organisation and order.'[30] When people do not trust money, because of high inflation, revolution, or other rapid social change, it is a symptom of the general weakening of trust throughout society which often entails an abrupt transformation of political power too.

[26] Morgan, *History*, 13–16.
[27] Niall Ferguson, *The Ascent of Money: A Financial History of the World*, revised edition, London: Penguin Books, 2009, 31, 22.
[28] See Chapter 2, 'Sociologists on Trust'.
[29] Jorge Luis Borges, 'The Zahir', in his *Collected Fictions*, trans. Andrew Hurley, London: Allen Lane, 1999, 244; Dostoevsky, 'Zapiski iz mertvogo doma', *Polnoe sobranie sochinenii*, Leningrad: Nauka, 1972, iv. 17.
[30] Georg Simmel, *The Philosophy of Money*, London: Routledge, 1978, 179.

Inflation, indeed, is the great destroyer of trust in money. It breaches all Sztompka's preconditions for trust.[31] Only when inflation gets out of control do we notice how much we normally rely on the confidence that money will be worth tomorrow, next week, and, within a percentage or two, next year, what it is worth today. Without that confidence economic life descends to more primitive levels, in which people desperately seek for alternative repositories of value that they can exchange for what they need. Those who have such things hoard them; those who have not face abject poverty. The fabric of an advanced society, many of whose processes depend on money as lubricant, begins to rip apart. The economist John Maynard Keynes observed that 'As inflation proceeds . . . all permanent relations between debtors and creditors, which form the ultimate foundation of capitalism, become so utterly disordered as to be almost meaningless. . . . There is no subtler, no surer means of overturning the existing basis of society.'[32]

The German hyper-inflation of 1922–3 offers a terrible example. At its height a lifetime's savings would buy no more than a cup of coffee. A witness recalled: 'Dentists and doctors stopped charging in currency and demanded butter or eggs, but the farmers were holding back their produce. "We don't want any Jew-confetti from Berlin," a chronicler quotes a Bavarian farmer. The flight from currency that had begun with the buying of diamonds, gold, country houses, and antiques now extended to minor and almost useless items—bric-a-brac, soap, hairpins. The law-abiding country crumbled into petty thievery. Copper pipes and brass armatures weren't safe. Gasoline was siphoned from cars. People bought things they didn't need and used them to barter—a pair of shoes for a shirt, some crockery for coffee. Berlin had a witches' "Sabbath" atmosphere.'[33]

The reference to Jews and witches reminds one that what is involved is intense distrust, which needs to attach itself to an object. Money, when it is not a mediator of trust, becomes a powerful mediator of distrust, especially when it starkly divides the haves from the have-nots. Such distrust can become poisonous and destructive at times of crisis. Elias Canetti thought that the inflation was decisive in turning many Germans towards anti-Semitism: '[Jews'] long-standing connection with money, their traditional understanding of its movements and fluctuations, their skill in speculation, the way they flocked together in money markets, where their behaviour contrasted strikingly with the soldierly conduct which was the German ideal—all this, in a time of doubt, instability and hostility to money, could not but make them appear dubious and hostile.'[34]

This distrust arises from the nature of money as a symbolic system. Most symbolic systems create meanings which combine with each other to generate further meanings. This is how many advances are made in mathematics and the

---

[31] See Chapter 2, 'Sociologists on Trust'.

[32] J. M. Keynes, *The Economic Consequences of the Peace*, New York: Harcourt, Brace, and Howe, 1919, 220–33, quoted in Niall Ferguson, *The Cash Nexus: Money and Power in the Modern World*, London: Allen Lane, 2001, 209.

[33] From 'Adam Smith' (George J. W. Goodman), *Paper Money*, quoted in Kevin Jackson (ed), *The Oxford Book of Money*, Oxford University Press, 1995, 449.

[34] From Elias Canetti, *Crowds and Power* (1960), quoted in *The Oxford Book of Money*, 451.

sciences: through reflecting on how we interpret what we already know and linking it with other aspects of the same or another symbolic system. Money, however, is strangely impoverished and isolationist in this respect. It can beget a bewildering variety of financial institutions, but no meanings which refer to other symbolic systems. It is like an inert element which does not combine with other chemical substances. Money is the purest example of the tool, being highly versatile and applicable to almost any use. Neutral, precisely calculable, and infinitely fungible, it tends to reduce all our experience to a series of quantitatively conceived means without ends and without autonomous significance. In that way, when detached from the objects it enables us to exchange, it actually tends to drain other symbolic systems of their significance. In the words of Simmel, 'Money is everywhere conceived as purpose, and countless things which are really ends in themselves are thereby degraded to mere means.'[35] Or, in the more elegant words of Oscar Wilde, it encourages those people who 'know the price of everything and the value of nothing'.

Indeed it may be worse than that. When money completely detaches itself from other symbolic systems, it can become extremely dangerous. It metastasizes and takes control over them, implanting in them cancerous cells of its own value-neutrality. Those engaged in the business of money tend to assume that they are emancipated from ethics, from religion, and whenever they can manage it also from law. When they operate in the global economy, they also disdain the state as public risk manager. This is what Karl Marx was referring to when he wrote 'The bourgeoisie, whenever it has got the upper hand, has put an end to all feudal, patriarchal, idyllic relations . . . and has left no other nexus between man and man than naked self-interest, than callow cash payment.'[36]

In his 2011 Reith Lectures philosopher Michael Sandel offered examples of the incursion of money into areas of life where it reinforces inappropriate or even repugnant moral standards: buying, and therefore treating as a commodity, human body parts or babies for adoption, the right to pollute the atmosphere or to shoot an endangered animal. Such things have always been available for money in the form of illicit markets, usury, or bribery. But there has usually been a shifty, underhand air about them. Today, Sandel is probably right to suggest that such trades are closer to being considered legitimate than ever before: 'The era of market triumphalism has coincided with a time when public discourse has been largely empty of moral and spiritual substance.' When monetary values penetrate so deeply, they undermine community: 'People of affluence and people of modest means increasingly lead separate lives.' Since we tend to trust more readily those who are like us, this blatant inequality entails an increase in generalized social distrust.[37]

[35] Simmel, *Philosophy of Money*, 431.
[36] Karl Marx and Friedrich Engels, *Manifesto of the Communist Party*, with introduction and notes by Gareth Stedman Jones, London: Penguin Books, 2002, 222.
[37] Michael Sandel, *What Money Can't Buy: The Moral Limits of Markets*, London: Allen Lane, 2012, 202–3.

In one passage of his *Philosophy of Money* Simmel compares the power of money to the power of God. 'In so far as money becomes the absolutely sufficient expression and equivalent of all values, it rises to abstract heights way above the whole broad diversity of objects; it becomes the centre in which the most opposed, the most estranged and the most distant things find their common denominator and come into contact with one another.'[38] Devotion to money as an instrument for gaining power and ensuring security has the potential to subvert other symbolic systems. For all the benefits offered by money, we must never forget this danger. Money creates trust, but equally readily destroys it.

BANKING

From the earliest recorded times institutions sprang up to facilitate the use of money. In ancient Egypt, Greece, and Rome money-changers would help those who had the coins of another city or country. Money-lenders would advance cash to those who for the moment had not enough—though only against some kind of guarantee, while charging interest for the period of the loan. Banks would accept deposits and probably sometimes arranged credit transfers, though we know little about credit systems in the ancient world, perhaps because the documents recording them have not survived as coins have.[39]

Banking was highly developed in the medieval Middle East, where bankers played a vital role in the monetarization of the economy. They provided quite a number of different services, all dependent on clients' trust. They accepted money on deposit. They changed money from one currency to another. They weighed and assayed coins (a vital service when coins lost value if they were worn or clipped), then issued them in sealed purses certified to be worth a specified amount. They accepted payment orders (Arabic *ruq'a*), rather like the modern cheque, issued promissory notes, and discounted bills of exchange, which circulated more or less as cash. In this form they offered credit, helping to lubricate trade which would have become much more fitful if immediate payment in coins had always been expected.[40]

We know far more about the banks of late medieval Europe. That was when, starting in Italy, banks began to take on the variety of functions we associate with them today. Those functions also depend on trust: a bank accepts deposits from its clients, who entrust money to it since its vaults are safer than the family strong-box, let alone the mattress. The bank promises to pay back that money when the client needs it. All the same, in apparent contradiction, it lends out much of that money to other clients in need of a loan. In other words, it extends credit, which is another word for trust. This of course is risky: banks are borrowing short and lending

[38] Simmel, *Philosophy of Money*, 236: I have slightly modified the translation.
[39] Glyn Davies, *A History of Money from Ancient Times to the Present Day*, Cardiff: University of Wales Press, 2002, chapter 3.
[40] Goitein, *Mediterranean Society*, i. 230–62.

long. What if all one's clients turn up together to withdraw their deposits? In normal circumstances, though, that is extremely unlikely. An essential skill of banking is to be able to foresee when circumstances may become abnormal. In general, banks specialize in gathering information about the state of trade, the creditworthiness of their customers, and in assessing the risks inherent in lending money. That is how they stay afloat and earn the trust of their clients.

Gradually banks began to offer other services too. Carrying coins about in any quantity was inconvenient and risky. Much better to write a cheque drawn on a bank one trusted; or, as a variant for long-distance trade, with more than one currency involved, to write a bill of exchange. This convenient instrument would be given by banker A to customer B instructing bank C in another city and possibly in another country to pay an equivalent amount to B or his agent there. This of course could only be done if bankers A and C trusted each other and also customer B and his agent. But if such trust existed the bill of exchange was enormously useful. For one thing, since the journey from one town to another took an appreciable time, the bill in effect offered credit: thirty, sixty, or ninety days were customary, usually specified on the bill. One economic historian actually calls bills of exchange 'the most widely used credit instrument in the course of the thirteenth century'.[41]

Eventually too it became acceptable for customer B to endorse a bill of exchange, signing it on the reverse, so that he could use it for paying a third party. In that way the bill became a surrogate currency, though of course only if the payee knew and trusted B and probably A as well. This did not become a regular practice before the sixteenth century, but already earlier the bill of exchange functioned as a kind of money among a circle of colleagues who knew and trusted each other. In that way it increased the money supply and therefore the amount of trade that could be conducted with confidence.[42]

A logical extension of the bill of exchange was paper money, that is, a piece of paper issued by a bank promising to pay any bearer a certain sum of money in the accepted local currency. It was, if you like, a bill of exchange with universal applicability inside a particular territory or political unit. Paper is much lighter and easier to deal with than coins, which in any quantity are heavy. But for paper money to maintain its value and function properly, the society's trust structures must be both broad and stable. The first country where this condition was fulfilled was China, where already by the ninth–tenth century CE the emperors began to issue paper money. Under the Song dynasty this became a regular practice, and one that was taken over by the Mongols when they ruled over China.[43] Marco Polo, in his account of his travels to China, remarked that the Great Khan 'has mastered the art of alchemy' by issuing paper as a substitute for gold. 'With this

---

[41] R. S. Lopez, *The Commercial Revolution of the Middle Ages, 950–1350*, Cambridge University Press, 1976, 104.

[42] Peter Spufford, *Money and its Use in Medieval Europe*, Cambridge University Press, 1987, 254–6; Raymond de Roover, *L'Évolution de la lettre de change (xiv–xviii siècles)*, Paris: Armand Colin, 1953.

[43] Davies, *History*, 180–3; Denis Twitchett and Paul Jakov Smith (eds), *The Cambridge History of China*, v/1: *The Sung Dynasty and its Precursors, 907–1279*, Cambridge University Press, 2009, 748–9.

currency he orders all payments to be made throughout every province and kingdom and region of his empire.... All the peoples and populations who are subject to his rule are perfectly willing to accept these payments, since everywhere they pay in the same currency. With these pieces of paper they can buy anything and pay for everything.'[44]

In spite of Marco Polo's encomium, though, there is a problem about paper money. Since it has no intrinsic value, unlike gold or silver, governments, when in debt, will always be tempted to issue too much of it; as a result it becomes devalued and less trustworthy, and hence cannot function properly as money. During the first half of the thirteenth century, under pressure of war, disaster relief, and the corruption of officials, the Song court increased the note issue by a factor of twenty-five. The natural result was runaway inflation: money ceased to function smoothly as the lubricator of economic processes, and social breakdown resulted, ultimately fatal for the dynasty.[45]

Late medieval Italian city-states found better ways to augment the supply of money, while strengthening social trust rather than enfeebling it. They were small and constantly engaged in battles with each other, and with outside forces such as the papacy and the Holy Roman Empire. They were also self-governing, and their citizens created a variety of elective institutions of government, all subordinated to the commune, the citizen assembly. Small, self-governing, embattled communities have to generate a strong sense of internal cohesion if they are to survive, and that is what the Italian cities did. It is important not to misunderstand: I am not asserting that within their walls brotherly harmony always prevailed. On the contrary, there was constant feuding between lower-level trust networks: families, guilds, confraternities, and patron–client coteries. But when necessary they would drop these conflicts and reunite, if only temporarily, to defend the whole city, and they would then deploy their own armed militias for the purpose.[46] The interplay between these two types of solidarity exemplifies the distinction between routine 'thick' trust, towards one's own faction, and somewhat 'thinner' trust, towards the commune, which could be reanimated and mobilized in an emergency. It also illustrates that in a crisis it often makes sense to *broaden* the radius of trust.

In the economic sense this solidarity revealed itself in an important new practice: the floating of public loans among the citizens. Genoa and Venice were the first cities to do this. At first the loans were obligatory: citizens would form syndicates to make loans, and in return would be assigned the revenue from a tax category. Venice raised compulsory loans in this way from the twelfth century, and set aside a portion of the excise to guarantee repayment. That was no different from the practice of monarchs. In time, though, it occurred to the city fathers that they could offer an incentive monarchs could not, and hence compulsion was not

---

[44] *The Travels of Marco Polo*, trans. and introd. Ronald Latham, London: Penguin Books, 1958, 147–8.

[45] *Cambridge History of China*, v/1: 908–10.

[46] Edward Muir, 'The Idea of Community in Renaissance Italy', *Renaissance Quarterly*, 55 (2002), 1–18, especially 5–6.

necessary: if one paid annuities offering an attractive rate of return, citizens would subscribe voluntarily. After all, the loans were guaranteed by an elected body of one's own associates, who would suffer badly if their credit were impugned; not much in life comes in more trustworthy form than that. Some ingenious devices were adopted: in the mid-fifteenth century, for example, Florence created a 'bank of dowries', in which fathers could invest for up to fifteen years in order to provide for marriageable daughters at the end of that time. Some of these debts were tradeable, and in time many of them were consolidated and sold as bonds on the money market. The upshot was that citizens became accustomed to trading in securities, and to relying on them as a safe way of making a profit from spare funds.[47]

Faced by external threats, these wealthy, productive cities deployed the trust generated by their elective, self-governing institutions to raise credit that would not normally be offered except to trusted associates in times of danger. This credit then became the nursery of permanent financial institutions to mobilize and transfer funds for peacetime purposes, including long-term investment. Politics and economics reinforced each other in creating the conditions for stable companies to emerge.

Contrast this situation with that of monarchs. For all their potential sources of income, monarchs had difficulties in raising funds. The problem was that they could not be fully trusted. Lenders were reluctant to advance money directly to monarchs, since after all those monarchs controlled the law courts where those lenders might one day have to seek redress for non-repayment. Monarchs had to offer extraordinary security against such an eventuality: a common one was the right to collect taxes—tax-farming. But such a method was a grossly inefficient way of raising revenue, since much of it went into the pockets of the tax-farmers. It was also blatantly unjust: it usually meant that the poor paid taxes, while the rich did not.[48] Moreover, fear of royal default was not idle. In the seventeenth century a number of European monarchs did renege on their debts: France in 1648 and 1661, England in 1672, Denmark in 1660, Spain several times. City-state republics, as in Italy, Switzerland, and the Netherlands, were much more reliable, for they raised loans on the security provided by their own elected citizens' assemblies, law courts, and municipal banks, whose reputation would be much more damaged by a default than would that of a monarch.[49]

Yet monarchs had one crucial advantage: the size of their armies and of their taxable populations. In spite of the Italian cities' success, by the early sixteenth century, it looked as if the nature of warfare required resources on such a scale that only a large monarchy could mobilize them. In the late fifteenth and early sixteenth centuries the main Italian city-states were conquered by two absolute monarchies, France and Spain, which then proceeded to fight a long war over their territories.

[47] Louro Martines, *Power and Imagination: City-States in Renaissance Italy*, New York: Vintage Books, 1980, 240–4; James Macdonald, *A Free Nation Deep in Debt: The Financial Roots of Democracy*, Princeton University Press, 2006, 69–95.

[48] John Hicks, *A Theory of Economic History*, Oxford: Clarendon Press, 1969, 85–94.

[49] Martin Körner, 'Public Credit', in Richard Bonney (ed), *Economic Systems and State Finance*, Oxford: Clarendon Press, for the European Science Foundation, 1995, 525–31.

The only hope for cities was to create a league of several large ones. This is exactly what the cities of the Netherlands did in the late sixteenth and early seventeenth centuries. They managed to raise enough revenues to avoid the fate of the Italian cities, to throw off the rule of the Spanish monarchy, and then to defend their independence in a war lasting on and off for eighty years.

There were many reasons for the Dutch revolt, but a major one was the imposition of new taxes by the Spanish overlord. Yet, in order to fight Spain, the Dutch cities imposed on themselves levies which exceeded even the Spaniards' demands. The crucial difference was that these taxes were self-imposed and that they were supplemented by the floating of public debt on the Italian model. The annuities they offered found a ready market, not only inside the Netherlands, but abroad as well. The Dutch cities were able to incur ever mounting debts, yet borrow funds at relatively low interest rates.[50] By 1715, at the end of the French wars, the level of debt was probably around 200 per cent of annual GNP, yet investors were still willing to commit their money. As one economic historian of the period writes, 'Because the officers of the state themselves held large portions of their fortunes in government bonds, every public creditor could be sure that his investment was safe. The whole system was based on the kind of trust that was so conspicuously lacking in the credit arrangements of the monarchies.'[51] Each city had its own self-government and its own civic solidarity. In peacetime they frequently squabbled among themselves, and were often unable to mobilize resources for common purposes. To resist the Spaniards, however, they combined effectively as the United Provinces, with their own parliament, the Estates General, and their own quasi-monarch, the Stadholder.[52] As so often, it took an external threat to broaden the boundaries of mutual trust.

In the late seventeenth century, the Italian–Dutch system of public debt was adopted for the first time by a major European monarchy: England, soon to become Britain. The revolution of 1688–9 made possible the mobilization of public credit—i.e. public trust—on a hitherto unprecedented scale. As Fukuyama has pointed out, crucial to this achievement was that England already had a strong central state and a well-established rule of law (even if that law benefited only a small elite). After 1660 the government had also put in place customs and excise taxes which were relatively efficient, relatively uncorrupt, and drew on much of the country's real wealth in the form of manufacture and trade—though not yet land. What happened as a result of the 1688–9 revolution was that the English state added to its armoury the Italian–Dutch technique of public credit. It did so by supplementing the strong state and the rule of law with Fukuyama's third

[50] Augustus J. Veenendal Jr, 'Fiscal Crises and Constitutional Freedom in the Netherlands, 1450–1795', in Philip T. Hoffman and Kathryn Norberg (eds), *Fiscal Crises, Liberty and Representative Government*, Stanford University Press, 1994, 115–25; L. Neal, 'How it All Began: The Monetary and Financial Architecture of Europe, 1648–1815', *Financial History Review*, 7 (2000), 123.

[51] Macdonald, *Free Nation*, 156.

[52] Jonathan Israel, *The Dutch Republic: Its Rise, Greatness and Fall*, Oxford University Press, 1995, 185–6.

requirement for good governance: public accountability of the executive. The incoming monarch, William of Orange, Stadholder of the United Provinces, was prepared to make this concession as the price of securing England's support in his home country's life-and-death struggle against France. As a Dutch statesman, moreover, he knew about good public credit.[53]

Through the Bill of Rights of 1689, the great landowners and London merchants bound William to a constitutional style of rule in which they consented to being seriously taxed in order to establish trustworthy forms of public credit and to gain control over parliament, the army and navy, and the state budget. This was the first time the city-state method of raising public loans had been tried at the level of a sizeable power. Municipal trust structures now became operative at the level of a major European monarchy, drawing in landowners too, and broadening the radius of trust to an unprecedented extent. This could only be achieved by a constitutional monarchy, whose parliament could render credible the promise to make repayment of debt the first charge on the public revenues—since it represented the people from whom the money had been borrowed.

As a contemporary pamphlet explained, 'No Man whatever having lent his money to the Government on the Credit of the Parliamentary Fund has been defrauded of his Property. . . . The Goodness of the Publick Credit in England is the reason why we shall never be out of Debt. . . . Let us be, I say, a free Nation deep in Debt, rather than a Nation of Slaves owing Nothing.'[54]

The theorist of the new political settlement (his main work was written before but published after 1689) was John Locke. He believed trust was essential to political arrangements—indeed to all stable social life. Human beings, he asserted, 'live upon trust'. Ordinary people were bound by the law of nature to trust one another except where untrustworthiness was blatant, for only thus could society hold together. Locke was tolerant on principle in religious matters, but he made an exception for atheism, which he abhorred because he thought people who did not believe in God did not feel themselves bound by their undertakings. If people regularly broke their oaths and violated contracts, society would fall apart, or, to borrow a phrase from another thinker, life would become 'nasty, brutish and short'. Trust for Locke more or less replaced the untrammelled power of Hobbes's sovereign as the foundation of social stability. Governments, he believed, in particular depended on the trust of their subjects, and if they did not deserve it they became tyrannies; if they persisted in their folly they could legitimately be overthrown.[55]

Having the trust-generating guarantees of the Bill of Rights in place enabled the government to revive more successfully a method of taxation reminiscent of Charles I's fateful Ship Money, which had provoked rebellion and ultimately civil war. In

[53] Fukuyama, *The Origins of Political Order from Prehuman Times to the French Revolution*, London: Profile Books, 2011, 14–19, 413–20.

[54] *The Chimera, or the French Way of Paying National Debts Laid Open* (1720), 7–9, quoted in Macdonald, *Free Nation*, 3.

[55] John Dunn, *Locke*, Oxford University Press, 1984, 52–7; quotation on p. 52.

1692 it introduced a land tax, levied variously (depending on the level of military expenditure) on the imputed annual income at between one and four shillings in the pound.[56] It was to be raised each month in regular instalments by county committees and remitted to the Exchequer. A tax which in the 1640s had been rejected as tyrannical was now peacefully accepted as legitimate, even though it was to be levied at an even higher rate.[57] The crucial difference was that the system had meanwhile become constitutional, and this enabled a substantially higher level of trust in government. As the economic historian Martin Daunton has commented, writing about a later period, successful taxation depends on 'institutional procedures and social norms which sustain cooperative solutions to the problems of collective action, and provide some assurance that fellow taxpayers and the government may be trusted'.[58]

Another keystone of the financial-constitutional revolution was the creation of the Bank of England, on the model of the successful municipal banks of Italy and the Netherlands. Opened in 1694, with a large public subscription, it was the only chartered joint-stock bank, and remained so till 1826. Investors who purchased so-called 'gilt-edged' bonds from the Bank of England had their dividends or annuities guaranteed by parliament as the first call on tax revenues. The Bank had two main functions: (i) it managed the government's debt; (ii) it dominated the note issue, indeed from 1844 had a virtual monopoly over it, and was thus able to play the leading role in guaranteeing the value of the pound sterling. The paper money it issued extended the principle of bills of exchange as circulating currency. This currency, however, was now offered not only to trusted customers but was generally available, and it was secured not by an individual merchant or banker, but by an institution bearing the whole authority of the English monarchy.[59]

The Bank also acted as the focus of the credit system of the City of London. This function stemmed from the government's decision in 1693 to create a permanent debt which was transferable, that is to say, which could be sold at any time when investors wanted to recover their funds, just like shares in a joint-stock company. Government securities became just another form of investment, though an unusually secure one, and they proved immediately popular, for that reason. In fact a number of joint-stock companies bought up large tranches of what became known as the National Debt, which gave potential investors additional confidence in those companies—not always justifiably, as we shall see.

The Bank of England's orderly discharge of its two main functions gave wealthy people far more confidence in investing their money, not only in the Bank itself,

[56] A pound was twenty shillings.

[57] Thomas Ertman, *Birth of Leviathan: Building States and Regimes in Medieval and Early Modern Europe*, Cambridge University Press, 1997, 208–21; H. Roseveare, *The Financial Revolution, 1660–1760*, New York: Routledge, 1991, 33–4, 45.

[58] Martin Daunton, *Trusting Leviathan: The Politics of Taxation in Britain, 1799–1914*, Cambridge University Press, 2001, 10–11.

[59] H. V. Bowen, 'The Bank of England during the Long Eighteenth Century, 1694–1820', in Richard Roberts (ed), *The Bank of England: Money, Power and Influence, 1694–1994*, Oxford: Clarendon Press, 1995, 1–18; Larry Neal, 'How it All Began', 124.

but in the economy generally. Contemporaries argued that the Bank 'must be secure [because of] the great sums they have lent the government upon the faith of a British Parliament which is sufficient to keep them above failure'. By 1776 Adam Smith was able to declare, 'The stability of the Bank of England is equal to that of the British government.' Lord North called it simply 'a part of the constitution'.[60]

During the eighteenth century Britain fought numerous expensive wars. The National Debt enabled the Treasury to borrow on a previously unprecedented scale, laying the foundation of what has become known as the 'fiscal-military state'.[61] Holders of spare cash proved willing to invest in a so-called Sinking Fund, consisting of outstanding state debt, in return for dividends or annuities. Since confidence in the Bank was high, the Fund was fully subscribed early on, and the National Debt remained a permanent institution, almost a benefit, a way of attracting funds. Banks and insurance companies would place their spare funds there for periods, in the knowledge that they would retain their value and that they could be recovered at any time to meet an emergency (important for banks since in general they were borrowing short and lending long). As an investment, the National Debt generated returns more quickly than land, yet was still very secure. It helped to form the habit of investment among the middle and upper classes, who began to strengthen their confidence in the future by providing in this way against the risks of illness and old age, and making provision for dependants and heirs.[62] In this way the trust networks of the upper and middle class became more closely integrated with the state.

There were good reasons for trusting 'the funds'. All the same, the process did not run smoothly. The new techniques of making money also created new ways of losing it. Unfamiliar systems of trust cannot be built overnight, especially when they converge with old systems not yet completely outgrown—in this case royal monopoly companies. One of the first fruits of the British fiscal-military state was the South Sea Bubble. The South Sea Company was created from the opportunities engendered by the end of war in 1715 and in the expectation of attractive profits from the slave trade with South America. It was an old-style chartered monopoly, and like previous such companies it took on responsibility for much of the National Debt. The holders of relatively low-return Treasury bills were encouraged to exchange them for tradeable South Sea shares, which were expected to offer a much higher return. Many people saw this as both a lucrative and a patriotic venture, and they hastened to make the transfer, buoyed up by the new confidence in the money markets. It was considered smart and fashionable to be 'in the South Seas'. For a time there was very brisk business, and the price of South Sea shares rose dramatically. Half of the MPs bought them, as did a good many peers and

[60] Bowen, 'Bank of England', 13, 3.

[61] John Brewer, *The Sinews of Power: War, Money and the English State*, London: Unwin Hyman, 1989.

[62] Ron Harris, 'Government and the Economy, 1688–1850', in *The Cambridge Economic History of Modern Britain*, i: *Industrialisation, 1700–1860*, Cambridge University Press, 2004, 218; Peter Earle, *The Making of the English Middle Class: Business, Society and Family Life in London, 1660–1730*, London: Methuen, 1989, 146–51.

several government ministers, including the Chancellor of the Exchequer. According to one estimate, as many as three-quarters of the active investing public held shares at any one time.[63]

Actual returns, however, were disappointing, and the Company became to all intents and purposes a pyramid or Ponzi scheme, no longer paying dividends out of real profits, but using recent investments to pay off obligations to previous investors.[64] Eventually the public began to suspect what was happening, and in September 1720 the 'bubble' burst. South Sea share prices began to decline, and then fell sharply as investors tried to cut their losses. Dividends ceased, the shares became almost worthless, and many investors faced ruin, especially those who had been relying on Treasury annuities which they had surrendered for now worthless South Sea paper.[65] In the end, to avert a complete collapse of confidence, which would have affected all financial markets, the government decided to convert many South Sea shares back into Treasury bonds, whose modest returns by that time looked attractive when compared with total ruin. A parliamentary inquiry found that an inner circle of directors had made fraudulent statements, and had bribed officials, court favourites, and MPs to keep silent.[66] The whole episode illustrated the vulnerability to fraud of large-scale, trust-sustained finance, and the difficulty of judging the prospects of companies in open financial markets, especially when their interests became interwoven with those of the government. Trust had been augmented, but so too had risk. Distrust, when it came, was sudden, cumulative, and destructive—a pattern to be repeated many times later.

It is instructive to compare the South Sea Bubble, which in the end did not fatally harm British public credit, with the rather similar scheme launched in France by the Scottish banker John Law. Law thought public credit should be expanded in France by using English techniques. He persuaded the Regent to let him rename his bank La Banque Royale, with the power to issue paper money. He then amalgamated the Banque with his own new venture, the Mississippi Company, to form La Compagnie des Indes as a monopoly chartered company, which would make huge profits by developing the extensive French territories in the Mississippi valley. Its revenues were intended to clean up royal finances by paying off the royal debt and repurchasing venal offices. The profits, however, soon proved illusory. Law covered the mounting deficits by getting the Banque to issue ever more paper money, and by censoring press reports on the Company's activities. The resulting runaway inflation, combined with the throttling of information and discussion, only intensified investors' suspicions, and the Company soon crashed just like its South Sea equivalent. In France, though, the crash brought down the Banque Royale as well, and with

---

[63] Roseveare, *Financial Revolution*, 56–7.

[64] Such schemes are essentially confidence tricks, or what one might call 'trust scams'. They are surprisingly durable. The apotheosis of all such schemes was unmasked in December 2008, when a crooked financier with the implausibly Dickensian name of Madoff was revealed to have defrauded his clients of no less than $50 billion over a period of nearly half a century.

[65] Roseveare, *Financial Revolution*, 52–8.

[66] Larry Neal, *The Rise of Financial Capitalism: International Markets in the Age of Reason*, Cambridge University Press, 1990, chapter 5.

it France's entire financial system. Thereafter the French monarchy depended on hand-to-mouth expedients, such as short-term loans from tax-farmers and the sale of office, right through to 1789. This financial instability was one of the main causes of the French Revolution. The whole episode demonstrated first that a national currency-issuing bank needs to be independent of any commercial company, and second that stifling public discussion undermines the confidence essential to any system of credit.[67]

During the three decades after the South Sea fiasco and in spite of it, two First Lords of the Treasury, Robert Walpole and Henry Pelham, succeeded in consolidating the various categories of public debt in the form of Treasury bonds known as 'consols', and reducing the interest on them to just 3 per cent, remarkably low by the standards of the time. In practice, investors were prepared to forgo the higher rates available elsewhere and to buy 'consols', simply because they were absolutely trustworthy: with parliament's guarantee they could not fail, and interest on them was always paid on time.[68] In that way, at modest cost, the Treasury could run a mounting debt stretching indefinitely into the future—*provided confidence remained high*. On the whole—with a notable blip after the crash of the South Sea Company—it did so. By the 1730s Treasury bonds had become the normal way for wealthy people to place a substantial part of their spare money when they wanted a reliable return.[69] During the eighteenth century the Treasury took full advantage of this public trust: in 1688 the National Debt was about £1 million, but by 1698 it had risen to £15 million, by 1750 to £78 million, by 1770 to £131 million, and by 1790 to no less than £244 million. Then, during the Napoleonic wars it made another exponential leap, to £456 million in 1801, £745 million in 1815, and £844 million in 1819. Interest payments servicing this colossal debt often consumed more than half of public expenditure, yet the public proved willing to go on investing in Treasury bonds to help finance them.[70] In Martin Daunton's words, credit had 'shifted from reliance on personal reputation and obligation to a more impersonal nexus of financial institutions—and underpinning them was the government's involvement in the financial markets of London'.[71]

In this way, Britain's 'fiscal-military state' became far more efficient at raising both taxes and loans than Britain's great rival France, which was restricted to short-term loans and the sale of office. As a result, with more modest resources Britain was able to mobilize much greater economic power for war-making purposes.[72] This

---

[67] Thomas E. Kaiser, 'Money, Despotism and Public Opinion in Early Eighteenth Century France: John Law and the Debate on Royal Credit', *Journal of Modern History*, 63 (1991), 1–28; Paul Harsin, *Crédit Public et Banque d'État en France du xvii au xviii siècle*, Paris: Droz, 1933, 59–60.

[68] Roseveare, *Financial Revolution*, 61–3.

[69] Stephen Quinn, 'Money, Finance and Capital Markets', in *The Cambridge Economic History of Modern Britain*, i: 147–74; Peter Earle, *The Making of the English Middle Class: Business, Society and Family Life in London, 1660–1730*, London: Methuen, 1989, 146–51.

[70] Harris, 'Government and the Economy', 216–17.

[71] Daunton, *Trusting Leviathan*, 6.

[72] John Brewer, *The Sinews of Power: War, Money and the English State, 1688–1783*, London: Unwin Hyman, 1989; Patrick K. O'Brien, 'Fiscal Exceptionalism: Great Britain and its European Rivals from Civil War to Triumph at Trafalgar and Waterloo', in Donald Winch and Patrick

enhanced power resulted directly from the effective mobilization of trust, focused on national institutions.

Reflecting on the financial-constitutional revolution has given rise to a whole school of economics, the so-called 'institutional school'. In 1989 Douglass North and Barry Weingast asserted in a seminal article that the settlement of 1688–9 created institutions that in the long run made possible the development of industry and a modern economy; in particular they pointed to the secure judicial protection of property and contracts, which encouraged investment by providing redress against abuse. Ron Harris has shown that, in the formal sense, property and contract were less well defended in the courts than North and Weingast assumed, but that the new institutions, once consolidated, created vested interests which in some ways worked better than law in ensuring credible commitment.[73] The crucial point here, it seems to me, is not so much formal guarantees as the creation of habitual trust that institutions will work reliably.

Another way of both raising capital and providing stability was through insurance companies. These had first been launched in late medieval Italy: they provided cover against the risk of trading voyages going wrong—which fairly frequently occurred. As Shylock remarks caustically in *The Merchant of Venice*, 'Ships are but boards, sailors but men: there be land-rats and water-rats, water-thieves and land-thieves, I mean pirates, and then there is the peril of water, wind and rocks.' If any of these struck, you would receive compensation from the insurance underwriters; but because the risks were high, so were the premiums, and few traders could afford them.

Insurance was established on a regular and affordable basis only gradually during the eighteenth century when several prerequisites came together: statistics of disease, mortality, disaster, probability theory, and a regulated stock market. Only by combining these could a company calculate the likelihood of accident, illness, or death striking its various clients and link that likelihood to the probable returns from investment; consequently, only in that way could confidence in various kinds of insurance be fortified and sustained.[74] This was an unprecedentedly reliable method of assessing risk, providing security, and thus bolstering confidence in the future. Moreover, insurance funds not being used to compensate those who had suffered misfortune were available for investment. By the late twentieth century this was one of the main sources of investment finance.

K. O'Brien (eds), *The Political Economy of British Historical Experience, 1688–1914*, Oxford University Press for the British Academy, 2002, 245–66.

[73] P. G. M. Dickson, *The Financial Revolution in England: A Study in the Development of Public Credit*, Aldershot: Gregg Revivals, 1993; Douglass C. North and Barry R. Weingast, 'Constitutions and Commitment: The Evolution of Institutions Governing Public Choice in Seventeenth Century England', *Journal of Economic History*, 49/4 (December 1989), 803–32; Harris, 'Government and the Economy', 228.

[74] C. G. Lewin, *Pensions and Insurance before 1800: A Social History*, East Linton: Tuckwell Press, 2003, chapter 13; Geoffrey Clark, *Betting on Lives: The Culture of Life Assurance in England, 1695–1775*, Manchester University Press, 1999, 79–81.

In the course of the eighteenth century the new fiscal arrangements were gradually complemented by others, not directly dependent on the government or Bank of England, to facilitate the confident transfer of money from where it lay idle to where it could be activated for productive purposes. One of them was the Stock Exchange, as a forum for the buying and selling of securities. It took shape initially in the coffee houses around what became known as Exchange Alley in the City of London, where merchants, shipowners, and bankers would gather to exchange news about commodities, technical novelties, and commercial voyages. While drinking coffee at Jonathan's or Garraway's, buyers and sellers of securities could be brought together and matched. With the help of the latest information and of various colleagues' estimates of it, those involved could better assess the price one should pay for particular goods and services, and the risk one was assuming in undertaking certain types of transaction. The informal bonhomie of such establishments was very helpful, perhaps indispensable, in generating the mutual trust necessary for commercial and financial operations.[75] In recent decades this kind of background trust has become acknowledged as an essential aspect of 'social capital'. Institutions based on it reduce uncertainty and cut transaction costs; 'social capital' thus plays a crucial role in stimulating economic growth.[76]

At various sociable venues in Exchange Alley, then, industrial and commercial enterprises could sell shares to investors willing to risk their money in the hope of sharing in the profits. After a delay caused by the South Sea damage to the reputation of joint-stock companies, a formal Stock Exchange was finally established in its own building in 1773. At that time it had no monopoly on the trading of shares, so it had to establish a reputation for particular trustworthiness. Many of its transactions had to be carried out speedily, to profit by changing market conditions, and without immediate payment: inevitably, then, brokers and jobbers had to trust each other implicitly. Those found to be unreliable would be ruthlessly excluded. Well-fortified trust boundaries were erected: from 1801 only professional brokers and jobbers were allowed to trade on the Stock Exchange floor, and they paid a considerable subscription for the right to do so.[77]

For the kinds of very large project which characterized the later stages of the Industrial Revolution, family firms and most partnerships were too small to raise the necessary capital. This problem of scale first arose with the construction of canals, and then with the provision of gaslight and water in the towns. It became much more acute with the building of railways, which required huge capital investment before a penny could be earned in revenue. For such ventures the joint-stock limited liability company was necessary. This, however, was an innovation which alarmed many contemporaries. Economic historians have tended to

[75] Ranald C. Michie, *The London Stock Exchange: A History*, Oxford University Press, 1999, 20; Dickson, *Financial Revolution*, 590.

[76] Douglass C. North, *Institutions, Institutional Change and Economic Performance*, Cambridge University Press, 1990.

[77] Michie, *London Stock Exchange*, 34–43.

dismiss their objections as obscurantism, but actually very serious issues were involved—issues of trust. It is worth pausing to consider them.

The point was that partnerships bound the partners to the full personal responsibility that went naturally with ownership. Partners had equal rights over their joint property and the action of any one of them bound all the others. Those forming partnerships had therefore to know their colleagues well and to trust them completely. That implied that their customers could trust them no less confidently: a reputation for honesty constituted a kind of 'moral collateral' crucial to business success.[78]

The joint-stock company, on the contrary, normally limited the liability of shareholders and moreover allowed shares to be transferred at will from one owner to another. Many contemporaries feared that a commitment thus limited and transferable would engender irresponsible behaviour. The directors would be tempted to reckless expenditure, knowing that the money they spent was not their own and that extravagant display attracted its own kind of trust—unthinking trust in power and wealth. 'The faster we can spend, the more we're trusted', as a satirical play of 1870 put it. It would be difficult for individual shareholders to monitor the company's performance effectively and hold the directors to account for reckless or even fraudulent conduct.[79]

The Times warned of 'societies in which friendship, ability, knowledge, education, character, credit, even monied worth is in a great measure disregarded, and money, the mere amount and value of the shares standing in the name of each, is the sole bond of connexion between the proprietors'.[80] The banker J. W. Gilbart put it more succinctly: companies, he charged, had no conscience and could not go to heaven![81]

Economic historians tend to dismiss such warnings as anti-progressive, even though the hero of modern economists, Adam Smith, famously warned that the directors of a joint-stock company 'being the managers of other people's money than of their own, it cannot be well expected that they should watch over it with the same anxious vigilance with which the partners in a private co-partnery frequently watch over their own. . . . Negligence and profusion, therefore, must always prevail, more or less, in the management of the affairs of such a company.'[82]

In the light of the Enron collapse in 2001 and the general financial crisis which began in 2007, such old-fashioned caveats now look prophetic. Directors and company executives reward themselves with outsized pay and bonuses, essentially robbing shareholders of their legitimate returns. A modern American economist

[78] James Taylor, *Creating Capitalism: Joint-Stock Enterprise in British Politics and Culture, 1800–1870*, Woodbridge: The Boydell Press, 2006, 24–5. The phrase 'moral collateral' comes from Stefan Collini, *Public Moralists: Political Thought and Intellectual Life in Britain, 1850–1930*, Oxford: Clarendon Press, 1991, 106.
[79] Taylor, *Creating Capitalism*, 34–6. Fukuyama, *Trust*, considers how the problem of transferring trust from a personal to an institutional relationship was handled in different countries.
[80] Quoted in Taylor, *Creating Capitalism*, 27.
[81] Taylor, *Creating Capitalism*, 29–30.
[82] Smith, *The Wealth of Nations*, Oxford 1976 edition, ii: 741.

has recently reiterated the warnings: 'American corporations (and those of many other countries) are only nominally run by the shareholders. In practice, to a very large extent they are run by and for the benefit of management.... Management effectively appoints most of the board, and it naturally appoints people who are likely to serve their interests most effectively. The board decides on the pay of management, and the "company" provides good rewards for its board members. It's a cosy relationship.'[83]

The Joint Stock Companies Act of 1844 was intended to minimize these risks. It made joint-stock status automatic on condition that all joint-stock companies should register with an official Registrar, giving full details of their capital and shareholders, and thereafter produce twice-yearly returns and undergo an annual audit. These precautions were intended to ensure that potential and actual investors had maximum information on which to assess the company's reliability.[84] Limited liability became automatic in 1855, on the grounds that it tended to promote economic development by relieving investors of unlimited exposure to risk. It was maintained thereafter in the face of considerable financial instability, notably the collapse of the Overend & Gurney bank (recently refloated as a limited liability company) in 1866. One satirical journal suggested that 'in future limited liability companies be designated as *Unlimited Lie-Ability Companies!*'[85]

By the mid-nineteenth century the keystone trust structures of modern commerce and finance were all in place in Britain: a professional tax-collecting bureaucracy, parliamentary oversight over state budgets, a funded national debt under parliamentary control, a central bank with a partial or complete monopoly over the note issue, established insurance companies, and a stock exchange listing joint-stock companies under more or less effective supervision.[86] During the nineteenth century these characteristics of modern capitalism, most of which were first adopted in Britain, spread to many other European countries and to North America. They proved unprecedentedly effective in generating economic growth. With the creation of more progressive tax systems, moreover, they were able to broaden a sense of solidarity to very large masses of the population from different social classes.

In alliance with a strong constitutional state, then, capitalism can deliver great benefits to the population at large. All the same, capitalism has two fundamental weaknesses. First, as we have seen, it is liable to both manias and panics, that is, to booms and busts. That characteristic derives from the nature of trust. We tend to trust beyond—sometimes well beyond—the point at which sober reason would suggest we should be more cautious. Money is a powerful symbol of trust, and therefore of the power to get things done and to provide security. But trust is not infinite: it eventually yields to serious evidence that something is wrong. It can then metamorphose into intense distrust with alarming speed.

---

[83] Joseph E. Stiglitz, *Freefall: Free Markets and the Sinking of the Global Economy*, London: Allen Lane, 2010, 154.
[84] Taylor, *Creating Capitalism*, 135–42.   [85] Taylor, *Creating Capitalism*, 172–3, 182.
[86] Ferguson, *The Cash Nexus*, 287.

That is exactly how financial markets operate. In Britain the first crisis to reveal their nature was the South Sea Bubble, as we saw above. Similar wild oscillations accompanied the building of railways. As one railway paper reported in autumn 1845, 'It was so easy to draw a pencil on a map, to get a few names as provisional directors, to pay a few fees for provisional registration, and a few pounds for advertisements—the stake was so small, the prize so great . . . that the temptation to manufacture prospectuses was nearly irresistible. It is reckoned that £100 spent in this manner is sufficient to realise £10,000 to an adroit swindler.'[87] Letters of allotment and scrip certificates were bought and sold, the sellers wishing to divest themselves of risk, the buyers hoping for large profits by selling later on an upswing of the market. In short, financial documents themselves became the object of speculation, an inescapable accompaniment to capitalism, which benefits from, and sometimes manipulates, short-term movements of trust and distrust.

Before the risks and opportunities of railways could be soberly appraised, the result was a series of 'bubbles', scandals, and crashes, notably the panic of October 1845. Since similar bubbles also lay behind the financial crash of the late 2000s, it is worth considering their nature. Typically a bubble begins to form when a new and apparently lucrative opportunity presents itself: it may be a new invention, the opening of a new market, the discovery of hitherto unknown resources such as minerals, or the end of a war. In response investors find ways to mobilize existing funds or raise credit to take advantage of the possibilities. Bankers, brokers, and other intermediaries will usually help them, for that is how they earn their livelihood. The price of a commodity or the shares of a company rise sharply in response to ballooning demand, and an extra impulse is imparted by speculators hoping to profit by the upswing. Trust is highly contagious. A fever or 'mania' results, in which investors pile aboard, not wanting to be left out or outdone by rivals. Eventually, some event or even just a rumour casts doubt on the long-term prospects. One or two major investors calculate that the commodity or share price no longer matches the risk, and begin to sell. News spreads that something is wrong. Distrust is equally contagious. Panic sets in and feeds on itself; the price plunges. Investors sell out hastily, without even pausing to make fuller enquiry, lest delay lose them even more money. Overstretched investors, those who borrowed heavily to buy on the upswing, are ruined, firms go bankrupt, and even banks may collapse.[88] Exaggerated trust turns to equally exaggerated and destructive distrust.

The second defect of capitalism is its tendency to encourage irresponsible behaviour, to reinforce and make obvious social and economic inequality, which in itself weakens generalized social trust. Long before Karl Marx made this the central point of his analysis of capitalism, many moralists and opposition politicians were horrified at the mountains of debt being piled up by the Treasury, in apparent

---

[87] R. W. Kostal, *Law and English Railway Capitalism, 1825–1875*, Oxford: Clarendon Press, 1994, 36. This process forms the main plot of Anthony Trollope's novel *The Way We Live Now*; the fictitious railway which fraudently attracts investors is located abroad, hence its absence is more difficult to detect.

[88] Charles P. Kindleberger, *Manias, Panics and Crashes: A History of Financial Crises*, London: Macmillan, 1978, chapter 2.

disregard of the burden thus being imposed on later generations. The philosopher David Hume complained of the tendency 'to mortgage the public revenues, and to trust that posterity will pay off the incumbrances contracted by their ancestors. . . . It would scarcely be more imprudent to give a prodigal son a credit in every banker's shop in London, than to impower a statesman to draw bills in this manner upon posterity.'[89] Similarly, in his *Rural Rides*, William Cobbett highlighted capitalism's victimization of the poor, inveighing against 'the Debt, the blessed Debt . . . hanging round the neck of this nation like a millstone'. Interest on this debt was paid out of the highest tax rates in Europe, most of which was customs and excise, and so inflicted the greatest hardship on the poorest people. In this way, as Cobbett charged, the debt was a 'vortex drawing wealth into great masses . . . for the gain of a few'.[90] The wealthy and powerful, it seemed, were able to provide each other with lucrative opportunities for making money while the poor and future generations were left to bear the cost.

The only long-term way to ease this problem is for the state to deploy taxation as a means of spreading risk, sharing burdens and reducing inequality. The introduction of income tax and various forms of property taxes in most advanced countries has achieved a good deal in this respect, and has also made it possible to finance or subsidize infrastructure projects and also social services available to all who need them, such as police, armed forces, education, health care, and welfare payments. As a result, the general population has become healthier, better educated, better protected against crime, illness, and poverty—all of which benefits tend to promote generalized social trust and hence economic development too.[91]

The imposition of such taxes did not happen without formidable political struggles in most European countries. In Britain, for example, the passage of Lloyd George's 'People's Budget' of 1909 only became possible after a major constitutional crisis and far-reaching reform of the House of Lords. But it did happen, and thereby the nation-state became the generally accepted 'public risk manager', a function I examine further in Chapter 6. To formulate such taxes, collect them, and distribute them fairly required a considerable enhancement of the state's capacity to collect information and therefore an extension of its powers which made it more imperative than ever that the population could trust it. The appearance of fairness, efficiency, and probity became crucial. Martin Daunton, in his major history of British taxation, asserts that 'the creation of a high degree of trust in the state and public action permitted a shift in attitudes, away from criticism of the state as prodigal to acceptance of the state as efficient'.[92]

The dangers of capitalism are thus embedded in the nature both of trust and of money. Capitalism is a complex and delicately calibrated system of trust resting on

[89] David Hume, *Writings on Economics*, ed. Eugene Rotwein, Edinburgh: Nelson, 1955, 90–2.

[90] Quoted in Ferguson, *The Cash Nexus*, 200.

[91] Peter H. Lindert, *Growing Public: Social Spending and Economic Growth since the Eighteenth Century*, vol. i, Cambridge University Press, 2004.

[92] Martin Daunton, *Trusting Leviathan: The Politics of Taxation in Britain, 1799–1914*, Cambridge University Press, 2001, 178. See also the conversation between Bo Rothstein and the Russian tax inspector in the Introduction, above.

a symbolic system which can all too easily be disconnected from our other values. The defects of capitalism cannot be eradicated altogether: it is the function of the state to mitigate them and ensure that the huge benefits it brings are distributed widely and are connected to other values. Without such regulation capitalism tends to generate repeated economic crises, to plunge the mass of the people into poverty, and to devalue other values. That is why a strong state is not an enemy of the free market, but on the contrary vital to its successful functioning.

Money as a mediator of trust has immense potentiality; indeed it is the keystone of our current economic, social, and political stability. But money is an isolationist symbolic system, one which tends to disengage completely from other systems and then to colonize and enfeeble them, including religion, law, culture, and everyday codes of ethical behaviour. That is why Islam and the medieval Catholic church condemned usury. This cancerous tendency of money comes to the fore in financial institutions and permanently threatens to destabilize capitalism, of which those institutions are the mainstay. As a result, capitalism has a constant tendency to break away from its moorings in trust. Without vigilant regulation under a strong state it becomes self-destructive. The crises of trust of recent years are the result not of an over-mighty state, but on the contrary of the state's weakness. I shall argue this further in Chapter 6 when examining the financial crisis which began in 2007.

5

Promised Lands
Nations and Symbols of Trust

In a public lecture of 1882 at the Sorbonne the French thinker Ernest Renan asked the question 'What is a nation?', and he suggested several obvious answers, only to reject them all. Is it perhaps a race of people? he suggested. No, since modern nations have many racial origins: the French, for example, are Celtic, Iberian, and German. Is it the speakers of a common language? No, for otherwise the populations of Spain and much of South America would form one nation, while Switzerland would form several. Religion would also not qualify as a determining factor, since most nations contain several confessions; indeed religion had by the late nineteenth century become largely an individual or family matter in most European countries. Nor would shared economic interests or economic union explain nationhood: 'A Zollverein is not a fatherland!' Geographical features, such as rivers or mountain chains, sometimes form national boundaries, but more often they do not. We shall see later that all of these features have their significance, but Renan was right in asserting that none of them is conclusive.

His conclusion was that 'A nation is a soul, a spiritual principle. Only two things, which are actually only one, constitute this soul, this spiritual principle. One is in the past, the other in the present. One is the common possession of a rich legacy of remembrances, the other is the present-day consent and wish to live together, the will to continue to value the common heritage. . . . A nation is a great community of solidarity constituted by the sense of the sacrifices which one has made in the past and which one is ready to make again. It presupposes a past, but all the same in the present it comes down to a palpable fact: the agreement and clearly expressed desire to continue the communal life.'[1]

Renan's proposition is as apt and relevant today as it was in 1882, even though our economies and our communication systems are far more interlinked and globalized. Indeed, millions of people have in the meantime confirmed Renan's assertions by displaying their readiness both to kill and to die for their nation. National wars have not only occurred frequently since the late nineteenth century; they have proved even more destructive than dynastic ones. That is because nations create both strong solidarities and also rigid boundaries. A major component of

---

[1] John Hutchinson and Anthony D. Smith (eds), *Nationalism*, Oxford University Press, 1994, 17. I have modified the translation on the basis of the French text in Ernest Renan, *Qu'est-ce qu'une nation? Et autres écrits politiques*, Paris: Imprimerie Nationale, 1996, 223–43.

national feeling is the sense of the Other, the certainty about who one is *not*, whom one tends to distrust, or certainly trusts less readily. Here nations obey the same general tendencies which we have seen to operate in other contexts of trust and distrust: the stronger the feelings of mutual trust, the more rigid the boundaries around them. It is not clear in which direction the causal arrow points—probably both ways simultaneously—but in any event solidarity and boundaries are closely correlated. This helps to explain how the term 'trust' can be applied to an entity as large and complex as a nation. That trust is much easier to inspire among masses of people at a time of national danger or war. Then the boundaries are clearer, the need for solidarity and mutual trust much greater and more obvious.

As I shall argue in Chapter 7, even in peacetime, most contemporary peoples have a much stronger will to live together in nations than in international or global associations. We trust our fellow countrymen more than we do outsiders, even though, given the size of most nations, we cannot know personally the overwhelming majority of our co-nationals; that trust is inevitably very thin. In Britain a political party founded with the sole purpose of articulating that sentiment, the United Kingdom Independence Party, was by 2013–14 doing well in local, national, and European polls. The core of its appeal was that it wished the United Kingdom to limit immigration and to withdraw from the European Union. Similar parties exist in most European countries, as I shall show in Chapter 7. Even the Germans, the most internationalist in outlook, at a time of crisis tended to distrust the European Union more than they trusted it.[2]

The appeal of the nation is so attractive and powerful that many people have been ready, even willing, to sacrifice their lives for it. The Italian historian Alberto Banti suggests why. Explaining the response of many Italians to the nationalists of the Risorgimento (we are talking of several tens of thousands of people), he asks, 'What did the watchwords mean in the name of which, in the first half of the nineteenth century, many people decided to act dangerously, risking exile, prison, or even life?'[3] His answer posits 'the existence of an articulated series of "deep images" positioned at the very heart of the discursive mechanism of nationalism'. By 'deep images', he explains, 'I mean those systems of images, allegorical constructions, and narrative constellations that embody the fundamental values of nationalist discourse.'[4] In the Risorgimento Banti suggests that images of kinship and sacrifice combined with the figurative constellation of love/honour/virtue to generate an enthusiastic mass response to images of the nation.

The power of kinship derives from our early experiences as children, when the matrix of trust/distrust is fixed as a permanent driving force in our emotions, attitudes, and relationships. That is when we learnt to trust our parents, close

---

[2] By 59 to 41 per cent: *The Guardian*, 25 April 2013, 1.

[3] Alberto M. Banti, *La nazione del Risorgimento: parentela, santità e onore alle origini dell'Italia unita*, Turin: Einaudi, 2006, 3; Banti applied his ideas more generally in his *L'onore della nazione: identità sessuali e violenza nel nazionalismo europeo dal xviii secolo alla Grande Guerra*, Turin: Einaudi, 2005.

[4] Alberto Mario Banti, 'Reply', in the debate on his interpretation of Italian Risorgimento nationalism, *Nations and Nationalism*, 15/3 (2009), 449.

relatives, and those near to us in the community.[5] Kinship was the major source of social solidarity in tribal societies, along with strong military leadership, and it retains a powerful appeal within more complex social formations. In national discourse it generates the images of 'fatherland' and 'motherland', the idea of the warriors of the nation forming a 'brotherhood' and its heroes and founders becoming 'fathers'. The image of women as guardians of hearth and home, preservers of a normal and family-based way of life, constitutes another of this cluster of kinship images underpinning trust in the national community.

The ideal of sacrifice combines both military and religious imagery. It can be found much earlier than nationhood, in the symbolic repertoire of tribal societies and city-states. It inspires trust, since readiness for self-sacrifice, in battle or at the stake, suggests the ultimate in courage and reliability. Moreover, both religion and war demand that we trust those placed in political or spiritual authority over us, to the point if necessary of self-sacrifice, especially if they display honour or courage. Honour and courage are trustworthy characteristics, associated with persons, which we readily project onto the nation, especially if it is threatened. If a person is honourable and courageous we are likely to trust him or her as someone to be relied upon in difficult or dangerous circumstances. These forms of trust attachment can all be transferred to the ethnos or nation, even if we have to exercise Renan's forgetfulness about the less virtuous or creditable episodes of our national history.

Banti describes his 'deep images' as deriving from 'a discursive continuum which is centuries-old, in some cases more ancient still', but reconfigured to suit the contexts of specific historical periods.[6] I suggest that we may reformulate Renan's 'desire to continue the communal life' and Banti's 'deep images' by positing that the most important factors binding nations are the symbolic systems which strengthen faith and confidence in the national community—by and large those which I identified in Chapter 2. They derive from historically previous experience of human community life, in tribes, city-states, kingdoms, and empires.[7]

SYMBOLS OF NATIONHOOD

Anthony D. Smith indicates the most important symbolic systems when he defines a nation as 'A named human population sharing a historic territory, common myths and historical memories, a mass public culture, a common economy and common legal rights and duties for all members.'[8] The various elements of Smith's definition mostly correspond to trust-inducing symbolic systems or

[5] See Chapter 2, 'Trust, Society, and the Individual'.

[6] Alberto Mario Banti, 'Conclusions: Performative Effects and "Deep Images" in National Discourse', in Laurence Cole (ed), *Different Paths to the Nation: Regional and National Identities in Central Europe and Italy, 1830–70*, Basingstoke: Palgrave/Macmillan, 2007, 220–9; quotation on p. 223.

[7] I exclude science from the list of such symbolic systems. Science is inherently international; if anything, it acts as a restraint on the appeal of nationhood, not a support of it.

[8] Anthony D. Smith, *National Identity*, London: Penguin Books, 1991, 14.

institutions. Indeed his approach is commonly referred to as 'ethno-symbolism'.[9] It offers an account of the reasons why the idea of nationhood has such mass support among populations, especially but not only in Europe. It clarifies the essence of the nation as a set of institutions and symbolic systems whose function is to take advantage of shared ethnic identity and of the strong modern state to attract and deploy the trust of its members. Their effect is to create or give shape to what Benedict Anderson has called an 'imagined community'—'imagined' because we cannot possibly know the great majority of our co-nationals.[10] Smith's approach does not tackle directly the question of nationalism, that is, of how national identity hooks into politics, and how politicians manipulate it in order to gain or hold power, but it certainly helps us to understand how nationalism enables them to claim the allegiance of so many ordinary people.[11]

Let us briefly examine the constituent elements in Smith's paradigm. A territory or homeland is where people feel secure and have confidence in the future. It provides the means of life, and also a sense of belonging. Their forebears are buried there. It has air, water, and land: people breathe it, drink it, grow food on it, and conduct their everyday lives on it. They must look after it so that they can continue to do all those things and thus have confidence in their future. They are accustomed to the landscape and the visual culture of the towns and villages; they may not consciously value them while they live there, but many exiles have singled out the loss of these familiar features as one of the most painful aspects of loss of homeland, since without them a sense of continuity and hence an inborn and spontaneous confidence in the future are undermined. Territory also has borders, which mark the boundary between 'us' and 'them', the trusted and the less trusted. Defence of the territory's integrity and of its frontiers is always seen as a crucial priority in maintaining the nation's identity and ensuring its survival.[12]

Myths and historical memories are linked, but they are not the same. They are the stories people tell about a shared past, both personally experienced and conveyed from an earlier or 'great' past. They provide common reference points which enable members of the nation to communicate more readily. They intensify the sense of belonging to a community which will support one through difficult times, which has existed for a long time and is likely to continue to do so, and can thus underwrite our confidence in the future. The importance of such longevity is revealed in the tendency among romantic nationalists to attribute to their nations 'primordial' qualities which have existed since time immemorial. National memories tend to be selective: nations 'forget' the less creditable elements of their past, the periods when they were oppressors or committed atrocities. As Renan remarked, 'every French citizen must have forgotten St Bartholomew and the

[9] Athena Leoussi and Steven Grosby (eds), *Nationalism and Ethnosymbolism: History, Culture and Ethnicity in the Formation of Nations*, Edinburgh University Press, 2006.

[10] Benedict Anderson, *Imagined Communities: Reflections on the Origin and Spread of Nationalism*, revised edition, London: Verso, 1991.

[11] John Breuilly, *Nationalism and the State*, 2nd edition, Manchester University Press, 1993.

[12] Jan Penrose, 'Nations, States and Homelands: Territory and Territoriality in Nationalist Thought', *Nations and Nationalism*, 8/3 (2002), 277–99.

thirteenth century massacres in the Midi [in the Albigensian crusade]'.[13] The invention of tradition[14] is not possible, but its exaggeration, selection, and partial falsification certainly are. For that reason some degree of continuous monitoring of memory is necessary to social solidarity, to ensure that repressed bitterness or grief do not fester among those slighted by selective or distorted memory, and that the present does not blatantly contradict our understanding of the past. There is also danger in using memory to shift blame to others or to foster distrust of outsiders. In more closed societies, where there is no mechanism for the continual monitoring and correcting of memory, official versions of memory arouse distrust among many people, and have to be supplemented or corrected by unofficial sources transmitted through family, friends, or outsiders. Post-1945 Central and Eastern Europe suffered particularly from this problem.[15]

Smith's 'mass public culture' includes regular customs and ceremonies which bring people into contact with each other in shared activity, enable them to get to know each other better, and strengthen the sense of community. It links with myth and religion. It is often, but not invariably, expressed in a shared language (it may be couched in dialect, or in an elite language not usually spoken by the majority of people). It includes such taken-for-granted features of everyday life as dress, food, music, and body language. According to Jürgen Habermas, since the eighteenth century, ideally, a mass public culture offers a 'public space' in which diverse parties and currents of opinion can exchange knowledge and ideas within a shared consensus on non-violent contestation.[16] The shared culture enables individuals to communicate with each other, even when they disagree, much more easily and peacefully than in its absence, and thus to lay a bedrock of mutual trust.

A 'common economy' refers to the dense web of trade—the exchange of goods and services—which tends to concentrate within national boundaries. Smith does not perhaps sufficiently emphasize the importance of the state or public authority which provides a stable framework for the peaceful functioning of the common economy and the peaceful exercise of common legal rights and duties. We saw in Chapter 4 how crucial the state has been in underpinning trust in the currency, as well as in guaranteeing the legal and law-enforcement system. In the absence of a strong public authority the wealthy are able to exploit and victimize the poor with much less restraint. Similarly, while the modern state exercises what Max Weber called a 'monopoly of legitimate violence', pre-modern or weak states cannot securely defend their frontiers or prevent the wealthy, powerful, or seriously

---

[13] Renan, *Qu'est-ce qu'une nation?*, 228.

[14] As evoked in Eric Hobsbawm and Terence Ranger (eds), *The Invention of Tradition*, Cambridge University Press, 1983.

[15] Barbara Misztal, *Trust in Modern Societies: The search for the bases of social order*, Cambridge: Polity Press, 1996, 139–44. See also Misztal, *Theories of Social Remembering*, Maidenhead: Open University Press, 2003, and Maurice Halbwachs, *On Collective Memory*, ed., trans., and introd. Lewis A. Coser, University of Chicago Press, 1992.

[16] Jürgen Habermas, *The Structural Transformation of the Public Sphere: An Inquiry into a Category of Bourgeois Society*, trans. Thomas Burger and Frederick Lawrence, Cambridge: Polity Press, 1989 (first published 1962).

discontented from attempting to impose their will by force, and thereby destroying the confidence which people have in territory and community.

A nation often, though not invariably, has a core ethnicity, or what Smith calls an 'ethnie'. An ethnie in his view has similar features to a nation, but lacks a state, common legal rights, and a common economy. As he sees it, nations did not exist in pre-modern times, but a kind of national identity did, even in the ancient world, in the form of ethnies.[17] I believe that modern nations have inherited from those ethnies powerful symbolic systems promoting mutual trust and solidarity.

The political scientist Henry Hale sees ethnic identity as a means of 'uncertainty reduction': 'ethnic markers become convenient cognitive shorthand for rapidly inferring a wide range of information about a person one has never actually met before'.[18] As we have seen, a common language, similar bodily gestures, shared assumptions about the community, its history, and culture, make such rapid inference possible. In the modern urban world of mass communications and complex economic activity, where encounters with unknown people are frequent, shared ethnicity enables us readily to build relationships with strangers and thus bolsters generalized social trust. On the other hand, as is usual with trust, what increases trust within one group of people can also intensify their distrust towards other groups, those whose ethnicity is distinct. One begins to imagine threats and conspiracies which may not exist but are difficult to verify.[19] Ethnicity thus strengthens bonds of mutual trust within the ethnos, but also often intensifies reciprocal distrust around its boundaries.

RELIGION AND MYTH

Nations quite readily appeal to many of the emotions and attitudes characteristic of religion. They fulfil three of the functions I identified with religion in Chapter 3. They are *existential*: they form a major part of our identity as social individuals. They are *affective*: they make a strong appeal to our emotions. And they are *social-cultural* and *political* entities: they form institutional frameworks within which our routine social interaction can take place.

The religious aspect of nationhood is especially marked in the mythical complex of the 'chosen nation'. The paradigmatic case is ancient Israel: the image of a nation selected for a special mission by God, freed from bondage, provided with a Promised Land, and bound by a covenant. 'Ye have seen what I did to the Egyptians, and how I bore you on eagles' wings and brought you unto myself. Now therefore, if ye will obey my voice indeed and keep my covenant, then ye shall be a peculiar treasure unto me above all people; for all the earth is

---

[17] Anthony D. Smith, *The Ethnic Origins of Nations*, Oxford: Blackwell, 1986, chapter 1, especially pp. 7–13.
[18] Henry E. Hale, *The Foundations of Ethnic Politics*, Cambridge University Press, 2008, 243.
[19] Hale, *Foundations*, 259.

mine: And ye shall be unto me a kingdom of priests and an holy nation.'[20] The covenant contained a number of trust-inducing motifs: deliverance from slavery, assurance of divine protection, the knowledge of being chosen, even consecrated, for a special mission. These motifs were underpinned by the Ten Commandments, which laid out the basic requirements for an upright, ethical, and trustworthy communal life. Through the Commandments trust could be upheld both within the community and through its exclusive link with God. One special feature of the covenant was that God bound himself to human beings, not just by oath and contract, but also from love. Whenever disaster struck, Israelites could interpret it not as a sign of complete failure, but as a sign that they had sinned, had not kept their own side of the covenant, but were still loved, and so should strive even more resolutely to fulfil the Commandments and be worthy of their status. This remorseful but determined re-dedication to their mission ensured that they did not fall apart, as many ethnies did, after serious setbacks.

During the long centuries when, having been driven from the Promised Land, the Jews lacked a territorial homeland and lived dispersed among other peoples, the symbolic complex of the covenant held them together as an identifiable community. It was transmitted to later generations through their scriptures, notably the Torah, and the Hebrew language in which they were written. The bearers of the tradition were learned men, rabbis, committed to studying, interpreting, and transmitting those scriptures together with the associated legal texts. In consecrated buildings, synagogues, Jewish congregations could meet and conduct rituals in which the reading of scriptural texts held a central place. The Jews thus exemplify aptly the symbolic and institutional elements needed to maintain confidence in a continued national identity for centuries against very heavy odds, including the normally fatal loss of a homeland: they had a distinctive religious mission, strong religious–legal traditions, holy sites, rituals, a written language, a myth of origin, a tradition of suffering and sacrifice, and a detailed, recorded, frequently monitored history. (The monitoring goes as far as the questioning of fundamental elements, as in the work of Shlomo Sand[21]—which, paradoxically, gives one renewed confidence in the vitality and resilience of Jewish identity.)

Later nations have consciously adapted the Jewish myth for their own ends. When threatened by Spanish invasion in the sixteenth century, the Dutch invoked the Israeli myth of election. Dutch Protestants fleeing across the rivers from the Spanish army in 1574 saw parallels with the ancient Jewish experience of fleeing from Egypt across the Red Sea, and combined it with evocations of their newly flourishing economy to reformulate their own self-understanding. The historian Adriaan Valerius's *Netherlands Anthem of Commemoration* of 1626 exclaimed: 'Oh Lord, when all was ill with us, You brought us up into a land wherein we were enriched by trade and commerce, and You have dealt kindly with us, even as you led the Children of Israel from their Babylonian prison; the waters receded before

---

[20] Exodus 19: 4–6.
[21] Shlomo Sand, *The Invention of the Jewish People*, trans. Yael Lotan, London: Verso, 2009; *The Invention of the Land of Israel*, trans. Geremy Forman, London: Verso, 2012.

us and you brought us dry-footed even as the people of yore, with Moses and with Joshua, were brought to their Promised Land.' Valerius also drew moral conclusions from the tacit covenant and evoked the image of the nation as a family under a heavenly father: 'Oh Lord, you have performed wondrous things for us. And when we have not heeded you, you have punished us with hard but Fatherly force so that your visitations have always been meted out to us as a children's punishment.'[22] Sacrality, tradition, morality, and kinship with the divine were thus all invoked to construct a narrative framework reinforcing mutual trust, confidence in the future, and the determination to continue the national struggle.

Another, less well-known, 'chosen' nation, with a history almost as ancient as Israel, is Armenia. Its original location in eastern Anatolia was rugged and mountainous, cleft by deep valleys. This terrain made it a good heartland for maintaining independence from threatening outsiders, though it also impeded the task of sustaining internal unity. From the ninth to the sixth century BCE there was an independent proto-Armenian kingdom, known as Urartu, but thereafter the territory became a province, or provinces, of various empires: Persian, Hellenic, and Roman. Governors appointed from the metropolis tended, however, to assimilate to the local language and culture.[23]

The decisive turning point in the Armenians' history came when, in the fourth century CE, the Sasanid Persians tried to convert them to Zoroastrianism. In reaction their king, Trdat III, who had been educated in Rome, converted to Christianity, and so did many of the noble families. This probably occurred in 313, marginally after Constantine's conversion to Christianity, though most Armenians insist it happened in 301 and claim the proud and distinctive title of the first Christian nation. The church, itself headed initially by great nobles, jealously guarded its independence, not only from Persia, but also from the Armenian monarchy and from the ecumenical Christian church: it rejected the decisions of the Council of Chalcedon regarding the dual nature of Christ and also refused to acknowledge the primacy of the patriarchate of Constantinople. The claim of being the first Christian nation, and also a distinctive one, has imparted a powerful impetus to Armenians' status as a 'chosen people'.[24]

When the Sasanids tried to re-establish their dominance militarily, the Armenians resisted. Their army was defeated at the battle of Avarayr (451), but the people survived to benefit from a later softening of Persian policy. Their defeated troops were acknowledged as martyrs and their leader, Vardan Mamikonian, was elevated to sainthood. Thereafter Armenia acquired its own historian, Eghishe, who wrote the *History of Vardan and the Armenian War*. Movses Khorenatsi, author of a comprehensive history of Armenia up to the fifth century, integrated Armenia into biblical history, claiming that Haik, the legendary father of the

---

[22] Simon Schama, *The Embarrassment of Riches: An Interpretation of Dutch Culture in the Golden Age*, London: Collins, 1987, 98.

[23] Razmik Panossian, *The Armenians: From Kings and Priests to Merchants and Commissars*, New York: Columbia University Press, 2006, 32–42.

[24] Panossian, *Armenians*, 42–4.

nation, was descended from Noah, rebelled against Bel, the 'evil' leader of Babylon, and then returned to his native land around Mount Ararat.[25] Defiance in defeat and miraculous survival were thus recorded as a written history with its own religious interpretation.

Armenian 'chosenness' is different in some ways from that of the Jews, and Armenians have always had *some* homeland, however stunted and jeopardized. Their identity is more hierarchical and more ecclesiastical, but has many of the same elements: a myth of origin, a strong link with the divine maintained through an exclusive religious institution, a written language and history, a continuing legal tradition, and stories of sacrifice, suffering, and resistance to mighty enemies transmitted over many generations. As their homeland has been repeatedly curtailed and/or fragmented, many Armenians have lived in diaspora communities, where these symbolic ingredients helped them to maintain their distinct identity. Like the Jews, and for similar reasons, they have also tended to generate very successful financial and commercial institutions.

LANGUAGE AND CULTURE

Why is language important to the study of trust? The point is that in government, in law (see below, 'Law'), in culture, and in routine everyday interaction beyond family and immediate neighbours, a widely understood and clearly formulated language is a great aid to mutual confidence. When dealing with property, with contracts, or even just with the routine exchange of goods and services, concepts and descriptions need to be as precise and unambiguous as possible, otherwise misunderstandings will arise. If full communication with a potential counterparty in a deal is not possible, then uncertainty and probably a measure of distrust will remain. As economic life became more complex in the later middle ages the need for fuller and more precise communication was accentuated. A shared language facilitated clarification and possibly settlement of any disputes. In international trade also the use of a precise and well-formulated language aided the process of translation. The 'silk road' could only function at all because translators were always available at interchange points.[26]

In culture a degree of conceptual precision is also desirable, since it enables people to exchange complex ideas with maximum understanding. Beyond precision, culture also needs the evocation of rich associations of ideas, concepts, and images. Culture helps to deepen individuals' mutual knowledge and confidence because it supports and enriches our emotional and spiritual life, enables us to share it with those around us, and to gain greater insight into their ways of thinking and feeling. For the same reason, of course, it may harden boundaries against those who do not share the same language and/or cultural field. Connected with culture is the recording of the shared past, at first in the form of chronicles, which do little

---

[25] Panossian, *Armenians*, 44–51.
[26] Valerie Hansen, *The Silk Road: A New History*, Oxford University Press, 2012.

more than note down events almost as in an account book, so that they can be recalled with precision. At a later stage, history proper ventures into the field of understanding individuals and communities, interpreting the way they think, feel, and act, and enabling later peoples to see their concerns as part of a long continuum of community, as we have seen in the case of Armenia. All this contributes to the 'habitus of trust' encountered earlier.

Nowadays we take national languages for granted, but in the middle ages they scarcely existed. Language communication generally took place on one of two levels. For everyday interaction within a limited locality ordinary people used what we now call a dialect. Where comprehension over a wider area was required, as in a multi-ethnic empire or long-distance trade, an imperial, ancient, or elite language would be used: Persian, Greek, Latin, Sanskrit. Religious scriptures and ritual were usually couched in such a language. The same was true of law, which in Western Europe was couched in Latin for longer than most other written genres.

Armenia offers an unusually early example of the crucial contribution language can make to the formation of a distinct nation. To fix the language spoken by most Armenians and disseminate the scriptures, the king and Catholicos (church leader) commissioned a learned clergyman-scholar, Mesrop Mashtots, to create an alphabet in which it could be written. He accomplished this between 400 and 405 CE, and the written language was then used to translate the Bible and Greek scientific and philosophical texts. This facilitated the conversion of the mass of the people to Christianity, but also served to isolate them from the empires and peoples around them. It tended to render their cultural and religious borders very rigid.[27]

Much later, during the high and late middle ages, as long-distance trade picked up in Europe, it seemed desirable to have a non-elite language precise and clear enough to be relied on, or at least a small number of such languages, which could be used to describe products, reckon monetary amounts, and exchange contracts, oral or written. At the same time, for high culture, and that of royal courts and aristocratic residences, there was a growing tendency to put together language amalgams which might derive from a variety of dialects spoken over contiguous regions, perhaps with admixtures drawn from classical languages. This process would stimulate variegated and exuberant linguistic experimentation, such as that of Chaucer, Rabelais, or Shakespeare, out of which would ultimately emerge a precise, though also expressive, literary language. Its semantics and syntax could be relied upon because they were becoming codified in dictionaries and grammar books.[28]

From the mid-fifteenth century Johannes Gutenberg's invention of movable-type printing made possible the dissemination of texts of all types to a much larger audience of potential readers, soon extending far beyond those who could understand Latin. Printers and booksellers who wanted to tap this audience needed to encourage writers to use languages closer to those spoken by ordinary people.[29]

---

[27] Panossian, *Armenians*, 44–51.
[28] Benedict Anderson, *Imagined Communities*, revised edition, London: Verso, 1991.
[29] Anderson, *Imagined Communities*, 38–9.

The extension of monarchical power helped to spread the use of national languages. Germany offers a leading example. When we talk of 'Germany' in the late middle ages, we are guilty of an anachronism: there was no such country. What in the distant future did become a single country and a sovereign state was then a shifting confederation of territories under the canopy of a loose-limbed empire which also claimed territories elsewhere and which was not named German till 1512. Nevertheless, according to the most recent historian of German identity in this period, there did exist a certain feeling of being German, and it rested more than anything else on a common language, or at least on similar adjacent languages which were clearly distinct from those of their Latin and Slav neighbours. 'The Germans were, unusually in Europe, a people named from language; and language played a significant part in narratives of who they were.'[30] This shared language, with initially unstable usages, first emerged in princely courts in the twelfth and early thirteenth centuries; they were centres of patronage for chivalric epics, romances, and lyric poetry. In very different mode, it was then used for land registers, manorial documents, and financial accounts, by princely stewards, and increasingly also in the cities for local laws and regulations. Low German entered common use in the cities of the Hanseatic League. The first *Landfriede* in German seems to have been that issued at Mainz in 1235, and thereafter similar princely attempts to encourage law and order were increasingly promulgated in a form of German.[31]

The Reformation added extra impetus to this tendency. The reformed religions required that believers, of whatever social station, should be able to read and understand the scriptures in their own language. Martin Luther translated the Bible and established a consensus around the Middle High German of the Lower Saxon region. Between 1520 and 1540 three times as many books were published there as in the previous two decades, many of them by Luther. Between 1522 and 1546 no fewer than 430 complete or partial texts of his Bible translation appeared. New forms of religious faith, community, and hence loyalty were taking shape. In reformed churches trust was to be mainly horizontal, vested in congregation and pastor, while in the Catholic church it was directed upwards, towards a hierarchical and universal church headed by the Pope. Such a transformation was inconceivable without a dignified vernacular language in which the scriptures were written and could be discussed. The congregational singing of hymns in German confirmed and extended ordinary people's understanding of their language and their identification with it.[32] This language was crucial in enabling Germans to generate their own sense of national solidarity well before they had a national state.

As, during the nineteenth century, nations urbanized, industrialized, and introduced mass primary education and military conscription, the concept of 'nation' as a unit of solidarity had to broaden from a relatively small educated elite to the mass

[30] Len Scales, *The Shaping of German Identity: Authority and Crisis, 1255–1414*, Cambridge University Press, 2012, 495.

[31] Scales, *Shaping*, 487–504.

[32] See further Geoffrey Hosking, 'The Reformation as a Crisis of Trust', in Ivana Marková and Alex Gillespie (eds), *Trust and Distrust: Sociocultural Perspectives*, Charlotte, NC: Information Age Publishing, 2008, 29–47.

of the people. At this point the term 'trust network' can no longer apply directly to a nation. Whereas the elites of a nation may know each other quite well and constitute a large network formed from the interconnection of smaller ones, there is no way members of a mass nation can know more than a tiny proportion of their fellow countrymen and -women. A modern nation has to be an 'imagined community'.

To help most of the populace imagine it, mass literacy and a widely shared language became newly important, so that within the nation people of different regions, social origins, possibly of different ethnic or religious identity, could communicate easily with one another. At this stage, too, previously oppressed or marginalized peoples outside the core nation felt the need to have their own conscious culture and a language in which to give it shape, so as to mark out their own ethnic boundaries against 'outsiders' who were trying to assimilate them and efface their distinct identity. Theorists like the German linguist and philosopher Johann Gottfried Herder began to articulate the idea that the essential spirit of each nation—a category which for him included peasants as much as nobles—was to be found in its vernacular language and folk culture. For smaller and previously subordinate peoples, this was a call to action: either create your own language and use it to rescue your folk culture before it dies out, or soon you will not have a nation at all! The danger was that local trust structures based on a spontaneously imbibed culture would simply be swallowed up by those of larger and politically more dominant peoples.

During the 1820s and 1830s Elias Lönnrot, a district health officer in the Finnish region of Karelia, travelled extensively in the large area for which he was responsible, collecting oral poetry recited by local bards. He then assembled the miscellaneous material as a connected narrative in a synthesis he called the *Kalevala*. On the title page of the first edition (Helsinki, 1835) Lönnrot called it 'Old Karelian poems about ancient times of the Finnish people'. The text consisted of epic narrative, lyric reflections, magic spells, and ritual incantations, cast in a language which represented a synthesis of the various dialects which he had heard in recitations. The *Kalevala* was an immediate success among the small but growing Finnish educated public; Lönnrot had not actually invented a national language and culture, but he *had* recast the raw materials of one in a form viable for the modern world, yet bearing the hallmarks of antiquity.[33]

In 1809 the Finns (having for centuries been part of the Swedish kingdom) had fallen under Russian rule, though as a semi-autonomous Grand Duchy, with the Tsar as Grand Duke. The change of status stimulated interest in their native traditions as a reaction against the two more powerful nations that dominated them. The Russian authorities actually encouraged the Finnish cultural revival at first as a way of sundering the Finns from their Swedish past. By the end of the nineteenth century, however, when the authorities tried forcefully to Russify the

---

[33] *The Kalevala: An Epic Poem after Oral Tradition by Elias Lönnrot*, trans. and introd. Keith Bosley, Oxford University Press, 1989, introduction; see also Miroslav Hroch, *Social Conditions of National Revival in Europe*, Cambridge University Press, 1985, 62–75.

Finns, they found that the nation's trust structures had become extraordinarily resilient and tough. When attempts were made to conscript young Finnish men into the Russian army, local inhabitants hid and protected them. Finns boycotted all Russian institutions and drew up a Great Address, signed by no less than one-fifth of the population, which was borne to St Petersburg by a Great Deputation of 500. The Russian authorities, who were well accustomed to crushing violent resistance to their rule, had no way of dealing with such cohesive and widely supported non-violent civil resistance.[34] Here the Finns' consciousness of having their own institutions (their Grand Duchy), and their own Lutheran church, together with a strong demotic culture and language, combined to generate the high degree of national solidarity required to make peaceful civil resistance successful. We have already seen how analogous symbolic systems and institutions enabled the Jews and Armenians to resist absorption into powerful surrounding empires for centuries.

Similar efforts were made during the nineteenth century in many European countries by literary scholars, antiquarians, linguists, and ardent collectors of folk tales, songs, and dances. They were reworked by Romantic symphonists, recorded in multi-volume publications deposited in national libraries, or enshrined in images and artefacts placed in national museums. Such creations bear witness to nationalists' need for both their own literary language and a venerable past as a vehicle for easy communication and mutual understanding.

The impulse to revive, fix, and give literary durability to an existing but threatened oral culture was widespread among the smaller ethnies of Europe. Of particular interest to the student of trust is one blatant forgery this impulse produced, *The Works of Ossian*, published in English 'translation' by the Scottish poet James Macpherson in 1760–5. Macpherson claimed that Ossian had been an ancient blind Gaelic bard, whose work he had collected as both manuscript and oral material during travels in the Highlands; he then published it in English, he explained, so that it would reach a wide audience. The book was an immediate success and was translated into numerous European languages; among its admirers were Diderot, Napoleon, Jefferson, and Goethe, and it became one of the keystones of the Romantic preoccupation with national identity. In Britain itself it gave powerful impetus to a growing interest in oral Celtic cultures, both among Scots anxious to promote their own national identity, and among English pleased to discover that they ruled over a territory of diverse and thriving peoples.

Macpherson, however, came up against a redoubtable adversary: Dr Samuel Johnson. Johnson was a doughty proponent of honesty and sociability, and of a reliable and vigorous language as their guarantee. He considered both truth and trustworthiness indispensable foundations for society to function at all. 'Whoever commits a fraud,' he once said, 'is guilty not only of the particular injury to him whom he deceives, but of the diminution of that confidence which constitutes not

---

[34] D. G. Kirby, *Russia and Finland, 1808–1920: From Autonomy to Independence*, London: Macmillan, 1975, 76–81.

only the ease but the existence of society.'[35] Johnson's concern with language and culture as indispensable prerequisites of civilized human intercourse took on tangible form in his *Dictionary of the English Language*, the product of many years' labour. It was not the first, but it was the most successful, attempt to lay down correct English lexical usage, with due attention to the history of the language. Its author's concern for the moral foundations of society was reflected in the way he chose quotations so as to impart ethical and religious teachings.[36]

From the time the first 'Ossian' publications appeared, Johnson was suspicious of their authenticity, a suspicion fuelled by the fact that no original Gaelic manuscript, or indeed any Gaelic text of any kind, was ever forthcoming. He admonished Macpherson to deposit the originals in an Aberdeen college library; 'and if the professors certify the authenticity, then there will be an end of the controversy'.[37] So troubling were Johnson's suspicions that he undertook a journey to the Highlands, partly in order to learn more about the history and culture supposedly underlying Macpherson's publications. He acquired considerable knowledge of Gaelic culture, and was converted from his previous opinion that the language was that of a rude and barbaric people; in fact he subsequently helped to sponsor the publication of a Gaelic Bible. Nothing, however, shook his conviction that *The Works of Ossian* were a forgery.

Subsequent scholarship suggests that there was a connection between old Gaelic legends and some of the material in *The Works of Ossian*, but that most of Macpherson's 'translation' was a fabrication.[38] The whole episode testifies to the strong need European intellectuals felt at the time to rescue threatened languages and cultures as a guarantee of the authenticity and durability of national sentiments.

LAW

Another attractive feature of a strong state is that it can ensure universal and impartial law. One might ask whether law has any place at all in a study of trust. After all, if one invokes the law in dealing with someone, that surely means one no longer trusts him or her. In his book on trust Marek Kohn roundly asserts that 'Contracts are substitutes for trust.'[39] That may be true of relationships between individuals who know each other well and can readily assess each other's trustworthiness: law has no place between close friends and is often impotent in dealing with bitter enemies. But in relationships with the overwhelming majority of humanity law can strengthen social trust. Such relationships are full of

---

[35] Thomas M. Curley, *Samuel Johnson, the* Ossian *Fraud, and the Celtic Revival in Great Britain and Ireland*, Cambridge University Press, 2009, 57. See Chapter 2, 'Sociologists on Trust'.

[36] Robert Demaria, Jr, 'Johnson's *Dictionary*', in Greg Clingham (ed), *The Cambridge Companion to Samuel Johnson*, Cambridge University Press, 1997, 85–101.

[37] Curley, *Samuel Johnson*, 102.   [38] Curley, *Samuel Johnson*, chapter 1.

[39] Marek Kohn, *Trust: Self-Interest and the Common Good*, Oxford University Press, 2008, 63.

unpredictable contingencies and hence of potential conflict with people one knows slightly or not at all. Such contingencies crop up almost every day, concerning relations with neighbours, goods and services, property and contract, buying and selling, and they are aggravated periodically by crime—drug-trading, fraud, burglary, assault. Without any law, and a legitimate authority to enforce it, social life can easily become more or less what Hobbes dreaded, a condition of constant low-level war, in which the strong and the cunning exercise enduring dominion over the weak and guileless. Law, then, strengthens the predictability of social relationships, confidence in their stability, and the possibility of individual acts of trust. It is more the existence of law—the confidence that in the last resort one can appeal to it—which has this effect, rather than its specific provisions and procedures. Where it does not exist, or is only partial, social trust will tend to reconfigure itself in narrower and more exclusive groupings, with boundaries of distrust, hence latent conflict, around them.

All societies need some kind of law. The Russian revolutionaries of 1917 were initially opposed to law on principle, as a bourgeois prejudice designed to bolster the power of the capitalist ruling class. They intended to abolish it and to rely on 'revolutionary class consciousness'. In practice, though, once they had been in power for a few years, they realized that laws and law codes were essential for any kind of social stability, including their own.[40]

The concept of law, then, or at least of right and justice, is more or less universal, but the content and procedures differ greatly from one society to another. In many societies law is not differentiated from religion, myth, tradition, and morality, and it has no institutions of its own. In others it is sharply set apart from other symbolic systems and has a lush profusion of its own distinctive institutions and their associated experts.

What are the main factors in ensuring that law will in fact underwrite generalized social trust? I would single out three.

1. Law needs to be durable, to be generally known, to be applied in a predictable and consistent manner, and to affect all members of society if not equally, then at least in accordance with known and settled hierarchies. Where certain social groups feel they are persistently and arbitrarily discriminated against, the rule of law does not arouse general trust and is therefore stunted or distorted. Conflicts are then more likely to be settled by violence.

2. Law must be seen as consistent with the basic moral values of the society. Law and morality are not identical, but they must not be too far apart, in order for law to meet with general acquiescence.

3. Law's reliability is greatly strengthened if there is an overarching authority, above contesting parties, which is viewed as legitimate and is able to back up the judicial system by maintaining the integrity of the courts and enforcing verdicts and sentences; this is especially important in countries where

---

[40] Robert Sharlet, 'Stalinism and Soviet Legal Culture', in Robert C. Tucker (ed), *Stalinism: Essays in Historical Interpretation*, New York: W. W. Norton & Co, 1977, 155–79.

separatism or warlordism have been prevalent in the recent past, challenging the legitimacy of that central authority. That is one of the main contributions of the state, when it is functioning effectively, towards grounding generalized social trust.

From a very early stage in recorded history, societies were beginning to frame their judicial practices in codes of law which would generate principles or at least rules helpful to judges dealing with particular cases. One of the earliest was the Code of Hammurabi, king of Babylon around 1750 BCE. This was written on a tall stone column in Akkadian, the language of the educated class, so that at least the literate should know and be regularly reminded of their rights and duties. Presenting the law in such a way bore the implication that it was permanent, i.e. would outlast the lawgiver who formulated it, and that it applied to everyone. The code made specific provision for the punishment of each offence, often very harsh by modern standards, such as death or disfigurement. Perhaps the draconian provisions were intended to deter potential malefactors in a society not accustomed to any unified law or centralized coercion. At the top of the stele was an image of Hammurabi receiving the law from Shamash, the sun god; this implied that the law reflected the fixed state of the universe.[41]

In relatively undeveloped societies, law is part of an undifferentiated continuum which includes religion, myth, tradition, and morality. It is part of the community way of dealing with conflict and with destructive or deviant behaviour, and thus of upholding confidence in the community's overall stability. Its aim is reconciliation and the continuation of community life rather than punishment, though the latter may be thought necessary as a deterrent to future transgressors. It is not written but oral, and it is 'discovered' rather than decreed and recorded. It is decided and administered not by professionals but by elders or respected members of the community in accordance with their experience, their knowledge of the persons involved, and the community's norms.[42] This kind of law generates trust because it conforms to the values of the community and is administered by its most respected members.

In ancient Rome, up to the mid-fifth century BCE the law was unwritten: it consisted of rulings in accordance with custom, delivered by the college of pontiffs, who were patricians responsible for public cults. The plebeians—citizens who did not come from the aristocratic patrician families—felt that as a result the law was both unpredictable and probably biased against them. On both grounds they could not trust it, and so demanded that its main principles be written down and permanently put on view in a public place. They backed up their demand by a *secessio plebis*, withdrawing from the city, so that workshops and public services ceased operation. Deprived of the amenities of normal life, the patricians gave

[41] J. H. Breasted, *Ancient Times or a History of the Early World*, Boston: Ginn & Co, 1935, part 1, 141; Marc van de Mieroop, *King Hammurabi of Babylon: A Biography*, Oxford: Blackwell, 2005, chapter 8.

[42] H. Patrick Glenn, *Legal Traditions of the World: Sustainable Diversity in Law*, 2nd edition, Oxford University Press, 2004, chapter 3.

way. The outcome was the Twelve Tablets, carved in bronze and displayed in the Forum. They are now lost, but, as far as scholars have been able to reconstruct them, they briefly stated how crimes should be dealt with and how civil disputes should be conducted in matters such as debt, family relations, inheritance, and property.[43] This was the beginning of a long process of creating a stable, known, and equitable law, backed up by a Roman state which could be considered legitimate by all its citizens. Roman law evolved into a complex system of written provisions, classified in various categories and backed by legal experts able to advise on how to apply those provisions to particular circumstances. In this way the legal profession arose as a body of trusted and impartial experts.

The ultimate product of this development was the *Corpus Juris Civilis*, the 'body of civil law' compiled under the Emperor Justinian in the sixth century CE. This was the most complete and lucidly expounded juridical amalgam of its time, and it was to play a major role in the subsequent gestation of law in European countries, as we shall see.

To grasp the importance of law to social trust, it is especially illuminating to see how it functioned in the absence of a strong state. Without an effective overarching authority, in the middle ages many local communities had to improvise their own methods for upholding peace and order. They would usually endeavour to create intermediate associations to deal with criminals and disturbers of the peace. Tenth-century London, for example, had a 'peace-guild', to which both nobles and ceorls (freemen of the lowest rank) contributed funds. They gave pledges to act as 'of one friendship and one enmity' in pursuing felons and disturbers of the peace. In villages it was customary to form groups of ten or twelve freemen, known as 'tithings', who would take oaths of good behaviour and of loyalty to the king. They would stand surety for each other: that is, they would guarantee that none of their number would commit an offence or that, if he did, the others would deliver him up for justice. If they failed to do so they could be jointly fined. To avoid this it was crucial to apprehend an offender as soon as possible, and for this purpose to raise a 'hue and cry', a collective manhunt. This system of peacekeeping and mutual policing was known as 'francpledge'. It could not operate unless the tithing members knew a lot about each other, and that knowledge in turn implied that they had to some extent to trust each other or at least to know the limits within which they could do so. Special peaces were declared for church festivals, certain meetings, and certain public places. Behind all this was the ideal of the *landfriede*, originally proclaimed by King Athelstan, though not yet effectively enforced by royal authority. It was later reiterated in the 'great peace' of William I.[44]

As social and especially economic life became more developed and complex in Western Europe in the tenth–twelfth centuries, communities felt the need to have law more clearly defined, since in many cases the state of the law on a given issue

---

[43] Peter Stein, *Roman Law in European History*, Cambridge University Press, 1999, 3–6.

[44] John Hudson, *The Formation of the English Common Law: Law and Society in England from the Norman Conquest to Magna Carta*, London: Longman, 1996, 62–6; Alan Harding, *Medieval Law and the Foundations of the State*, Oxford University Press, 2002, 79–81.

was unclear, or had never been ascertained. In eleventh-century Germany attempts were made to 'fix' customary law and record it for future consultation. This was done at the village level by drawing up *Weistümer*: formal legal questions would be put to authoritative persons within the community and their answers would be written down. In France a similar *enquête par tourbes* was held in the thirteenth century, in which persons of high repute were asked to 'say between whom they observed that custom, in what case, in what place, if there was a court decision and in what circumstances'. Their answers were summarized, recorded, and sealed.[45]

Since even such methods left large gaps in the law, European societies around this period also sought outside themselves for a source of consistent and comprehensive law. In some cases, especially where trading was involved, they borrowed their laws from a neighbouring town or one with which their merchants were in frequent contact. Thus in much of Central and Eastern Europe Magdeburg or Lübeck Law was adopted, or the Saxon law code known as the *Sachsenspiegel*.[46]

Most popular of all, though, was Roman law, interest in which was nourished by the rediscovery of Justinian's Codes in a library in Pisa. The use of Roman law was paradoxical, since the circumstances of life in medieval European societies were very different from those that had pertained in the Roman Republic and Empire. There were a number of reasons for this apparently incongruous adoption of the legal precepts of a completely different society. Since law is a distinctive symbolic system, with its own internal articulation, its gaps are best filled and its confusions best clarified by borrowing from other more developed legal systems; this helps to explain how it is that not only individual laws but whole law codes can be transferred to societies very different from those of origin. When law has to be changed, clarified, or supplemented, 'the resulting law will usually be borrowed from a system known to the legal elite, often with modifications, to be sure, but not always those deemed appropriate after full consideration of local conditions. The input of the society often bears little relationship to the output of the legal elite.... Legal development depends on the lawyers' culture.'[47] Law, like other symbolic systems, has its own internal logic, which often overrides other considerations.

There is a danger, though, in this fencing-off of law. It can easily become an out-of-bounds enclosure, whose language, institutions, and procedures, however necessary, are arcane, cumbersome, and inaccessible to ordinary people. Law can become the monopoly of a professional corporation which charges heavily for admission to its secrets. Then the law operates ineffectively, creates new inequalities, and generates powerful distrust. This was the situation depicted by Charles Dickens in his novel *Bleak House*, where we see the fog-bound Court of Chancery, its members 'tripping one another up on slippery precedents' and 'groping knee-deep in technicalities'. In Dickens's vision, this is a place where trying to obtain justice 'so exhausts finances, patience, courage, hope; so overthrows the brain and breaks the heart, that there is not an honourable man among its practitioners who

---

[45] Alan Watson, *The Evolution of Law*, Oxford: Blackwell, 1985, 60–1.
[46] Watson, *Evolution of Law*, 74.   [47] Watson, *Evolution*, 117.

would not give . . . the warning, "Suffer any wrong that can be done to you rather than come here!" '[48]

During the eleventh to thirteenth centuries another powerful source of law arose: the canon law of the papacy, which was developing its own ambitions of earthly sovereignty as a guarantor of social peace superior to monarchs.[49] The Pope's legal advisers studied Justinian's Codes and elaborated some of their provisions. Many of our modern notions of law on marriage, family, inheritance, education, poor relief, and even the use and abuse of credit derive from medieval canon law. The very notion of law as the province of specialists trained in its study and interpretation was mediated from Rome through the Vatican, which was the first medieval authority to create a corpus of such specialists. Such was the reputation of canon law that many secular rulers appointed ecclesiastical lawyers as advisers.[50]

The creation of background peace within a given territory, so that routine transactions could be carried on with confidence, was perhaps the most effective way of creating generalized social trust. The ideal of *Landfriede* inspired the efforts of Holy Roman emperors to establish the rule of law in their territories. We have seen in Chapter 4 how the church tried to put into effect its own version of this concept, both in cooperation and in rivalry with the secular state. Emperors found it difficult to do so, as their territories were so extensive and diverse, and their authority could only be transmitted through intermediate rulers. In 1235 Frederick II called an assembly at Mainz, at which a new peace was sworn and old rights confirmed. The resulting document, the *Constitutio Pacis*, contained the familiar peace pledges, but also added a good deal of criminal law. The emperor's mission was proclaimed to be 'to curb the lawlessness of the wicked and establish judgements for the people in matters of life and death'.[51]

In practice, though, emperors had to rely on their subordinate princes to enforce justice, and in doing so, those princes became de facto sovereigns in their own territories. When Maximilian I in 1495 tried to institute an 'eternal *Landfriede*' as part of his reform of the Holy Roman Empire's constitution, the estates of the *Reichstag* refused to consent to having royal officials enforce it.[52] Nevertheless, during these centuries the term *status regni* was beginning to imply the peace and good order of the kingdom. This is the root from which the modern term 'state' originates.[53]

Both the English and French monarchs, unlike those in Germany, did succeed in slowly but surely gaining a grip on law enforcement from the centre of sovereign authority. They did so by gradually establishing the principle that the king's court should have exclusive jurisdiction over certain very serious crimes, such as murder, and that it should also be the ultimate court of appeal, especially in matters concerning keeping the peace and the ownership of land (an area where they not

---

[48] Charles Dickens, *Bleak House*, chapter 1.   [49] See Chapter 3, 'Peace of God'.

[50] Harold J. Berman, *Law and Revolution: The Formation of the Western Legal Tradition*, Cambridge, Mass.: Harvard University Press, 1983; Joseph R. Strayer, *On the Medieval Origins of the Modern State*, Princeton University Press, 1970, 20–4.

[51] Harding, *Medieval Law*, 96–8.   [52] Harding, *Medieval Law*, 106–8.

[53] Harding, *Medieval Law*, 82–93.

infrequently came into conflict with the church, which claimed authority over inheritance). At the Assize of Clarendon in 1166 an unjust *disseisin* (seizure of property) was declared to be a breach of the king's peace, and a procedure was laid down for reversing it by royal authority.[54] The king would achieve this by sending out circuit judges to consult with local juries—assemblies of sworn 'best people'— to examine evidence in disputed cases and reach reasoned decisions, which would then be recorded in writing, so that they could act as guidance for future cases.[55] This procedure proved very popular, so much so that in the end the royal judges could not cope, and had to hand back some powers to local elites to act as Justices of the Peace—an institution which has survived to the present day.[56] Nevertheless, the principle had been established and widely accepted that the king should be the ultimate guardian of law, order, and peace.

In France the analogous process came later and took longer, since the French kingdom was much larger and more diverse, but it developed in the same general direction. When Louis VII returned from crusade in Compostela in 1155, and faced the growing Angevin threat, he decided to do what he could to strengthen the solidarity of magnates, clergy, and people. He called a great peace council at Soissons, at which he ordained a ten-year 'peace of the whole realm', implying that it was now mainly the responsibility of the king, rather than that of the church, to uphold it. His principal vassals, secular and ecclesiastical, swore to obey and support him in doing so.[57] To enforce the peace by regulating disputes, and also to collect taxes, the French king dispatched his own *baillis* (in the north) and *sénénechaux* (in the south). They consulted with sworn jurors and reached verdicts that were recorded in writing, so as to give their judgements the 'strength of perpetual stability' (*perpetuae stabilitatis robur*). Philip Augustus reaffirmed that it 'pertained to his office to restore peace and, as the promoter of justice, give everyone his due'.[58] We should not imagine that the process was smooth. It was repeatedly contested: the church and local secular elites were partly allies and partly rivals in enforcing order and fostering social solidarity. All the same, this was the path by which the monarch made his power acceptable and even trusted by the majority of his subjects.

By the late middle ages, then, a start had been made to establishing the principle that a 'state' was a stable authority over a fixed territory in the hands of a sovereign who had the right to secure peace and order by means of law and impersonal institutions. *Fides*[59] was still important, but it was now partly replaced by written

[54] W. L. Warren, *Henry II*, new edition, New Haven: Yale University Press, 2000, chapter 9.

[55] J. R. Strayer, *On the Medieval Origins of the Modern State*, new edition, Princeton University Press, 2005, 39–42; Richard W. Kaeuper, *War, Justice and Public Order: England and France in the Later Middle Ages*, Oxford: Clarendon Press, 1988, 154–9.

[56] Kaeuper, *War, Justice*, 175–9.

[57] Harding, *Medieval Law*, 113; Kaeuper, *War, Justice*, 149–50; Aryeh Grabois, 'De la trêve de Dieu à la paix du roi: étude sur les transformations du mouvement de la paix au XII siècle', in Pierre Gallais and Yves-Jean Riou (eds), *Mélanges offerts à René Crozet*, Poitiers: Société d'Études Médiévales, 1966, 585–96.

[58] Harding, *Medieval Law*, 119–23.   [59] See Chapter 3, 'Medieval Western Christianity'.

law and the monarch's authority. The state thereby provided a durable and reliable framework for the trust and loyalty of the king's subjects.[60] Along with the capacity to defend the realm, this still remains the rationale for the existence of the modern state and its basic claim to legitimacy.

A further stage had to be reached, though, before the state could be fully trusted: gaining assurance that the state would *itself* observe the law. This was the subject of complex political—and sometimes military—conflicts in all European states, conflicts which reflected contending views about the relationship between the state and the people.[61] The outcome was crucial: as we have seen in Chapter 4, constitutional states, i.e. those in which the government observed the law, found it far easier to raise credit on money markets, and thus to lay the foundation for economic growth and to finance ventures of all kinds, economic or military. Before the state could become constitutional, however, it had to become an effective and legitimate state at all.

THE STATE

Nowadays when we speak of a nation, we normally assume that it will have a strong centralized state. The existence of such a state is the cardinal criterion which, in Anthony Smith's conceptual scheme, distinguishes a nation from an ethnie. According to John Breuilly, moreover, the nation is 'a modern political and ideological formation which developed in close conjuncture with the modern territorial, sovereign and participatory state'. Why should nation and state go together? We have already seen that an overarching authority can augment confidence in the law and its enforcement by overriding localized strongmen and applying more objective and professional standards of justice. But the state has many other functions conducive to social solidarity among large numbers of people, for example taxation and military organization, which can only be achieved 'through a process of negotiation between the ruler and the political community of the core territory under his sway'.[62]

To be effective the modern state needs to be legitimate; that is, it needs to be trusted. Senator Patrick Moynihan warned Richard Nixon, just before the latter took office as US President in 1969, that 'the sense of institutions being legitimate—especially the institutions of government—is the glue that holds society together. When it weakens, things come unstuck.'[63] Legitimacy depends on the relationship between the state and its subjects or citizens. Smith has suggested

---

[60] This is the basic thesis of Strayer, *Medieval Origins*.

[61] See the next section.

[62] John Breuilly, 'The State and Nationalism', in Monserrat Guibernau and John Hutchinson (eds), *Understanding Nationalism*, Cambridge: Polity Press, 2001, 32; and his *Nationalism and the State*, 2nd edition, Manchester University Press, 1993, 373–4.

[63] Quoted in Lawrence Stone, *The Causes of the English Revolution*, London: Ark Paperbacks, 1986, 79.

three types of public culture which shape this relationship and thus underpin the state's legitimacy.

1. **Hierarchical**: The ruler is God's representative on earth, and has received from Him the right to issue laws and commands, which are transmitted through a priesthood and/or aristocracy to the mass of the people. The ruler also acts in God's name in making arrangements for defence of the realm's territory; the people man his armed forces under the command of nobles. Society is divided hierarchically into those who fight, those who pray, and those who work. Trust is thus vested in a divinely ordained ruler, whose commands reflect the nature of the cosmos; those who carry out those commands play their part in the trustworthy design.

2. **Covenantal**: The deity chooses a whole community to carry out his will, but by means of a covenant or agreement which binds both him and his people, as we have seen in the case of Israel. He marks it out from other communities and imposes on it moral and ritual obligations, as a model for other peoples; in return for observing those obligations he will continue to acknowledge them as his chosen ones. A particular leader or small religious community acts as intermediary in concluding the covenant and transmitting its ordinances to the people. Trust is now mainly vested in the community as a whole because it is an instrument of the divine will and has a specific agreement with God.

3. **Republican**: The people themselves, or at least the free citizens (however defined), come together to constitute themselves as a self-governing polity, without any divine intervention. They decide on their own fundamental principles and make their own laws, and they appoint officials to ensure that those laws are observed. This act of self-constitution can be based on a religious idea which consecrates it, but it can also be purely secular, based on ideas of human freedom and responsible autonomy. Trust is vested in the community as a self-justifying collectivity which has freely chosen to constitute itself and to make its own laws. Typically that community is imagined in kinship terms, as a 'brotherhood'.

These are all ideal types: that is, there has probably never been any single community which conforms entirely to one paradigm. Moreover, many communities have elements from two or three of them—whose admixture can lead to serious conflict. Nevertheless these types can function as models against which to measure the characteristics of particular societies. In particular, they help in considering the features of different public cultures and the kinds of trust they promote.

1. **Hierarchical** The hierarchical model derives from ancient empires, which contained relatively strong states, even if by modern standards they did not do much more than exercise sporadically effective dominance over a kaleidoscope of tribes, city-states, and principalities. Nevertheless they, and especially Rome, offered the model for later European authority-holders. For good reason: the Roman Empire had provided centuries of relative peace and order over very extensive territories with diverse populations, and in its later stages it had also become a Christian polity. Through physical power, legality, cultural example, and from the fourth

century moral teachings, it had created a uniquely broad radius of trust. In Europe both rulers and populations had thereafter the sense that creating a peaceful, orderly, culturally cohesive, morally upright, and enduring political community was possible, even if they could not achieve it themselves. The Byzantine polity, closest to being a legitimate heir, called itself simply 'Rome'. The precursors of Germany claimed the title of 'Holy Roman Empire' long before they added 'of the German nation'; Charlemagne and subsequent emperors were crowned by the Pope. And the Grand Duchy of Muscovy, or at least many of its churchmen, thought of itself as the Third Rome. These claims were shadowy and impossible to substantiate, but they were buttressed by legend and ceremony.

Even at times of maximum political anarchy this ideal remained attractive. The tribal kingdoms which had emerged from the ruin of the west Roman Empire— Lombards, Vandals, Visigoths, Ostrogoths—were initially temporary coalitions of armed men who had confidence in a successful leader or a succession of them. They had their own ancestor myths, customs, laws, ceremonies, and arrangements for averting feuds between powerful families, but these were flexible and could be combined with Roman practices which had stood the test of time. Tribal leaders and post-Roman elites often worked together to save what could be saved from the long-established trust-inducing institutions of the Roman Empire. Some of these new political communities were short-lived, but, in the words of one historian of the period, 'Others managed to survive beyond the lives of their founders, to absorb other, rival groups, and to create a unifying myth of peoplehood, a myth that projected the people back into a distant, glorious past and justified claims for a great and powerful future.' In that way by the eighth–tenth century ethnic barbarian identities were being replaced by political post-Roman identities over most of Europe.[64] Some of those identities formed the kernel of later nation-states.

It has been suggested that the distinguishing characteristic of medieval proto-nations was that they were political communities, that is, communities which could afford their members physical security, in return for which they were bound to obey the laws and customs of the community and to contribute when necessary to its defence or survival. 'Medieval kingdoms and city-states seem to have been perceived as political communities and to have developed an ethnic consciousness that transcended local differences of custom and sometimes ignored differences of language. . . . There was little argument either about the myths or about the nature of the political communities to which they related: it seems to have simply been assumed that kingdoms, lordships or city-states were natural, given communities.'[65]

France offers a clear example of divinely ordained hierarchical kingship. Its rulers traced its special status back to the papal coronation of Charlemagne in Rome in 800. Charlemagne sent his *missi* (agents) round his realm to administer

---

[64] Patrick J. Geary, *The Myth of Nations: The Medieval Origins of Europe*, Princeton University Press, 2002; quote on pp. 171–2.
[65] Susan Reynolds, *The Middle Ages without Feudalism: Essays in Criticism and Comparison on the Medieval West*, Farnham: Ashgate Variorum, 2012, xi. 22.

an oath to all free men aged 12 and over. Each was to take an oath before a saint's relics: 'I affirm I am a faithful servant of our lord and most pious emperor Charles, son of King Pippin and Queen Bertrada, as a man lawfully ought to be towards his lord, for his kingdom and for his right. And this oath which I have sworn I shall willingly keep to the best of my knowledge and ability, from this day forth, so help me God, who created heaven and earth, and these relics of saints.' In this way Charlemagne explicitly recognized that coercion was not enough to constitute legitimacy: he hoped to promote moral behaviour and social trust—*fides*—by means of an oath. His *missi* were to record the names of all who had taken the oath and report back.[66]

When Louis IX (1226–70) led a crusade to reconquer the Holy Land (unsuccessfully), the Pope referred to him as 'the most Christian prince, ruler of a devoted people', and he became generally known as Louis the Pious. Rheims cathedral and the chapel of St Denis became royal shrines. Louis built the Sainte Chapelle in Paris as a worthy setting for the relics of the True Cross which (he claimed) he brought back from the Holy Land. Philip IV (1285–1314) declared himself to be 'the most Christian king... shield of the faith and defender of the Church', even when he was in conflict with the current Pope. Guillaume de Nogaret, his councillor, reaffirmed that 'It is a proven truth well-known throughout the world that the kings of France are holy and very Christian princes.'[67] Chroniclers began to intimate that the French people had been chosen, like the ancient Israelites, by God. The monastic preacher Guillaume de Sauqueville called the king of France a new Moses and claimed that: 'God chose the kingdom of France from among all other peoples.' During the wars with England Joan of Arc declared: 'All those who make war on the said realm of France make war on Jesus the King.'[68] These and other quotations passed into the chronicles and later official histories of France.

Russia offers another example of divinely ordained kingship. The sixteenth-century Muscovite ruler (known as Tsar—Caesar or Emperor—from 1547, beginning with Ivan IV) claimed to be the heir of both the post-Mongol khans who had ruled the Eurasian steppes and the Byzantine emperor, overthrown by the Ottomans in 1453. The Tsar was revered as the culmination of a series of successful rulers who had greatly enlarged Muscovy's territory and wealth; that success was held to prove his status as bearer of God's purpose. The Orthodox church, not without internal conflict, had become his ally and guarantor of his godly standing. When it broke away from other Orthodox churches in refusing to reunite with Rome at the Council of Florence-Ferrara, it assumed, in its own eyes, a unique status as guarantor of the one true Christian faith. In the formulation of a monk from Pskov, Filofei, the first two Romes had fallen, the first because of its 'pride and ambition', the second through 'the violence of the sons of Hagar [Muslims]', but 'the third stands, and there will be no fourth'. The writings of the leading cleric Metropolitan Makarii filled out this heritage with lives of the saints, sermons,

---

[66] H. R. Loyn and John Percival (eds), *The Reign of Charlemagne: Documents on Carolingian Government and Administration*, London: Edward Arnold, 1975, 74–5, 81–2.

[67] Colette Beaune, *Naissance de la nation française*, Paris: Gallimard, 1985, 224.

[68] Beaune, *Naissance*, 215, 229.

epistles, and excerpts from historical documents, arranged so that they could be read from the pulpit on each day of the ecclesiastical calendar. In the Gold Room of the Kremlin palace and in the Archangel Cathedral frescoes and icons depicted Ivan IV as the heir of a long line of princes going back to Roman and Byzantine emperors, and ultimately to Solomon and David of ancient Israel. His rule was thus pictorially justified as righteous, strong, and traditional, hence able to attract trust through its moral qualities, its physical strength, and its ancient provenance.[69]

Monarchical authority as a principle could remain attractive even to a people who rejected many of the measures a specific monarch was trying to impose. The example of the Netherlands is illuminating: it shows how attractive the ideal of legitimate authority remained even as its provinces were beginning to rebel against alien rule from Spain. They had traditionally welcomed the authority of the Duchy of Burgundy and later of the Hapsburgs, and indeed celebrated it in 'joyous entries', when the duke would ride into Dutch cities in a richly apparelled cortège and join leading citizens in a feast. When in the sixteenth century the Netherlands were on the point of rebellion against Philip II of Spain, city elites were reluctant to break altogether with their legitimate sovereign, even though he was blatantly overriding their traditional rights and privileges by imposing religious conformity through the Inquisition. The petition presented by the nobles to Margaret of Parma, his regent, in 1566, called for the suspension of the Inquisition and the moderation of the heresy laws, as they violated 'ancient privileges, franchises and immunities'. In other respects, though, the petition reiterated the nobles' loyalty to the monarchy: it was presented during a Catholic festival and after a solemn procession in festive costume, with the purpose, they declared, of 'maintaining the king in his estate and keeping order and peace'.[70] In this way the trust-inducing emblems of authority were simultaneously subverted and confirmed. The later leader of the rebellion, William of Orange, was widely accepted by the rebels as 'father of the fatherland' partly because he had originally been appointed stadholder by Emperor Charles V.[71] Even rebellion aspired to the mantle of traditional authority.

2. **Covenantal** We have already seen that ancient Israel and Armenia offer examples of the covenantal type of public culture. This type was revived after the Reformation, when the study of the Old Testament received new impetus, and the example of Israel was revered with a new intensity.

A chosen nation regards itself as morally superior to other nations. In its own eyes it may not always be worthy of its destiny, but because it is chosen it always has the opportunity to repent of its errors, to return to righteous paths, and to recover its sacred mission. This obligation falls not just on the leaders, but on the people as a whole; hence they must all participate in fulfilment of the mission. This is what

---

[69] Geoffrey Hosking, *Russia: People and Empire, 1552–1917*, London: HarperCollins, 1997; *Russia and the Russians*, 2nd edn, London: Penguin Books, 2012, 99–111.

[70] E. H. Kossmann and A. F. Mellink (eds), *Texts concerning the Revolt of the Netherlands*, Cambridge University Press, 1974, 60–1.

[71] Peter Arnade, *Beggars, Iconoclasts and Civic Patriots: The Political Culture of the Dutch Revolt*, Ithaca, NY: Cornell University Press, 2008, chapters 6–7.

gives chosen peoples such internal cohesion, endurance, and resilience. By the same token, they mark themselves off from other peoples, seen as alien and profane, by especially strict boundaries. Those others will usually be outsiders, but the boundaries can be invoked against insiders who are considered to be betraying the mission; they may be symbolically or actually expelled from the community. This is how social trust operates, as we have already seen.

Perhaps the first modern nation to constitute itself through a covenant was Scotland, where by the late sixteenth century a Calvinist model of church organization was already predominant in the lowlands. In Calvinist political theory authority within the community should be exercised by magistrates chosen for their experience and moral standing; they should cooperate closely with the church elders in enforcing both law and moral discipline. Such rule by the 'elect' was not democratic, but all the same it was certainly inconsistent with hierarchical monarchical government, which Charles I was trying to restore. His attempt to enforce the full doctrine and ritual of the Church of England on Scotland prompted nobles, gentry, ministers, and burghers in 1638 to gather at the Grey Friars' Church in Edinburgh and sign a National Covenant agreeing to behave 'as beseemeth Christians who have renewed their Covenant with God', and to support the king 'in the defence and preservation of the ... true religion, liberties and laws of the kingdom'. They were still attached to monarchy, then, but only to a 'covenanted king' who agreed to uphold 'the true reformed religion' and rule according to the laws as defined by parliament. The document was opened to public signature and dispatched around the country for that purpose. Within a few months it held thousands of signatures from people of all social classes, some of whom, according to a nineteenth-century Scottish historian, 'did draw their own blood and used it in place of ink to underscribe their names'. Throughout the lowlands people took part in fasts and huge prayer meetings.[72]

The attempt to form a covenanted nation was extended a little later to the 'three kingdoms' of the British Isles as a whole. When the parliamentary side in the English civil war was in difficulties in 1643 it concluded a treaty with the Scottish covenanters, whereby both pledged themselves to defend the rights of parliament and the true liberties of the kingdom and to preserve the reformed religion 'according to the Word of God and the examples of the best-reformed Churches'. This was to be achieved by preserving peace between Scotland and England and working together to extirpate 'popery, prelacy, superstition, heresy, schism, profaneness and whatsoever shall be found to be contrary to sound doctrine and the power of godliness'. In subsequent civil war in England, Scotland, and Ireland, soldiers of parliament took an oath 'according to the heads sworn by me in the Solemn League and Covenant of the three Kingdoms'.[73] This, then, was an attempt to constitute a *British* nation on covenantal principles.

---

[72] John Mackie, *A History of Scotland*, 2nd edition, Harmondsworth: Penguin, 1978, 203–4; Ian Gentles, *The English Revolution and the Wars of the Three Kingdoms, 1638–1652*, Harlow: Pearson Longman, 2007, 9–13.

[73] Mackie, *History of Scotland*, 211–13; Michael Braddick, *God's Fury, England's Fire: A New History of the English Civil Wars*, London: Allen Lane, 2008.

After the civil war the Commonwealth brought to power rulers who believed in the covenantal origin of nations. They were fortified by their victory over monarch and bishops, and they ruled through the militant and God-fearing New Model Army which had gained that victory. Their model was the Israeli nation of the Old Testament. As their leader, Oliver Cromwell, proclaimed to the Barebones Parliament in 1653, at the high point of his success: 'Truly you are called by God as Judah was, to rule with Him and for Him.' He continued by quoting the book of Isaiah: ' "This people," saith God, "I have formed for Myself, that they may show forth My praise." '[74] John Milton, the most eloquent proponent of this version of nationhood, wrote in *Areopagitica*, 'Consider what Nation it is whereof ye are, and whereof ye are the governors; a Nation not slow and dull, but of a quick, ingenious and piercing spirit. . . . Why else was this Nation chos'n before any other, that out of her, as out of Sion, should be proclaim'd and sounded forth the first tidings and trumpet of Reformation in all Europe?'[75] In short, the Scottish–English revolution suggested a new vision of the nation as a community in which all could have faith because it was chosen by God in partnership with human beings as part of his design.

The implications of the covenant, if not its practice, were decidedly non-hierarchical. According to the ideal, all Englishmen were to be members of the nation. The 'True Levellers', also known as 'Diggers', insisted on this point. Gerrard Winstanley, their leader, asserted that parliament's function was 'to declare England to be a free Commonwealth. This law breaks in pieces the kingly yoke, and the laws of the Conqueror, and gives a common freedom to every Englishman, to have a comfortable livelihood in this their own land, else it cannot be a Commonwealth.'[76] Cromwell's practice was less democratic: the Diggers were forcibly evicted from the land they claimed.

The Afrikaners of South Africa were another covenantal nation, and one which drew even more rigid boundaries around themselves. The Dutch colonists who formed their original kernel came from a country imbued with its own sense of divine mission in having resisted the domination of Catholic Spain. The Afrikaners' experience in South Africa served to dramatize and redouble their inherited fervour. As they trekked into the veld to escape British imperial domination and win the right to their own land, the Bible was their moral guide and their religious practices resembled those of the US frontier.[77] They could readily imagine themselves as Israelis escaping slavery in Egypt and marching to the Promised Land which they would conquer from heathen tribes. As the *voortrekkers* in the 1830s Great Trek prepared for decisive battle against the Zulus at Blood River, they took an oath put before them by the lay preacher Sarel Cilliers: 'My brethren and fellow countrymen, at this moment we stand before the Holy God of heaven and earth to

[74] *Letters and Speeches of Oliver Cromwell*, London: Methuen, 1904, ii. 291, 296.
[75] *The Works of John Milton*, New York: Columbia University Press, 1931, iv. 339–40.
[76] Paul L. Hughes and Robert F. Fries (eds), *Crown and Parliament in Tudor-Stuart England: A Documentary-Constitutional History, 1485–1714*, New York: Putnam, 1959, 244.
[77] See Chapter 6.

make a promise, if He be with us and protect us, and deliver the enemy into our hands, so that we may triumph over him, that we shall observe the day as an anniversary in each year as a day of thanksgiving like the Sabbath, in His honour.'[78]

At the start of the first Anglo-Boer War of 1881, Paul Kruger, leader of the Boers, took up the idea of the special relationship with God when addressing some 10,000 Afrikaners who had assembled at Paardekraal: 'I stand here before you called by the People. In the voice of the People I have heard the voice of God, the King of Nations, and I obey!' Having achieved the victory of Majuba Hill, Kruger reiterated his message, now addressing those gathered as 'God's People', to whom God had restored their freedom. Ten years later, at the annual celebration of Covenant Day, he affirmed that 'It is for God that we have prepared the feast in His honour. . . . In the Old Testament, God said to Abraham: "The covenant which I made with you and your descendants, excluding none, shall remain before you and your seed from now to eternity." '[79]

Like all intense embattled trust communities, the Boers drew rigid boundaries around their identity, both against the British and also against the indigenous black tribes. Their covenant had a racial dimension: it invoked not only the Promised Land, but also the *seed* of Abraham and Isaac; many (though not all) Boer Afrikaners regarded the indigenous blacks as an inferior and heathen race, incapable of productive use of their territory and hence destined by God to work for their betters. This outlook, supported by the Dutch Reformed Church, was the basis of the twentieth-century doctrine of apartheid. Members of the Broederbond, formed in 1918, worked for the survival of a separate Afrikaner nation, using their positions in the media and in public office, and offering welfare benefits to poor Afrikaners. It played a leading role in the formation of the National Party, which in 1948 launched the policy of apartheid, placing rigid boundaries between the races and subordinating blacks to whites.[80]

3. **Republican** The republican model of legitimacy is ostensibly different from the covenantal one. Its prototype is the Constitution of the United States of America, whose preamble reads: 'We, the people of the United States, in order to form a more perfect union, establish justice, ensure domestic tranquility, provide for the common defense, promote the general welfare, and secure the blessings of liberty to ourselves and our posterity, do ordain and establish this Constitution for the United States of America.' Here there is nothing about the Almighty, no suggestion of any contract with a supreme being.[81] The initiators of the social contract are 'We, the people', who have taken a decision together to promote the trust-generating institutions of government. At the same time, the articles of the

[78] Bruce Cauthen, 'The Myth of Divine Election and Afrikaner Ethnogenesis', in Geoffrey Hosking and George Schöpflin (eds), *Myths and Nationhood*, New York: Routledge, 1997, 107–31; quotation on pp. 125–6; Donald H. Akenson, *God's Peoples: Covenant and Land in South Africa, Israel and Ulster*, Ithaca, NY: Cornell University Press, 1992, 47.

[79] Cauthen, 'Myth of Divine Election', 129–30; Akenson, *God's Peoples*, 69.

[80] Akenson, *God's Peoples*, 88–96.

[81] The 1776 Declaration of Independence does contain a reference to the 'Creator', but only as a bestower of rights, not of obligations, and there is no suggestion of a covenant.

Constitution set out the arrangements for ensuring that no government can become *too* strong and override the will of the people as expressed through its elected legislators.

In practice, though, many American citizens, both before and since, have not adhered strictly to republican principles. The view which they have of their nation, and which politicians have frequently evoked, is that it possesses special and unique virtues conferred on it by God, and that its mission is to spread those virtues to the rest of the world. John Winthrop, first governor of Massachusetts, declared in a sermon that 'We must consider that we shall be as a City upon a Hill. The eyes of all people are upon us; so that if we shall deal falsely with our God in this work we have undertaken, and so cause Him to withdraw his present help from us, we shall be made a story and a by-word through the world.... We are entered into a Covenant with Him for this work.'[82]

The idea of the covenant and the sense of worldwide mission tends to recur in US history at times of crisis, even if in routine circumstances it is far from Americans' minds. In the form of 'Manifest Destiny' it was utilized in the mid-nineteenth century to justify the USA's advance westwards to the Pacific, the uprooting and deportation of the native peoples, and its annexation of Texas and California. A painting by John Gast (1872) sums it up: it portrays Columbia as a goddess, clutching a school book, pushing natives and bison into the western gloom, while accompanying her from the luminous east come white pioneers, followed by railroads and telegraph wires. The ideal was invoked by both sides in the supreme crisis of the civil war: each was convinced that their struggle fulfilled biblical prophecy and that the Almighty was on their side. President Abraham Lincoln in the Gettysburg Address (November 1863) combined republican and covenantal themes: 'Four score and seven years ago our fathers brought forth on this continent a new nation, conceived in Liberty and dedicated to the proposition that all men are equal.' Now the civil war was testing whether this nation could long endure; the dead were the sacrifice made in this great test. 'We here highly resolve that those dead shall not have lived in vain—that this nation, under God, shall have a new birth of freedom—and that government of the people, by the people, for the people, shall not perish from the earth.'[83] Although Lincoln fought the war in order to save the Union, at Gettysburg he spoke rather of the 'nation'. According to historian David Reynolds, afterwards Americans less often said 'the United States are', replacing it with 'the United States is'.[84]

Something of this covenantal spirit has survived into the twentieth and twenty-first centuries to animate the US Cold War fight against Communism and thereafter against Islamist terrorism. When Barry Goldwater accepted the Republican nomination for the presidency in 1964, for example, he declared, 'The good Lord raised this mighty Republic to be a home for the brave to flourish as the land

---

[82] David Reynolds, *America, Empire of Liberty: A New History*, London: Allen Lane, 2009, 33.

[83] Steven B. Smith (ed), *The Writings of Abraham Lincoln*, New Haven: Yale University Press, 2012, 417.

[84] Reynolds, *America*, 205.

of the free—not to stagnate in the swampland of collectivism, not to cringe before the bully of Communism.' It is of course important to notice that Goldwater suffered a heavy defeat in the subsequent election: not all the US population subscribes to this version of divine election. All the same, something of this spirit certainly inspired the US campaign against Communism in Vietnam in the 1960s and 1970s.[85] The 9/11 attacks on New York and Washington in 2001 seem actually to have reinforced the sense of a special destiny by suddenly providing an obvious enemy against whom war could be waged, the 'war on terror' which George W. Bush initially called a 'crusade' (though he later retracted the word). At the National Cathedral he declared, 'Our responsibility to history is clear: to answer these attacks and rid the world of evil ... This will be a monumental struggle between good and evil. But good will prevail.'[86] US rulers at least can easily persuade themselves that social cohesion and generalized social trust can be enhanced by such rhetoric. Not all Americans subscribe to this vision, however; many continue to see their nation through a strictly secular republican lens.

France is another nation whose origins are impeccably republican on the surface. Indeed it has claims to be the purest type of republic. During the Revolution it initially transferred the divine right of monarchy to the people. During the late seventeenth and eighteenth centuries a gradual shift had taken place in the way educated French people thought about their society and the bonds which held it together. Secular or deist Enlightenment thinkers rethought concepts like *public*, *nation*, and *patrie*; they now saw the *nation* as an intense spiritual and political community engaging as a *public* in affairs of state and living in a sacred homeland, the *patrie*. Their campaigns were directed against absolute monarchy, aristocracy, and the Catholic church, which in their view encouraged tyranny and obscurantist superstition. They were inspired by the pre-Christian examples of the civic solidarity of the ancient Athenian city-state and the Roman Republic, as was symbolized by Jacques-Louis David's 1784 painting *The Oath of the Horatii*: it depicted the oath taken by three brothers to save Rome from invasion by offering to fight against three brothers from the rival city of Alba Longa.[87]

The theorist who lauded the Roman Republic as a model for modern France was Jean-Jacques Rousseau, whose *Social Contract* evoked in idealized form the city assemblies of Sparta, Athens, and republican Rome. In those assemblies, Rousseau asserted, all the citizens met together freely, made their own laws, and took their own decisions through discerning and acting on the 'general will'. In this concept he tried to elide the difficulty of transferring the will of one person, the monarch, to a large body of citizens. The nation-sovereign, he believed, was more trustworthy than the monarch-sovereign because it was not vulnerable to the whims of one person or to the intrigues of selfish and faction-ridden courtiers. Only in the

---

[85] Bruce Cauthen, 'Covenant and Continuity: Ethno-Symbolism and the Myth of Divine Election', *Nations and Nationalism*, 10/1–2 (2004), 19–34.

[86] Bob Woodward, *Bush at War*, New York: Simon & Schuster, 2002, 45, 67; *Keesing's Contemporary Archives*, 2001, 44334.

[87] David A. Bell, *The Cult of the Nation in France: Inventing Nationalism, 1680–1800*, Cambridge, Mass.: Harvard University Press, 2001.

people's 'general will', Rousseau believed, could true freedom be made real while the state remained stable and reliable. In this way he replaced the sovereignty of the monarch with the sovereignty of all the citizens.[88]

Significantly Rousseau himself, in the later stages of writing his *Social Contract*, came to the conclusion that those principles would not prove effective unless reinforced by a 'civil religion', consisting of 'those social maxims which everyone would be bound to acknowledge'. It taught that a benevolent deity exists, that there is life after death where the just will be rewarded and the wicked punished, that the laws and the social contract are sacred, and that sectarian intolerance is prohibited. This religion was to be protected by draconian provisions: those who did not sign up to this creed were to be banished, while those who did sign up but then violated it were to be punished by death.[89]

The full transfer of the national myth from monarchy to people took place after the revolution of 1789, and was enshrined in the Declaration of the Rights of Man and Citizen. A series of consciously crafted festivals was held to 'fix' the new collective identity symbolically and to link it to certain elements of the old one, in order to bind diverse and partly incompatible social groups in a unified consciousness of nationhood. Called Festivals of Federation, they were intended to represent the unity of people of different genders, regions, and social origins, and more specifically of the old royal army and the new post-revolutionary National Guard. The culmination was the celebration in Paris in July 1790 of the first anniversary of the fall of the Bastille. It was held on the Champ de Mars, former training ground of the royal army, and it contained religious as well as secular images. Delegates from the provinces bearing Roman-style banners filed past the 'Altar of the Fatherland', where Talleyrand, patron of the constitutional clergy (those prepared to take an oath of loyalty to the new regime), led the celebration of a mass combining Catholic and patriotic rites, while Lafayette, commander of the National Guard, administered the oath of loyalty to the new nation. Louis XVI, now constitutional 'King of the French', swore himself to 'employ all the power delegated to me by the constitution to uphold the decrees of the National Assembly'.[90] Many symbolic elements came together here: declarations of patriotic loyalty, oath-taking, civic and republican law-making, religious ritual, references to the Roman Republic (the enduring symbol of the French Revolution would be the Phrygian bonnet worn in ancient Rome by freed slaves). They all suggested that the new nation was the conscious and deliberate creation of patriotic citizens, a product of self-liberation and civic solidarity, more worthy of veneration than the dusty relics of saints. The narrative was intended to underpin mutual trust and confidence in a shared national future on a new civic basis.

---

[88] Keith Michael Baker, 'The Transformation of Classical Republicanism in Eighteenth-Century France', *Journal of Modern History*, 73 (2001), 32–53.

[89] Christopher Bertram, *Rousseau and the Social Contract*, London: Routledge, 2004, chapters 6 and 9.

[90] Simon Schama, *Citizens: A Chronicle of the French Revolution*, London: Penguin Books, 1989, 500–13; Mona Ozouf, *Festivals and the French Revolution*, trans. Alan Sheridan, Cambridge, Mass.: Harvard University Press, 1988, chapter 2.

It proved not to be enough, however. Robespierre, as later revolutionary leader, felt bound in wartime emergency to bolster civic ritual with a 'civil religion' on Rousseau's model. The Supreme Being, whose worship he ordained, was conceived as an all-seeing deity, able to see into everyone's hearts and souls, and to determine their virtue or otherwise. De Payan, one of his supporters, claimed that every good citizen would henceforth feel 'incessantly surrounded by a beneficent God, who reads in his heart, sees all his actions, and can wisely distinguish him from the corrupt man', while the bad citizen would feel 'incessantly surrounded by a powerful and terrifying witness, who sees him, who watches over him, and from whom he cannot escape'.[91] Worship was not enough in itself, however: the Law of 22 Prairial decreed that those suspected of being 'enemies of the people' should be arraigned before a Revolutionary Tribunal operating an accelerated procedure and able to consider 'moral' proofs even in the absence of material evidence; there was to be no counsel for the defence and no appeal. The Tribunal could decide between only two outcomes: acquittal or death.[92] As we saw in Chapter 1, the attempt to create total trustworthiness by means of maximum distrust can only lead to paroxysms of terror. The Law of 22 Prairial was repealed by the regime which took over after 9 Thermidor, and Robespierre himself was executed.

If Rousseau's and Robespierre's versions of civil religion were an unsatisfactory guarantee of social unity, then the threat of foreign invasion was to prove much more effective. In the face of monarchies arming themselves to crush the new revolutionary nation, the National Assembly in August 1793 issued a decree which declared the country to be in mortal danger from its enemies, and until they could be driven out commanded *la levée en masse*, the mass mobilization of the nation for war. It painted a picture of the nation as a huge family, each of whose members had his or her function. 'Young men will go off to fight; married men will forge weapons and transport supplies; women will make tents and clothes and serve in hospitals; children will tear up old underwear for bandages; old men will be borne to the public squares to stimulate the courage of the warriors, the hatred of kings and the unity of the Republic.'[93] Even a huge nation, it turned out, could be portrayed as a family.

Throughout the nineteenth century, the image of the motherland in danger and *la levée en masse* proved the most potent impetus to national solidarity, and not only for Frenchmen. Throughout Europe the image of the nation in danger was powerfully evocative and for many it supplanted a more traditional faith. Most nineteenth-century European wars were fought primarily over issues of national unity, sovereignty, and self-determination. This is especially striking, since war ran counter to the logic of economic development and international trade, which were also powerful motives in nineteenth-century political behaviour. As John Stuart Mill observed in his *Principles of Political Economy*, industry and trade were

---

[91] Dan Edelstein, *The Terror of Natural Right: Republicanism, The Cult of Nature, and the French Revolution*, University of Chicago Press, 2009, 231–7.

[92] Edelstein, *Terror*, 249–53.

[93] J. M. Thompson, *French Revolution Documents, 1789–94*, Oxford: Blackwell, 1948, 256.

boosting the attractiveness of positive-sum games compared with an earlier era: 'Before, the patriot . . . wished all countries weak, poor and ill-governed but his own; he now sees in their wealth and progress a direct source of wealth and progress to his own country. It is commerce which is rapidly rendering war obsolete.'[94] Alas, Mill was wrong. Mass primary education and the growing practice of universal conscription helped to spread and popularize compelling symbolic images of the nation. The mass media did the same, while often preaching simple-minded nationalism in the face of threatening Others. Because urbanization and industrialization were weakening immediate genuine kinship ties, the synthetic kinship of the nation became more appealing. In this way nations became the fundamental unit of European life, destabilizing empires and leading to a competition for domination, which, through the 'security dilemma'—the fear that rivals are preparing to attack—generated an unrestrained arms race and ultimately the war of 1914–18.[95]

Between the late middle ages and the nineteenth century in Europe the nation, and then the nation-state, became an increasingly important focus of faith and trust among ever wider sections of the population. It absorbed symbolic elements which had sustained confidence in earlier political formations, such as tribal kingdoms, city-states, and empires. It sponsored more conscious and systematic religious belief. It fortified inherited symbolic motifs through a national language drawn from the dialects of its ethnic core, a language which articulated its national myths, culture, and history, while an expanding educational system brought more citizens into contact with them. It restrained internal conflict and created a large zone of peace; it systematized law and did much to free it from partisan exploitation by local elites. The nation combined these symbols with the risk-bearing capacity of the organized and effective state to provide a stable framework for internal trade and manufacture, and much international trade too. At the same time its armies, drawn from the young male population, defended national borders and protected national homelands.

In these ways the state played a crucial role in stabilizing the nation and enabling it to realize its potential. Its relationship with the common people rested on the legitimacy created by hierarchical, covenantal, or republican types of public culture, or a mixture of them.

By the late nineteenth century international trade was doing much to sustain and improve the livelihood of European peoples. One might, therefore, have expected national loyalties to have faded and been gradually if only partly replaced by confidence in the international economy and international law. Instead of that, in the twentieth century national attachments reached a new intensity and generated extremely destructive wars. Why that should be so I examine in Chapter 7.

---

[94] Azar Gat, *War in Human Civilization*, Oxford University Press, 2006, 538, quoting from John Stuart Mill, *Principles of Political Economy*, New York: Kelley, 1961, book 3, chapter 17, no. 5, 582.
[95] Gat, *War*, 536–41.

6

God and Mammon
Trust in the Modern World

'God is back!' the authors of a recent book have announced.[1]

At first sight, this is odd. Until the late twentieth century it was widely assumed that modernization entailed secularization. As recently as 1992 Francis Fukuyama's *The End of History and the Last Man* predicted that, along with democracy, the rule of law, and the free market economy would come universal secularization. As nations became economically more advanced they would abandon superstition and become rational, tolerant, and dedicated to improving life on this earth rather than seeking salvation beyond the grave. Most people would turn away from religion and place their trust in science, reason, and economic development to combat life's ills.[2] That has indeed been the trajectory of most advanced European nations, even though religion played the residual role of bearer of nationalism in those nations which still lived under foreign hegemony, such as Ireland in relation to Britain or Poland under Russian and Soviet domination.

In the last two decades, though, the assumption of secularization has come under a serious challenge. It has become clear that in the modern world Europe is in many ways an exception.[3] In the USA and most other parts of the world, including China, which is making rapid economic progress under an avowedly atheist regime, religion in its various guises is spreading and gaining ever greater numbers of adherents. Controversies over veils and headscarves, and over crucifixes in schools, mass sectarian murders in India, and a series of suicide bombings launched by Al-Qaeda and its associates have brought religion right back into the centre of public attention, even in Europe. Trust in science, reason, and economic development has proved inadequate for many people: they still place their primary trust in religion and direct their distrust, with equal fervour, across the boundaries of their religion against adherents of other faiths.

The secularization theory has, however, been restated in modified form by Pippa Norris and Ronald Inglehart. Their thesis illuminates the ways in which people place their trust in times of economic and social transformation. Drawing on the World Values Survey launched by Inglehart in 1981, they assert that secularization

---

[1] John Micklethwait and Adrian Wooldridge, *God is Back: How the Global Rise of Faith is Changing the World*, London: Allen Lane, 2009.

[2] Francis Fukuyama, *The End of History and the Last Man*, London: Penguin Books, 1992.

[3] Grace Davie, *Europe—the Exceptional Case: Parameters of Faith in the Modern World*, London: Darton, Longman & Todd, 2002.

is indeed taking place where modernization has brought prosperity and security to people's lives. However, the population is growing faster in countries where everyday life is still beset by poverty, unemployment, disease, poor education, and sporadic health care; in those countries confidence in the future is precarious, and hence religious beliefs and practices remain at a high level. Paradoxically, therefore, the number of active religious believers is increasing even as secularization advances.[4] They accept that the USA, where prosperity is high, appears to be an exception, but they explain it by the fact that (i) there are a large number of relatively recent immigrants from poor countries in Central and South America, who bring their religious traditions with them, and (ii) the socio-economic welfare safety net is less comprehensive in the USA than in most advanced countries, and hence confidence in the future is more vulnerable.[5]

Callum Brown's study of British religion provides preliminary confirmation for this view. He suggests that the decline of Christian faith and practice in Britain took place quite abruptly in the 1960s, when—though he does not point this out—the first generation fully protected by welfare services was coming to adulthood.[6] Those able to put their trust in the state had less need of trust in God.

Trust in God, in fact, is related to trust in the economy. Here our two symbolic systems meet. The enormous growth in new forms of trade, manufacture, and services in the later decades of the twentieth century and their spread to most of the globe have brought with them far-reaching changes in every society they have touched. People have moved away from their families, home villages, and small towns into mega-cities where every day they rub shoulders with hordes of unknown people. Millions have moved much further than that, becoming immigrants in countries whose languages they do not speak and with whose customs they are unfamiliar. In both cases many newcomers lead a threatened and poverty-stricken existence, in shanty towns plagued by crime, alcoholism, drug trafficking, and epidemics. In these conditions to retain self-respect, lead a normal family life, and maintain some confidence in the future is immensely challenging.

Stability and normative coherence, two of Sztompka's preconditions of trust, have been comprehensively disrupted by economic and social upheaval; as for his other two preconditions, openness and redress, immigrants usually have great difficulty in benefiting from them, even if the institutions guaranteeing them exist in their new host society. In those circumstances they desperately need someone and something to trust.

Let us take an example. Veronica was an illegal immigrant, living in Texas; so at least the *New York Times* reported in December 2006. She had a good job, a pleasant home, a car, a loving husband, and two growing children. Her life was far better than it had been in her first home, a shanty town in Mexico, where she was

---

[4] Pippa Norris and Ronald Inglehart, *Sacred and Secular: Religion and Politics Worldwide*, Cambridge University Press, 2004.

[5] Norris and Inglehart, *Sacred and Secular*, 225–6.

[6] Callum G. Brown, *The Death of Christian Britain: Understanding Secularisation, 1800–2000*, London: Routledge, 2001, chapter 8.

unemployed. Things were not altogether easy, all the same, because she was afraid of any encounter with federal, state, or municipal officials, who might demand to see her papers. For the same reason, she avoided contact with doctors and drove the car very cautiously, so as not to be involved in an accident. Any brush with officialdom could land her in squalor and despair back 'at home'.

To cope with risk and uncertainty, Veronica said, she turned to God. She 'speaks about God with the passion of a new convert. It is her way of fending off the uncertainty at home and the longing she feels for her family in Monterrey. When her days seem too tenuous, Veronica prays, usually alone in her bedroom with her Bible. She asks God to protect her family from harm, to keep her strong, to help her relatives in Mexico buy a hot-water heater. She asks that her husband's boss stay faithful to him. She prays that her children stay far from drugs and sex.'

She found God when she had a pain in her uterus that would not go away. Being depressed and anxious, she went to a little evangelical church nearby, a tiny place of worship in a converted garage, where she could pray to God together with fifty or so other Latinos, 'many of them also one slip from misfortune. . . . This is her community, and she dresses up for it, with highlights in her hair, a long, tight-fitting skirt and an elegant black top.'[7]

This is a story that could be repeated millions of times over throughout the world, a story of people daily facing the possibility of poverty, serious illness, loss of job, loss of home, family breakdown, or natural disaster. Foresight, caution, and rational action can stave off or moderate some of these potential setbacks, but not all of them. To deal with life at all, to face its sometimes terrifying uncertainty and complexity, people have to trust in something, even, perhaps especially, when difficulties seem insurmountable. Without trust suspicion, anxiety, and depression could become overwhelming. Veronica found trust in God, but was also able to place trust in the people of her congregation, to support her and help her to the best of their abilities if things went wrong.

Religions are well placed to meet her need and that of millions like her. It is no accident that nineteenth-century USA, the first land of concerted economic development combined with mass immigration, pioneered the kinds of churches and religious movements which appeal to the newly uprooted. The frontier was a site of individualism and competition, but those who had arrived there needed some sense of community, some way into the mutual cooperation which was essential to cope with the hazards and dangers of the environment. In the absence of settled parishes, religious services would be improvised in so-called 'camp meetings', to which families would come from miles around, often camping out in order to attend. Freed for a while from daily routines, they would participate full-heartedly. The Methodist preacher William Burke reported that at Carr Ridge in Kentucky hundreds fell prostrate on the ground before him and lay in agonies of distress, from which sporadically someone would leap up and emit shouts of triumph.[8]

---

[7] *New York Times*, 20 December 2006, A26–7.

[8] Bernard A. Weisberger, *They Gathered at the River: The Story of the Great Revivalists and their Impact upon Religion in America*, Chicago: Quadrangle Books, 1958, 28–34.

Such a setting encouraged a spontaneous, emotional style of religion, unencumbered with scriptural learning. Pastor and people could come together on a basis of near equality to sing and celebrate. Religion also fostered a certain moral rigour, necessary to restrain the vices and excesses of frontier life. The congregation rather than the sheriff or law court dealt with drunkenness, brawling, stealing, and wife-beating, all ubiquitous in remote settlements.[9] In this way, religion provided a modicum of social cement and a means of sustaining mutual trust in a harsh and precarious environment.

Similarly, newcomers to American cities needed help with settling in, especially if they came from abroad. In the nineteenth century Catholic priests would sometimes meet immigrants from Italy, Spain, or Poland at the docks, then help them to find food, work, and a local community of co-ethnics in which to settle down. A church with services in a familiar language (the ethnic vernacular or, for Catholics, Latin) would enable the recent arrival to regain some of the lost togetherness of his original homeland. In the twentieth century Chinese churches in New York's Chinatown would help Chinese immigrants in the same ways, providing a kind of parallel welfare state while they found their feet in their new environment.[10] In return, a good many immigrants practised their faith more ardently in their new home than they had done in the ancestral lands from which they had come.[11]

In Philadelphia today nearly all churches provide some help for the poor, sick, aged, and recent immigrants. Some help the homeless and families of prisoners; one church even allows them to live in the church for a limited period while they sort themselves out. Some give counselling to the unhappy or organize visits to lonely, elderly homebound folk. Some give free vaccinations and a limited repertoire of medical care—a great boon in a country where normal medical treatment can be prohibitively expensive. Black churches have been at the centre of the life of African-Americans, helping them to create schools, banks, credit unions, insurance companies, housing projects, and funeral parlours. Since state welfare provision is relatively meagre, these facilities are not only a lifeline for many people, they also come with less red tape and form-filling than their secular equivalents.[12] In such ways the churches promote generalized social trust within marginalized communities, and help the victims of social change to face the future with a degree of confidence even in very adverse circumstances.

In modern prosperous US suburbia religious adherence also remains strong, for related though rather different reasons. People are separated from each other by long distances, even if they have cars to traverse them. Mothers with small children can feel very isolated and face practical problems with child-care, at the very time that their husbands, working hard to pay the mortgage and keep a valued job or

---

[9] Gregory H. Nobles, *American Frontiers: Cultural Encounters and Continental Conquest*, London: Penguin Books, 1998, 112–13.

[10] Micklethwait and Wooldridge, *God is Back*, 73, 235.

[11] Philip Jenkins, *God's Continent: Christianity, Islam and Europe's Religious Crisis*, Oxford University Press, 2007, 52–3.

[12] Micklethwait, *God is Back*, 162–5.

gain promotion, are less often at home. Mega-churches create social bonds for otherwise potentially atomized suburban dwellers. Churches also perform a lot of social work: rehabilitation for addicts, counselling and emotional support for people who are grieving or going through marital problems, help for battered women, temporary aid for people with financial problems. They are 'anchors in a mobile society and life rafts for the distressed'.[13]

The style of religion best adapted to the recently uprooted or socially isolated is one that is intellectually straightforward, offers certainty, stability, strong feelings, warm relationships, and a way of life that promises improvement in this life and salvation in the hereafter. Evangelical religions best meet these requirements. They propose conversion as a spiritual equivalent to the arrival in a new society, they offer a personal relationship with Jesus, and through his crucifixion suggest that disaster and suffering may be the way to salvation. They also encourage absolute confidence in a sacred text, the Bible, and in a congregation which is supportive in adversity. This kind of fundamentalist religion emerged in the late nineteenth century in reaction against Bible criticism and modernist theology, and against the spread of science as a rival trust-generating symbolic system.[14] It offers its own symbolic rewards in strengthening self-esteem, self-reliance, and a tough moral code within a robust community; it helps to promote confidence in the future.

In other countries also, rapid modernization, far from bringing about decline in religious belief and practice, has stimulated their growth. In South Korea, for example, starting in the 1960s, as urbanization and industrialization took off, there was a remarkable upsurge in the beliefs and practices of Protestantism and, more gradually, Catholicism and Buddhism. Urbanization was exceptionally fast: towns accounted for 28 per cent of the population in 1960, but 74 per cent in 1990. Many of the newcomers had to live in slums, where life was insecure, and traditional asceticism and family-centred collectivism no longer seemed to work. Everywhere western values—individualism, rationalism, materialism—challenged traditional Korean ones.

Protestantism first arrived in Korea in the late nineteenth and early twentieth centuries, when the country was in deep crisis following Japanese invasion and occupation. Koreans hated the Japanese, but many also felt that Chinese Confucianism, for centuries their religious mainstay, had let them down. They were therefore predisposed to welcome western—and specifically American—ideas. Early Protestant missionaries promoted both education and medical services, and thus gained the trust of many, especially from the lower classes, and also provided them with a new symbolic paradigm for regaining confidence in themselves and in society.[15]

[13] Micklethwait, *God is Back*, 144–5.

[14] Richard Kyle, *Evangelicalism: An Americanized Christianity*, New Brunswick, NJ: Transaction Publishers, 2006, 10–15.

[15] Yong-Shin Park, 'Protestant Christianity and its Place in Changing Korea', *Social Compass*, 47 (2000), no. 4, 507–25.

The aftermath of the Korean War (1950–3) impelled a further explosive growth of Protestantism and, to a lesser extent, of Catholicism. Christianity appealed to those looking for spiritual support against the terrible new threat of North Korean Communism. The most successful churches, the Unification Church of Sun Myung Moon, and the Full Gospel Church, preached vehement nationalism and anti-Communism. They provided welfare services for the poor, but also preached a gospel of moral self-improvement leading to self-enrichment, through strong families, self-discipline, and a strict reading of the Bible. By the 1990s Seoul had 7,000 churches and 40 per cent of the population was said to belong to one or other of them. The Full Gospel Church's huge building could accommodate 7,000 believers; yet every Sunday morning it had to hold successions of services, with believers bussed in from all parts of Seoul, and television relays for those not able to get inside. At its 'Prayer Mountain' outside Seoul, people in crisis could go to say their prayers and receive counselling and help.[16] The Protestant churches thus used their own symbolic system plus modern technology to offer Koreans trust in God, in their country, and confidence in themselves as moral agents.

In China, the economic reforms initiated by Deng Xiaoping in the late 1970s transformed the lives of millions of Chinese, who had to move from village to city, and to wean themselves from dependence on the state to find jobs or themselves become entrepreneurs. A wholly new religious movement, Falun Gong, emerged during the 1990s, probably the decade of maximum upheaval resulting from Deng's reforms. It grew out of the revival of *qigong*, a traditional Chinese healing and meditative practice, after the catastrophic failure of the Cultural Revolution of the 1960s. *Qigong* had been practised in the redemptive societies which offered a message of hope during the terrible hardships of the warlord period, the Japanese occupation of the 1930s–1940s and then the extremely dislocating social revolution instigated by the Communist government after 1949. The societies had interpreted these events as the apocalypse through which humanity had to pass before reaching ultimate redemption. In the meantime they provided some degree of social welfare. Some societies were involved in counter-revolutionary risings, but most were non-violent in orientation. The People's Liberation Army tried to suppress them all, but many survived semi-underground in the villages to revive in the 1980s.[17]

Falun Gong was launched by a charismatic *qigong* teacher, Li Hongzhi. He claimed to have learnt from Dao and Buddhist masters, but he also imparted a greater moral emphasis to *qigong*. He taught that through the cultivation of truthfulness, compassion, and forbearance—all required for trust in the trustworthy—one could come into contact with one's true self and with beneficent forces in the cosmos. He believed that the modern obsession with wealth and

[16] Nathalie Luca, 'La conquête de la modernité par les nouveaux mouvements chrétiens coréens', *Social Compass*, 47 (2000), no. 4, 525–39.

[17] David Ownby, *Falun Gong and the Future of China*, Oxford University Press, 2008, 38–43. I am grateful to Professor Stephen Smith for letting me see his unpublished article, 'Redemptive Societies and the Communist State, 1949 to the 1980s'.

fame, as well as the fascination with western science, and the widespread addiction to drugs and alcohol, indicated that humanity was in a period of decline, had become disconnected from the gods, and was now a prey to demons. Humanity, he prophesied, will go through an apocalyptic period, after which rebirth and growth can occur, provided at least some human beings have stayed in touch with their own deeper natures and with cosmic good.[18] Falun Gong thus seems to promote embattled mutual trust in an environment where potential disaster is perceived as imminent. No doubt the persecution inflicted by the Chinese state intensifies this trust within religious communities.

Religions, then, offer trust in many forms. But they also sow distrust, in especially virulent forms, up to and including mass murder by suicidal terrorists, as was dramatically exemplified in the 9/11 attacks on the USA by Islamist terrorists.

What lay behind these horrific attacks was not the inherent nature of the Islamic religion, but rather the perception of many Muslims that during the past two centuries or so the Christian West has persistently degraded, humiliated, and exploited them. The destruction of the Ottoman Empire and the Caliphate, the western quasi-colonial takeover of the Middle East after 1918, the distortion of its economies for western needs and profits, and then the creation of the state of Israel in Palestine, all taken together, have generated among Middle Eastern Muslims a sense of instability, normative incoherence, and a lack of openness and accountability. Resentment and distrust followed naturally from these perceptions, and at first engendered Arab nationalism. After gaining independence from the colonial powers, however, secular nationalism's achievements proved disappointing, and Islam, as a supranational faith, began to seem a more satisfactory focus of trust. The 1979 Islamic revolution in Iran was the first sign that resentment at US and western domination was taking a religious form. Ayatollah Khomeini deepened distrust of the West by pointing to both material deprivation and symbolic desecration. He declared that 'The foul claws of imperialism have clutched at the heart of the lands of the people of the Koran, with our national wealth and resources being devoured by imperialism . . . with the poisonous culture of imperialism penetrating to the depths of our towns and villages throughout the Muslim world, displacing the culture of the Koran.'[19]

In similar spirit in December 2006 Ayman al-Zawahiri, close associate of Osama bin Laden in Al-Qaeda, posted a video on the internet, offering a black-and-white choice of polarized absolutes, of total distrust and total trust.

> O my Muslim Umma, you must choose between two choices: the first is to live on the margins of the New World Order and international law and under the control of the enemies of Islam, dishonoured, humiliated, plundered and occupied, with them meddling in your beliefs and true religion, sticking their noses in all your domestic and foreign affairs, and you living the life of a vassal, lowly, disgraced and defiled.

[18] Ownby, *Falun Gong*, 93–109.
[19] John L. Esposito, *Unholy War: Terror in the Name of Islam*, Oxford University Press, 2002, 62.

And the second choice is that you rely on your Lord, renew your *Tawheed* [worship of the one God], rise up with your true faith, follow the revealed religion of Allah, and stand with it in the face of the arrogant criminals, as your truthful and trustworthy Prophet (peace be upon him), his righteous companions and his purified family (Allah was pleased with them all) stood in the face of the world, inviting, giving the good news, warning and performing Jihad in order that Allah's Word be made the highest and the word of the infidels the lowest. And there is no third choice.[20]

Such polarized evocations of the symbolism of trust and distrust evidently have resonance among at least some Muslims. In the Middle East many people felt after the US–UK invasion of Iraq that suicide bomb attacks against westerners were justified. In a Pakistani opinion poll, 65 per cent of respondents were reported as regarding Osama bin Laden favourably, and in Jordan 55 per cent.[21] In 2006 people in the West were surprised when Hamas won a majority in the Palestinian parliament. Yet the electors' reaction can easily be explained by their intense distrust of Israel, as a result of the poverty and insecurity created by Israeli settlement and occupation policies. They needed to place their trust in another entity which could both speak for them and offer them some hope and a modicum of social welfare. Hamas emerged in 1987 as the Palestinian branch of the Egyptian Muslim Brotherhood. Its charter declares that 'there is no solution for the Palestinian question except through jihad', interpreted as war against the infidel. It also offered social welfare through libraries, sports clubs, and charitable associations such as the Orphan Care Society, and education through schools usually attached to mosques. In that way it provided physical help and a sense of community such as constitute primary nodes of trust. Through those same institutions, on the other hand, it also laundered money and intensified distrust by socializing young people into a culture of violent anti-Israeli and anti-western activity up to and including suicide bombings.[22]

Europe, then, does seem to represent an anomaly, in that nearly all forms of religious belief and practice are declining there except in communities of relatively recent immigration. Does this confirm the Norris–Inglehart view that in more stable, affluent societies secularization *is* still the dominant trend? The sociologist Grace Davie, who has examined this question closely, came to the conclusion that it does, but in a distinctive form. In most European countries the modernization shock was less abrupt than elsewhere, since industrialization and urbanization took place relatively gradually and on the basis of social structures generated internally rather than imposed from outside. The disruption of traditional social structures was less abrupt and disorienting. In Europe, moreover, Christian churches had long existed, were institutionalized in pre-industrial society, and were closely identified with the state; they therefore had greater difficulty in adapting

---

[20] Quoted in Faisal Devji, *The Terrorist in Search of Humanity: Militant Islam and Global Politics*, New York: Columbia University Press, 2008, 37.

[21] Andrew H. Kydd, *Trust and Mistrust in International Politics*, Princeton University Press, 2005, 254–5.

[22] Matthew Levitt, *Hamas: Politics, Charity and Terrorism in the Service of Jihad*, New Haven: Yale University Press, 2006; quotation on p. 31.

to new social patterns, in contrast to the USA, where they arose more spontaneously. Thereafter in European Protestant countries religious practice gradually faded, while in Catholic ones secularization took place in polarized conflicts between the church and a militant secularism which had many religious features about it. In most European countries nowadays *belief* in some kind of supreme being or supernatural force remains quite high, but commitment to a church and regular attendance at it have declined markedly—what Davie calls 'believing without belonging'. In her words, Europeans tend to regard their churches as a 'public utility', which they can fall back on in case of need and to celebrate life-threshold events.[23] Trust in churches remains quite high, even while attendance in them is low. Even in Europe, then, secularization has been half-hearted. God is not dead, but held in reserve.

Davie thus on the whole confirms the Norris–Inglehart thesis, but adds additional features to it. I believe we can best understand the process as a transfer of trust from churches and congregations to the state, our 'public risk manager', and also to science, technology, and modern financial mechanisms—a change which has not taken place—or indeed has been reversed—in countries where modernization has been more abrupt and externally imposed or where, as in the USA, the state has not fully taken on the role of public risk manager. In those countries the role of public religion has intensified and taken on new symbolic forms in order to meet the need for at least a degree of generalized social trust.

MONEY AND COMMERCIAL TRUST

As we saw in Chapter 4, capitalism is a powerful magnet of trust, thanks to the symbolism of money and the institutions which mediate that symbolism. We have tended to take for granted that we can place our trust in them, not seeing that they are artificial and vulnerable creations, liable to crisis and change. In the early twenty-first century, however, their vulnerability has been cruelly exposed. The two cardinal defects of capitalism—its proneness to boom and bust, and its creation of blatant inequalities—have not gone away, and they are now reasserting themselves with destructive force. They have moreover combined in a toxic mixture with money's potential for the nihilistic devaluation of other symbolic systems.

The twentieth century provided us with egregious examples of all these tendencies and the disasters to which they can lead. In the 1920s the USA was gripped by financial fever, fuelled by technological advance and the opportunities offered by a fast-growing consumer economy. The most conspicuous new industry was the automobile, but there was also a rapid expansion of the market for household utilities and consumer durables, such as vacuum cleaners, irons, and washing machines. There was heavy demand for family homes and the land on which to build them. The price of shares in construction firms and in those manufacturing

[23] Davie, *Europe*, quotation on p. 138; see also Grace Davie, *Religion in Britain since 1945: Believing without Belonging*, Oxford: Blackwell, 1994.

and selling household consumer items rose sharply. Those firms both expanded their output and combined with each other under holding companies which could achieve economies of scale and greater control over the market. As the prices of shares rose, purchasers would borrow money to buy them, and their brokers would help them with new and inventive credit devices, so that they need pay up front only a fraction of the share price, with the remainder to follow 'on call', that is, held back till called for. Such 'buying on margin' became routine. Borrowers were confident that the tide would continue rising indefinitely, enabling them to sell at a tidy profit and pay back their debts with ease, whenever the 'call' came. The volume of shares on the New York Stock Exchange rose from $236 million in 1923 to $577 million in 1927 and $1,125 million in 1928.[24]

In October 1929 doubts began to arise about how secure the foundations of all this investment were. The sudden loss of confidence left many investors clawing at empty air as they tried to pay back debts that now considerably exceeded their assets. Wall Street lost some 40 per cent in a few weeks of late October and early November. Everywhere the economic certainties that had sustained confidence crumbled. Banks would not lend to each other, because they could not trust even well-known colleagues to pay them back. Some banks failed, brought down by loans which could not be recovered and by the decline in the value of assets held as collateral. In the autumn of 1930 a raft of regional banks crashed in the USA, culminating in the failure of the Bank of New York in December. As the USA was the financial power-house of the world, the contagion spread to other countries, where people also lost their trust in banks and queued up to pull out their deposits while there was still time. By the spring of 1931 the same was happening in Germany and Central Europe, and the key Austrian Creditanstalt closed its doors in May.[25]

Starved of credit and of customers, industries went on short time or closed down altogether; farms faced foreclosure, as their owners could no longer meet their mortgage payments; workers were laid off and crowded hopelessly around labour exchanges and social security offices. National governments made matters worse by cutting expenditure to balance budgets as required under the gold standard which had hitherto underpinned confidence in international trade. Social security was sharply reduced. The result was a vicious circle in which people had less money to spend, so demand fell sharply, dooming yet more businesses and leaving many workers without jobs and even less money at their disposal.

In response national governments eventually reasserted their role as public risk managers, but each did so only for its own nation, and thereby created international negative-sum games. Each raised tariff barriers to protect national industries from foreign competition and thereby degraded international trade still further. The

[24] Ronald E. Seavoy, *An Economic History of the United States: From 1607 to the Present*, New York: Routledge, 2006, 270–5; Arthur M. Schlesinger, Jr, *The Crisis of the Old Order, 1919–1933*, Boston: Houghton Mifflin, 1957, 68–9, 157; Charles P. Kindleberger, *The World in Depression, 1929–1939* (revised and enlarged edition), Berkeley and Los Angeles: University of California Press, 1986, 95–6.
[25] Kindleberger, *World in Depression*, chapter 7.

USA began the process. The Smoot–Hawley Tariff of June 1930 raised import tariffs to protect US agriculture; that had the effect of making it more difficult for other countries to export to the USA, previously the world's leading export market. Other countries reacted with comparable trade barriers to protect their own industries. In 1932, Britain, long the leading champion of free trade, imposed tariffs on imports coming from anywhere but the Commonwealth. At the end of 1932 the confidence which lubricates international trade had been so gravely impaired that trade was at barely one-third of its pre-crash levels.[26]

A World Economic Conference convened in 1933 broke up without agreement on any plan to coordinate national responses to the crisis. Trade was conducted largely on a bilateral basis, or within economic blocs such as the British Commonwealth.[27] Germany sought *Lebensraum* for itself in Central and Eastern Europe, then from 1941 in the Soviet Union. Japan set about creating a Greater East Asia Co-Prosperity Sphere, that is, a Japan-dominated economic bloc in China, Southeast Asia, and the Dutch East Indies. This competitive economic fragmentation was a major cause of the Second World War, the disastrous result of a narrowing and fragmentation of the radius of trust caused by the inherent instability of poorly regulated capitalism and by the understandable but short-sighted efforts of national governments to protect their own populations at everyone else's expense.

After 1945 international statesmen were determined to prevent a repeat of this disaster. They set about creating international institutions which would enable nations to share risk, to consult collectively to preserve peace, to face crises together rather than individually, and to provide some degree of global governance to underpin global commerce. In other words, they worked to create positive-sum games and to broaden once more the radius of trust up to the global level required by economic developments.

On that principle the United Nations was to provide a forum for the non-violent settlement of conflicts between nations of the kind which had led to the Second World War. The International Monetary Fund was to come to the rescue of nations in financial crisis, so that they need not engage in the negative-sum game of competitively devaluing their currencies or erecting tariff barriers to protect their industries. The General Agreement on Tariffs and Trade created a legal framework of procedures for global commerce, so that trade disputes could be peacefully resolved without serious disruption to it. The World Bank was to provide funds to encourage economic development in the world's weaker economies, so that they could provide a decent life for their peoples and participate effectively in international trade. The Bretton Woods currency agreement was intended to stabilize relationships between the world's various currencies, so that abrupt currency movements should not destabilize global commerce. All of these organizations aimed to create arenas where destructive rivalries could be restrained, risk could be

---

[26] Kindleberger, *World in Depression*, 123–7; Jeffry A. Frieden, *Global Capitalism: Its Fall and Rise in the Twentieth Century*, New York: Norton, 2006, 185.

[27] Harold James, *The End of Globalization*, Cambridge, Mass.: Harvard University Press, 2001, 128–33, 163–7.

pooled, and collective confidence upheld. In these ways trust in international trade was to be recreated and reinforced. The result was undoubtedly a great success: international trade grew no less than sixteenfold over the period 1950–1995.[28]

Other institutions were created for the same purpose. The European Economic Community, set up in 1957, was to pool risk and create positive-sum games between the nations of Europe, so recently engaged in murderous wars against each other. Through the Marshall Plan the USA diverted part of its own wealth to ensure that no European country would slip back into the poverty and mass unemployment which had given impetus to Fascism and which might now incline their populations to accept Soviet-style Communism. The USA provided $13 billion between 1948 and 1952, mostly in grants, to European countries, and made a major contribution to their post-war recovery. In Europe per capita incomes typically trebled or quadrupled from 1950 to the early 1970s.[29] The Plan also helped to engender trust relationships between West European nations and the USA. Since, however, the countries of the emerging Soviet bloc refused it—under Stalin's orders—the Plan also helped to entrench new boundaries of distrust across the middle of Europe. It is no accident that most of its beneficiaries subsequently joined NATO, the military alliance whose declared aim was to deter or if necessary repel a Soviet invasion.

Up to the 1970s each nation-state in the developed world played its part in sustaining this structure by pursuing sound fiscal policies, restricting capital movements, and regulating its banks and financial institutions so that they could not undertake risky and potentially disruptive experiments with the considerable funds at their disposal. They had also learnt from the 1930s bank crashes that they should guarantee ordinary banking customers' deposits, at least up to a certain level. The aim of all these measures was to reassure the public that the funds they had deposited with banks were absolutely safe, and hence so were their insurance policies and pension funds. They could undertake economic activity in the confidence that their livelihoods were secure.[30]

The levels of generalized social trust thus generated were economically very beneficial. The correlation between trust and a flourishing economy was pointed out in a pathbreaking study by Edward Banfield, published more than half a century ago. He ascribed the under-development of southern Italy to low levels of social trust above the level of the extended family, where he called such trust 'amoral familism'.[31] Robert Putnam found the same phenomenon several decades later and contrasted it with the economically developed Italian north, whose superior performance he traced back to civic institutions first set up there in the

[28] Tony Judt, *Postwar: A History of Europe since 1945*, London: Heinemann, 2005, 324–6.
[29] Judt, *Postwar*, 324–6; Barry Eichengreen, *The European Economy since 1945: Coordinated Capitalism and beyond*, Princeton University Press, 2008, chapter 2.
[30] Philip Coggan, *Paper Promises: Money, Debt and the New World Order*, London: Penguin Books, 2012, 88, 96, 126, 157.
[31] Edward C. Banfield, *The Moral Basis of a Backward Society*, New York: Free Press, 1958.

middle ages.[32] Some critics found the explanation unpersuasive, on the grounds that too long had elapsed for the factor to be still effective. But recent studies have tended to confirm Putnam's hypothesis, as we shall see.

In a similar vein, Francis Fukuyama attributed the poor performance of southern Italy to low levels of 'social capital', that is, 'the ability of people to work together for common purposes in groups and organisations'. If people cannot trust one another to pool their efforts and share their risks, if they fear the benefits are likely to be stolen by criminals, thwarted by bureaucratic obstruction, creamed off by a few of their own members for personal or family gain, or at best subverted by free riders, they are unlikely to commit themselves to a shared enterprise. Firms remain small, and centred in the family, which is therefore the core of economic life.[33]

This appears to be the case not only in Italy. A recent article based on worldwide data confirms that there is a low-trust poverty trap, and that broadly based social trust is closely linked to high levels of investment and economic growth. It suggests that generalized trust is negatively correlated with discrimination and with social distance between economic actors, but that trust is fortified by high levels of education, egalitarian distribution of incomes, and the effectiveness of formal institutions and social sanctions against cheating.[34]

The economist Guido Tabellini has examined a similar question in relation to the regions of Europe, and concluded that good economic performance is positively correlated not only with trust, but also with respect for others and the individual feeling that one is in control of one's life. The last two traits indicate attitudes which would encourage trustworthy behaviour and confidence in the future. Tabellini also gave a historical dimension to his research and found that these positive features correlated with good political and civic institutions established in the past, sometimes the distant past, as Putnam had suggested. Interestingly, though, Tabellini found that what explained current economic performance was not institutions as such, but rather the cultural dispositions associated with them.[35] The benefit of institutions is that they mediate trust in the trustworthy, and that effect can be remarkably durable.

POST-SOVIET RUSSIA

After the fall of the Soviet Union, the trust-corroding defects of the old Soviet system unexpectedly amalgamated with the equally trust-corroding defects of the new unregulated capitalism. Chapter 1 suggested why distrust was so rampant in

---

[32] Robert D. Putnam, *Making Democracy Work: Civic Traditions in Modern Italy*, Princeton University Press, 1993.

[33] Francis Fukuyama, *Trust: The Social Virtues and the Creation of Prosperity*, London: Penguin, 1996, 10 and chapter 10.

[34] Paul J. Zak and Stephen Knack, 'Trust and Growth', *Economic Journal*, 111 (2001), 295–321, especially 306 and 316–17.

[35] Guido Tabellini, 'Culture and Institutions: Economic Development in the Regions of Europe', *Journal of the European Economic Association*, 8 (2010), no. 4, 677–716.

the 1930s Soviet Union. Let us now examine the rather different factors which exacerbated generalized social distrust in the 1990s.

As we saw in Chapter 1, trust and distrust in the late Soviet Union tended to focus on quite small groups, or on patrons within the state-directed economy. Money also functioned idiosyncratically in the planned economy. Its major productive sectors used money in a vertically partitioned manner: that is, any enterprise received money as a unit of account from its ministry, to enable it to acquire the raw materials, spare parts, fuel, food, and so on required for production and workplace facilities, as well as the wages to pay its employees. But that money could not be spent outside the vertical partition, except to make the purchases envisaged in the five-year plan. If the enterprise needed supplies or services from elsewhere not foreseen in the plan—and most enterprises quite often did—then it had to turn to unofficial sources of supply and pay for them in some other way, typically by the exchange of goods or services, that is, by barter, a pre-monetary device.

Overall, then, money did not cut across boundaries of administrative authority, but rather reinforced them by serving as one means for the enforcement of that authority. As we have seen in Chapter 4, the vectors along which trust in money moves determine much about the nature of any society. In the Soviet Union money reinforced dependence—and therefore compulsory trust—on enterprise directors, ministries, and party secretaries, that is, on 'big men'. The easiest way to secure regular supplies of food and everyday consumer goods was to order them through one's workplace under the system of *zakazy* (orders) or *talony* (coupons awarded to especially favoured individuals). Nomenklatura hierarchs received especially favourable terms at *raspredeliteli*, literally 'distributors', special stores where scarce goods were not only regularly available, but very cheap.

An economy which deployed money and commodities in this manner was in no condition to assimilate the practices of western finance, as it tried to do very abruptly after the fall of the Soviet Union. Such concepts as property, contract, and money had very different meanings in the Soviet context from those taken for granted in most western economic theory—and those meanings could not be transformed overnight. The very word 'market' conjured up either flimsy peasant stalls on waste ground at the edge of town, or else the shady dealings of the black market, in which one engaged with foreboding, with the expectation of being swindled. In neither case was it possible to feel much trust.[36] Russians' ambivalence about the market expressed itself in a new form of distrust, directed against Chinese and also *kavkaztsy*, whether Chechen, Georgian, or Azerbaijani, in the belief that 'outsiders' were manipulating and distorting the market.[37]

The attempt to introduce the most radical western free-market ideas into these configurations of trust generated some bizarre practices. One result was an intense localism. The joint responsibility of the *kollektiv* took on even greater importance

[36] Caroline Humphrey, *The Unmaking of Soviet Life: Everyday Economies after Socialism*, Ithaca, NY: Cornell University Press, 2002, chapter 1.
[37] Caroline Humphrey, 'Traders, "Disorder", and Citizenship Regimes in Provincial Russia', in her *Unmaking*, 90–3.

when it was beset by the pressures of a raw and rapacious market economy. The individual enterprise remained for a time public risk manager for its employees; keeping it going for their sake became a new and demanding imperative. The familiar Soviet *tolkachi* ('pushers', informal traders) took on proliferating and even more urgently needed tasks, finding suppliers and offering them a mixture of cash and barter goods—whatever their enterprise had to spare at that moment. Employees who were not paid for months remained on the books of their enterprise to retain the social benefits it provided, even while to earn a little real money they engaged in various activities that had nothing to do with their nominal employment. Their loyalty was reminiscent of the late medieval manor, which in economic difficulties had provided back-up security while the peasants engaged in various alternative economic activities. Such practices formed part of what one scholar has called 'the transition from socialism to feudalism'.[38] In the long run, though, tough decisions had to be taken: eventually employees were laid off and usually had to resort to petty trade to keep going. Meanwhile, enterprises gradually handed over their social responsibilities to local government, which then had to pester Moscow for resources to shoulder them.[39]

Let us take a particular case. Tatiana was chief accountant of the 'spin-off' firm of a medium-sized industrial enterprise in Novosibirsk. 'Spin-off' firms were routinely set up to conduct transactions that the principal firm wished to conceal from the tax authorities. Besides doing that, Tatiana's firm provided discreet banking services for other firms: one of the basic rules of doing business at the time was to appear to have no funds or no profits, which would otherwise be heavily taxed, and so firms would deposit their money clandestinely with each other. In Tatiana's words: 'For example, somebody comes and asks me to keep some money at the bank, so that it wouldn't be kept at home. Not on deposit under his name (so that the client has to declare it), but just to keep it in the bank, say $1 million or so. Only I and one of my aides (just in case something happens to me) are going to know about this. This money is deposited in some company account, hundreds of millions [of rubles], simply on a handshake. There can't be any paperwork here, just trust. I pay them interest on this money. It's good for the bank and good for the client. Or, say, another typical service—to give a loan to a client with his own money. Someone comes to the bank and says: I'll put money in the bank and you give me a loan. A lot of businesses in Russia involve offshore companies and banks for storing money and for conducting financial operations, all of which imply an enormous measure of trust in people you deal with.'[40]

As Tatiana said, such dealings had nothing more to sustain them than mutual trust—strong thin trust squared. Enterprise managers would, however, try to alleviate the risks by forming circles of close acquaintance with whom to do most

[38] Katherine Verdery, *What was Socialism? And What Comes Next?* Princeton University Press, 1996.
[39] Humphrey, 'Traders, "Disorder", and Citizenship Regimes in Provincial Russia', 69–98; Kathryn Stoner-Weiss, *Resisting the State: Reform and Retrenchment in Post-Soviet Russia*, Cambridge University Press, 2006, chapter 4.
[40] Alena Ledeneva, *How Russia Really Works*, Cambridge University Press, 2006, 170.

of their deals.[41] In that way they attempted to create islets of high trust in a low-trust environment. Tatiana commented on the resulting paradox: 'While my trust in the state and in the business community overall is extremely low, trust in those with whom I do business is extremely high, because many deals go through without any documentation whatever.' She did not leave herself completely defenceless, though. If a business partner defaulted on a clandestine deal, she would appeal to an undesignated but clearly influential person known to herself or her 'above-ground' enterprise: 'The court system is still useless in many ways, but there are many situations where it takes just one call to the right person who would then get in touch with the client advising him to pay.'[42] 'Advising' was of course a euphemism: new trust structures were still being supplemented by older ones, including appeal to a personal protector or 'roof' (*krysha*).

In the absence of reliable state-backed law and order, many firms organized their own squads of 'heavies' for protection, the collection of debt, or the enforcement of contract, or they relied on armed bands hired to do so. In the 1990s there were many unemployed men in Russia holding surplus weapons and trained in the application of violence. They were happy to offer their 'services', which were essentially 'protection rackets': armed criminals would defend you as long as you paid them regularly, but would smash up your premises and possibly murder you if you did not. In some cases the police competed with them commercially: in 1994 foreign companies working in Moscow received from the city police a fax offering protection at the rate of 7,000 rubles (about $3) an hour for one policeman. In any event it was important to have a *krysha* in a dangerous and lawless world.[43]

Overall, then, since the state was not an effective public risk manager, people reconfigured trust at a much lower level. They looked to 'big men' to protect their interests rather than to police, law courts, banks, insurance companies, or state welfare systems. Patron–client networks re-emerged in a new form as the dominant political and economic sinews of society. Ironically international financial organizations reinforced the dominance of those networks by channelling investment through a small clique of reformers and businessmen whom they trusted, led by Anatolii Chubais.[44]

Banks were also not performing their normal function of guaranteeing sound money, providing deposit facilities, and transferring money from where it lay

[41] Vadim Radaev, 'How Trust is Established in Economic Relations when Individuals and Institutions are not Trustworthy: The Case of Russia', in János Kordai, Bo Rothstein, and Susan Rose-Ackerman (eds), *Creating Social Trust in Post-Socialist Transition*, New York: Palgrave Macmillan, 2004, 91–110; Christopher Woodruff, 'Establishing Confidence in Business Partners: Courts, Networks and Relationships as Pillars of Support', in Kordai, Rothstein, and Rose-Ackerman (eds), *Creating Social Trust*, 111–25.

[42] Ledeneva, *How Russia Really Works*, 170–1; see also Alena Ledeneva and Paul Seabright, 'Barter in Post-Soviet Societies: What does it Look Like and Why does it Matter?', in Paul Seabright (ed), *The Vanishing Ruble: Barter Networks and Non-Monetary Transactions in Post-Soviet Societies*, Cambridge University Press, 2000, 93–113.

[43] Federico Varese, *The Russian Mafia*, Oxford University Press, 2001, 55–68.

[44] Janine Wedel, *Collision and Collusion: The Strange Case of Western Aid to Eastern Europe*, Basingstoke: Macmillan, 1998, chapter 4 and 188–90.

unused to where it could be used profitably. The legal framework within which banks operated undermined their capacity to offer security both to depositors and to creditors. Disclosure requirements were inadequate, accounting and auditing procedures perfunctory, and central-bank regulation deficient, with the result that potential clients could not acquire information about banks whose services they might consider using. Law courts were often subverted by state institutions or powerful individuals, and did not offer reliable redress in defence of contract or title to property. For that reason banks could not be confident of being able to enforce agreements or collect debts; nor could they be sure that property offered as collateral was secure. Tax laws were complicated, inconsistent, and burdensome, and were enforced in such a way as to present state officials with a convenient pretext for legal action against enterprises that in any way inconvenienced them.[45] Only the old familiar state savings bank, Sberbank, could be trusted by most of the population.

Hyper-inflation and liberalization without stabilization enabled the best-situated banks to flourish as arenas for short-term money-making on a sensational scale. They did this by performing the exact opposite of banks' normal function: that is, by diverting capital away from the productive economy instead of providing capital for it. Those banks did best which had ready access to hard currency licences and foreign trade organizations, that is, usually those with the best political connections. In this way banks became disconnected from the productive economy and even harmful to it. Some of them bought up privatization vouchers, promising generous dividends, which were never paid, in operations reminiscent of the South Sea Bubble. Banks thus made huge profits while destroying trust in the market economy. They were instruments for the 'oligarchs' who in 1996 financed Yeltsin's re-election campaign in return for being allowed to take over cheaply state companies that were being privatized.[46]

To find a way round the money famine, many economic actors had recourse to 'veksels'. These represented a return to the monetary practices of medieval Europe, when traders would overcome the problems presented by barter and hazardous communications through issuing bills of exchange, accepted in settlement of debt by anyone who considered the issuer trustworthy. The veksel stood in for untrustworthy money, and also rendered complex barter chains unnecessary, provided that the reputation of the issuer was good—something that usually had to be established through chains of trusted acquaintances. Mutual payments societies sprang up, whose members agreed to accept veksels in settlement of debts. Banks and local authorities issued veksels to help customers cope with monetary bottlenecks. The veksel was thus a primitive form of money which functioned within reduced trust structures.[47]

---

[45] Most of this is taken from the World Bank report of 2002, presented in *Building Trust: Developing the Russian Financial Sector*, Washington, DC: World Bank, 2002, 1–47.

[46] David E. Hoffmann, *The Oligarchs: Wealth and Power in the New Russia*, Oxford: Public Affairs Ltd, 2002; Chrystia Freeland, *Sale of the Century: Russia's Wild Ride from Communism to Capitalism*, New York: Crown Business, 2000.

[47] David Woodruff, *Money Unmade*, Ithaca, NY: Cornell University Press, 2000, 149–61.

Such practices drastically curtailed the state's tax revenue. Veksels were difficult to tax, non-payment and barter altogether impossible; and late payment could only be taxed in inflated rubles. When tax inspectors tried to investigate the complex and interwoven transactions which kept the economy going, they encountered resistance not just from enterprise managers but also from local authorities, who continued to feel responsibility for the survival of the economic units on their territory. The consequence of low tax revenues was that the state could not pay pensions on time or in full, and the same applied to the salaries of the large number of professional people—doctors, schoolteachers, military personnel, officials—employed by the state. Pensioners, public employees, plus anyone in need of education or health care, could no longer fully trust the state, but had to look after themselves by taking second or third jobs, or setting up small businesses, to the detriment of their professional duties.

In the fiscal sense too, then, the state was no longer able to function as public risk manager. This massive degradation of its reputation and effectiveness undermined trust in all social processes. It also exacerbated a demographic decline which had set in during the last Soviet years: male life expectancy fell disastrously because of poor health care, increased stress, and continued poor diet and heavy drinking. The population fell from 149 million in 1991 to 142.8 million in 2006, at which point it was lower than that of Bangladesh.[48]

To cover the gaps in its budget the Treasury issued short-term bonds (GKOs) at favourable rates, which for a time were very popular abroad, and even enabled it to appeal successfully for IMF funds to continue its reform programme. In August 1998, however, the deficits became unbridgeable, and Russia defaulted on its debts. The ruble fell by some two-thirds, and the new middle class lost most of its savings. The proportion of the population living below the official poverty line leapt from around 20 per cent to over 35 per cent.[49] Trust in markets reached a new low.

This was a society in which the state could not properly fulfil even its basic function of guaranteeing social peace and creating the uncontested public space within which business transactions could take place. Top businessmen and state officials seemed unable or unwilling to distinguish national interests from their own personal and clannish concerns. The population responded accordingly: according to the respected polling institution, the Levada Centre, in 2006 61 per cent of the population said they did not trust the government. Distrust of politicians, business-men, and journalists was even higher, while 74 per cent felt that general social trust was declining. Forty-three per cent of the population agreed with the statement that 'our people always need a strong ruler', and a further 29 per cent with the statement that 'There are situations (like now) when power should be concentrated in one person'.[50] As I have said, total distrust is intolerable; hence it is understandable that,

[48] Liliia Shevtsova, *Russia—Lost in Transition*, Washington, DC: Carnegie Endowment for International Peace, 2007, 151.

[49] T. Gustafson, *Capitalism Russian-Style*, Cambridge University Press, 1999, chapter 6.

[50] Shevtsova, *Russia*, 77; L. D. Gudkov, B. V. Dubin, and N. A. Zorkaia, *Postsovetsky chelovek i grazhdanskoe obshchestvo*, Moscow: Moskovskaia Shkola Politicheskikh Issledovanii, 2008, 30–8.

at a time when few people feel they can trust the institutions and persons with whom they interact regularly, they should look to a strong figure to personify an ideal of social order. This helps to explain the subsequent relative popularity of Putin as President and Prime Minister from 2000. The ingenious devices adopted by Russian businessmen in the 1990s also illustrate the inexhaustible human need to trust someone or something, and to improvise arrangements to make it possible, even in the most unpromising milieu.

THE WESTERN FINANCIAL CRISIS, 2007–?

In the late 1990s most western commentators arrogantly concluded that Russia was hopelessly backward and in thrall to an ineluctable 'path dependency'. It had become clear that the Russian economy could not accommodate itself to 'correct' western economic nostrums, and it was therefore assumed to be stuck in a low-grade economic trajectory of its own making.[51] Less than a decade later, however, the most 'advanced' western economies found themselves in the grip of a crisis which sprang from the same roots: deep distrust lurking within its supposedly more stable financial systems.

The dangers had already been vividly exemplified by the American Savings & Loans crisis of the early 1990s. Savings & Loan Associations were mutual funds roughly equivalent to UK building societies, and they needed to remain trustworthy for the same reason, that they were lending large sums for unusually long periods to enable people to acquire and live in their own homes. For that reason the Associations had been strictly restricted in their market operations. During the 1980s many of the restrictions were removed: they were permitted to lend more and to buy riskier assets. When the property market declined, many of them got into serious difficulties. Eventually more than a thousand of them collapsed, with assets totalling some $500 billion. In order that savers should not lose their money, the federal government bailed the Associations out to a total by 1995 of $124 billion. One authority called it 'the greatest collapse of US financial institutions since the Great Depression'.[52] It should have sounded a warning of what was to come, but in the event it actually boosted 'moral hazard'—bankers' confidence that money trumped all ethical considerations, and that they could take big risks with the aim of making big profits, since, if they got into serious trouble, the state would rescue them.

The US Federal government made the problem worse in November 1999 by repealing the Glass–Steagall Act, which had separated investment banks from ordinary commercial and retail banks. While commercial and retail banks take deposits and issue loans in the ordinary way to individuals and firms, investment

---

[51] For a thorough statement of this position, see Stefan Hedlund, *Russian Path Dependence*, New York: Routledge, 2005.

[52] Timothy Curry and Lynn Shibut, 'The Cost of the Savings and Loan Crisis: Truth and Consequences', *FDIC Bank Review*, December 2000, 33.

banks underwrite firms' share issues and raise funds on the international markets for mergers and buyouts; what they are doing involves much larger sums and is much riskier. Separating the two had insulated 'ordinary' banks and their customers' deposits from the hazards of investment banking. It had made routine banking safer and more reliable.[53]

One consequence of deregulation was the rise of a 'shadow banking' system, which was not subject to even the most perfunctory regulation. 'Hedge funds' originated as a way of literally 'hedging' bets in the money markets by 'shorting' on shares expected to decline and 'going long' on shares expected to rise. Shorting means borrowing shares from a customer for a fixed period, for a fee, selling them and buying them back to return to the customer at the end of the period; if, as expected, their prices have fallen in the meantime, the result is a profit. Going long involves the simpler operation of buying shares at a lower price and selling them at a higher one. By balancing the two operations skilfully, funds can make profits whether the market rises or falls. By 2008, there were about 10,000 hedge funds, with a total capital of some $2 trillion.[54]

Funds can raise the stakes by leveraging, that is, borrowing large sums to make their purchases, and hope to make even larger profits before repaying the loan. That of course makes all their operations much riskier, as the ratchet can work both ways. A market that is generally falling can ruin them. Banks lend them large sums of money through their prime brokerage arms; they do it very willingly, since they make a lot of money by doing so, but they can get caught up in hedge funds' ruin—and their collateral can turn out to be worth less than was thought.[55]

Private equity funds service very wealthy investors, and are able to raise money without being quoted on the Stock Exchange. They buy existing companies, often when the latter are performing poorly though they have underlying assets. They then 'restructure' those companies, often by sacking some employees and selling off some assets, in the hope that the companies will perform better and start making profits again. If successful, they then sell them at a much higher price. Investments are locked in for several years, but provide high returns. The funds nearly always finance their purchases quite largely from debt, which enables them both to raise the money and to lower the tax burden (debt is tax-deductible in the UK and USA, and many smaller firms would suffer if it were not). Moreover they class their income as capital gains, which is taxed at a lower rate than income. One private equity veteran has confessed that he was paying less tax than his cleaner.[56]

Most hedge funds and private equity funds keep much of their money in 'shell' (fictitious) companies and bank accounts 'offshore', that is to say, in jurisdictions where their holdings are secret or disguised through intermediaries, hence unregulatable, and they pay very low tax or none at all. Offshore accounts can be used not

[53] Richard Roberts and David Kynaston, *City State: How Markets Came to Rule our World*, London: Profile Books, 2001, 70–1.

[54] Coggan, *Paper Promises*, 153–4.

[55] Philip Coggan, *The Money Machine: How the City Works*, fully revised and updated edition, London: Penguin Books, 2009, 82–7.

[56] Coggan, *Money Machine*, 87–90; *Paper Promises*, 189–91.

only to avoid tax but to protect underhand financial operations of all kinds, including terrorism and criminal operations. The Cayman Islands, Bermuda, and Jersey are all literally offshore; however, analogous arrangements are available in Switzerland, Luxembourg, and the City of London (whose regulations and practices are sheltered from those of the UK in general by ancient precedents).[57]

Offshore jurisdictions exemplify in hypertrophied form all the familiar paradoxes of trust. They are small yet politically stable entities, controlled by a tight oligarchy, whose members know each other well. They cultivate acquaintances among the wealthy and privileged around the world, engage in the same social round with them, and thus build up networks of trust. They learn to distinguish between 'one of us' and 'not one of us'. They practise both 'good' and 'bad' trust. 'Good' trust offers a safe return on assets and absolute discretion; 'bad' trust offers secret identities and readiness to break the law on clients' behalf. Insiders can set up companies with minimal documentation, whereas outsiders must undergo onerous verification. A code of silence, a kind of Mafia *omertà*, erects an impenetrable wall around their affairs. Investigators are met with intense suspicion and sometimes even a veiled threat of violence. One journalist was warned, 'If we discuss this with you, you will end up like Salman Rushdie. There are things here not to be discussed. I warn you.'[58] This reminds one of 1990s Russia more than of the secure and respectable financial world we used to think we were living in. 'Offshore' is the quintessential expression of money's tendency to emancipate itself completely from other trust-generating systems and then to prey on them.

The deregulation of the 1980s gave bankers, nourished by the offshore hinterland, far greater resources to play with—mostly other people's money, not their own—and created a much more competitive financial environment, in which they had little choice but to take risks, and every incentive to do so. Once one finance company devised an ingenious new money-making scheme, all their rivals were under pressure to emulate it or lose out. In any case, investment managers made huge sums for themselves through these transactions. US executives are today paid some ten times more in real terms than in the 1960s; at that time they earned 30–40 times the average wage, but now the ratio is 300–400 times.[59] Besides, the outcome of the Savings & Loan collapse implied that the state would bail them out if things went badly wrong. They had everything to gain and nothing to lose: a perfect recipe for untrustworthy behaviour.[60] Accordingly, they set about reckless borrowing: in large investment banks by 2004 the *average* ratio of assets to core capital was 40–1; in some cases it reached 80–1. In those circumstances a price fall of just 2–3 per cent could be seriously destabilizing.[61]

[57] Nicholas Shaxson, *Treasure Islands: Tax Havens and the Men who Stole the World*, London: Bodley Head, 2011.

[58] Shaxson, *Treasure Islands*, 219–23.

[59] Ha-Joon Chang, *23 Things They Don't Tell You about Capitalism*, London: Allen Lane, 2010, 148–50.

[60] Richard A. Posner, *The Crisis of Capitalist Democracy*, Cambridge, Mass.: Harvard University Press, 2010, 264.

[61] Joseph E. Stiglitz, *Freefall: Free Markets and the Sinking of the Global Economy*, London: Allen Lane, 2010, 163; *The Economist*, 10 September 2011, 79–80.

Up to 2007, however, most financial crises took place outside the advanced western world, in Asia, Russia, and Latin America, and we were able to persuade ourselves that we were immune from them. Moreover, international financial institutions dealt with those crises in ways which suggested that the interests of lenders would always be protected, no matter what the costs imposed on borrowers.[62] As a result, during the Asian financial crisis of 1998, in Indonesia the government was forced to cut food subsidies and social security for the poor, prompting riots on the streets of Djakarta and the resignation of President Suharto. In Thailand health expenditure was reduced, and the AIDS epidemic revived. The Pakistani government slashed its education spending, and as a result more children went to fundamentalist Islamic madrasas. Removing capital controls meant being vulnerable to sudden inflows and—much more damaging—outflows of investment funds. The measures adopted to end the crisis heightened the confidence of international financiers in the Asian countries, but at the cost of weakening the population's trust in foreigners, their own governments, and their own future.[63]

In order never to put themselves in such a vulnerable position again, Asian countries used their devalued currencies to expand exports and accumulate reserves. They invested those reserves in international financial markets, aggravating overinvestment worldwide, and fuelling the surge of financial bubbles in which prices lost contact with underlying assets.[64]

In western countries most of us were taking advantage of the bubble economy to take out loans in order to buy cars, consumer durables, and foreign holidays. The consumer society had its own inbuilt dynamic, which impelled purchasers to place themselves in the hands of bankers and financial companies who were only too happy to indulge them without asking too many questions. Consumers were motivated by greed and the desire to 'keep up with the Joneses', but also by a misplaced faith that, if bankers were prepared to lend them money, the deal must be sound. Both parties to these transactions were exercising flimsy forms of trust: consumers in bankers' competence and probity, bankers in ever-rising prices.

We were making use of the same financial conditions to provide against risk. Whereas in traditional societies people looked to family, friends, local community, or religious institutions to help them face life's risks, nowadays most of us put our trust in savings banks, insurance policies, pension funds, and state welfare systems. In 1963 pension and insurance funds owned 19 per cent of UK shares; by 1998 that was 65 per cent.[65] Managers of those funds were under constant pressure to generate maximum returns, which they had to report quarterly. In order to achieve this, they were investing all over the world on our behalf. Between 1980 and 1995

---

[62] George Soros, *The Crisis of Global Capitalism: Open Society Endangered*, London: Little, Brown, 1998; Robert Gilpin, *The Challenge of Global Capitalism: The World Economy in the 21st Century*, Princeton University Press, 2000, 142–62.

[63] Stiglitz, *Freefall*, 221–2; Joseph Stiglitz, *Globalization and its Discontents*, London: Allen Lane, 2002, chapter 4.

[64] Graham Turner, *The Credit Crunch: Housing Bubbles, Globalisation and the Worldwide Economic Crisis*, London: Pluto Press, 2008, 52–3.

[65] Jonathan Ford, 'A Greedy Giant out of Control', *Prospect*, November 2008, 22–8.

investments from mutual funds, insurance funds, pension funds, and such like grew tenfold, and much of this was foreign investment, which often offered better returns.[66] As a result, over the last thirty years or so most of us have, in many cases without even realizing it, been investing substantial resources in countries we have never visited and know nothing about—another example of strong thin trust on a massive scale. Total US pension fund assets rose astronomically from $0.2 trillion in 1975, to $3 trillion in 1990, $8 trillion in 1998, and $16 trillion in 2006.[67] Such investments have enabled us to feel confidence in our own future, to rest assured that in case of disaster—fire, storm damage, a serious illness—we would be able to cope, and that when we get too old to work we shall be able still to lead a decent existence.

All these funds depend on economic growth to remain reliable. When British Prime Minister Clement Attlee launched the National Health Service in July 1948, he remarked, 'All our social services have to be paid for, in one way or another', so that 'Only higher output can give us more of the things we all need.'[68] All western statesmen have periodically repeated this mantra. As I suggested above, it may be that the results have been good enough to partly replace religion as the provider of trust and security. As Robert Samuelson has remarked, 'The triumphant religion of the twentieth century was not Christianity or Islam but economic growth.'[69] Investment in economic growth became a panacea for all ills. Until recently this worked pretty reliably, but it also erected a new storey—in fact several new storeys—onto the already highly leveraged edifice of trust on which we base our lives.

Since the Second World War many people in advanced countries have also guaranteed their future by investing in urban real estate, not only in order to have a secure roof over their heads, but also because houses and flats offered a better and safer return than most other forms of investment. Placing trust in bricks and mortar has worked well for those who have been able to afford it, but, as *Financial Times* commentator Martin Wolf has pointed out, it also turned most of us into 'highly leveraged speculators in a fixed asset that dominates most portfolios and impairs personal mobility'.[70]

Moreover, the process also created a new underclass, the first-time buyers, the unemployed, and those on low pay, who had little hope of ever owning their own homes. In the UK they tended more and more to be isolated on large council-owned estates where few people were employed, crime was rampant, and there was a general atmosphere of hopelessness. Some banks and building societies,

[66] Gilpin, *The Challenge of Global Capitalism: The world economy in the 21st century*, Princeton University Press, 2000, 140–1.

[67] Michael J. Clowes, *The Money Flood: How Pension Funds Revolutionised Investing*, New York: John Wiley & Sons, 2000, 277; OECD statistics at <http://stats.oecd.org/wbos/Index.aspx?usercontext= sourceoecd>.

[68] David Kynaston, *A World to Build: Austerity Britain, 1945–48*, London: Bloomsbury, 2007, 284.

[69] Robert J. Samuelson, 'The Spirit of Capitalism', *Foreign Affairs*, 80/1 (January/February 2001), 205.

[70] *Financial Times*, 10 September 2008, 15.

especially in the USA, tried to find ways to offer access to the housing market for the disadvantaged by issuing so-called 'sub-prime' mortgages.

Investing in real estate generated a massive expansion in the mortgage market. Banks and building societies advanced their customers more and more credit (the financial term for trust) on easy terms. They were able to do this partly because prevailing interest rates were low, but partly because they no longer had to keep the accruing liabilities on their books: they split them up, repackaged them, and offered them as securities for other banks to buy. This was an attempt to spread and thus attenuate risk, but the mathematical models on which the securities were based were hopelessly inadequate: they only covered the experience of recent years, ignoring for example the 1930s depression, and hence did not take account of the possibility that one default might spark off a chain of others. They assumed that weakness in some funds would always be balanced by strengths in others. The trade in securities soared upwards: in the USA residential-mortgage-backed securities rose from $80 billion in 2000 to $800 billion in 2005. In the UK the rise was even more vertiginous: from £13 billion in 2000 to £257 billion in 2007.[71]

These paper bubbles bore little relation to the underlying assets, and on those grounds alone should have aroused suspicions. Since, however, the 'securitized' packages were apparently too complex for most dealers to understand, the resulting deals were based largely on trust—or, in this case, gullibility: trust in the untrustworthy. Booms are based on contagious trust, a surprisingly powerful force in the supposedly rational world of finance. As one senior figure in the Royal Bank of Scotland later explained, 'The problem is that in banks you have this kind of mentality, this kind of group-think, and people just keep going with what they know, and they don't want to listen to bad news.'[72] They were functioning on the 'auto-pilot' variety of trust.

Real estate prices rose steeply, by 105 per cent in the USA between 1997 and 2007, by 190 per cent in the same period in the UK.[73] As a result houseowners had greater assets to offer as collateral to raise further loans for cars, holidays, consumer durables, or yet more real estate. Non-houseowners, though, unless they could acquire sub-prime mortgages, saw the possibility of buying a home recede further and further into the distance. Nearly everyone took on more and more debt, supported or unsupported. In this way a world of socially divisive make-believe—or, if you prefer, weakly based trust—was created. UK private debt reached 328 per cent of annual GDP, the highest level in the world.[74]

---

[71] Gillian Tett, *Fool's Gold: How Unrestrained Greed Corrupted a Dream, Shattered Global Markets and Unleashed a Catastrophe*, London: Abacus, 2010, 52–9, 111–12; *Financial Times*, 12 December 2008, 11. Some banks probably did know what they were doing: the US Justice Department fined JPMorgan a record $13 billion for making serious misrepresentations to the public in selling mortgage-backed securities. *Guardian*, 20 November 2013, 2.

[72] Tett, *Fool's Gold*, 161.

[73] Graham Turner, *The Credit Crunch: Housing Bubbles, Globalisation and the Worldwide Economic Crisis*, London: Pluto Press, 26–7.

[74] Will Hutton, *Them and Us—Changing Britain: Why We Need a Fair Society*, London: Little, Brown, 2010, 354.

It is no accident that the current economic crisis began in 2007 with instability in the housing market. The epicentre was sub-prime mortgages, many of which the banks had granted with little or no enquiry into borrowers' ability to pay back the loans. During 2007–8 the spreading of risk, which had on the whole been benign, suddenly became malignant. Bad debts metastasized with breathtaking speed—and moreover in the darkness. No one knew whom they could trust any more.

The bubble began to burst in the UK in September 2007, when the British building society Northern Rock, overwhelmed by bad debts, approached the Bank of England for a loan. To understand the significance of this event, we need to look back at the history and function of building societies. They were first launched in Britain in the late eighteenth century to enable working families to borrow money to build or buy a home. They were mutual funds: that is, funded entirely by depositors, who received interest on the money they placed in the society. Rates of interest were modest but assured. Building societies needed to be extremely stable and trustworthy in the eyes of depositors, since they were lending large sums of money for much longer periods than ordinary banks considered prudent—up to twenty-five years. For that reason they were quite tightly restricted in how they could invest their funds. During the Great Depression of the 1930s they had been regarded as safe financial havens in a turbulent financial environment.[75]

During the 1980s, however, the British government lifted most of the restrictions. Many building societies then 'demutualized', that is, became public limited companies quoted on the Stock Exchange. They were thus enabled to attract investment from a wide variety of sources. This transformation violated the basic principles of the building-society model. It augmented their funds, but also exposed them to the risks of international financial markets, which operate on a much shorter timescale. At the head of the queue of reckless investors was Northern Rock, which embarked on an ambitious plan to secure for itself a greater share of the rapidly expanding UK mortgage market. It thus made itself more dependent than other building societies on international money markets, and in 2007 it suddenly found itself dangerously short of liquidity. Once its difficulties became known, thousands of depositors decided that the company must be in a seriously bad way, and they hastened round to their local branch to withdraw their deposits. This was the first run on a British bank since 1869. Eventually and reluctantly, the UK government had to abandon its free-market principles and nationalize Northern Rock, in order to prevent loss of trust spreading to other banks and building societies.[76]

Far worse things followed in 2008. Three of the five top US investment banks collapsed, largely as a result of overinvestment in mortgage-backed securities, many of which were by that time virtually worthless. Bear Stearns and Merrill Lynch were sold at minimal prices to rivals, but Lehman Brothers could not even manage

---

[75] Martin Boddy, *The Building Societies*, Basingstoke: Macmillan, 1980, chapter 1; Seymour J. Price, *Building Societies: Their Origin and History*, London: Franey, 1958, 408.

[76] Vince Cable, *The Storm: The World Economic Crisis and what it Means*, London: Atlantic Books, 2009, 10–14; Tett, *Fool's Gold*, 228–30.

that. On 15 September it filed for bankruptcy—the greatest corporate bankruptcy in history. Fannie Mae and Freddie Mac, two institutions which provided the financial backing for some 80 per cent of recent US mortgages, were placed under federal 'conservatorship', which meant that for the time being the US Treasury directly guaranteed their funding. AIG (American International Group), the world's largest insurance company, which insured mortgage-backed securities, was unable to meet its obligations, and the US Federal Reserve Bank had to prop it up with funding which over the following months totalled $182 billion. Meanwhile, the UK's largest mortgage lender, Halifax Bank of Scotland, was taken over by Lloyds TSB to prevent its collapse. Similarly, Royal Bank of Scotland became insolvent and more than half of its shares were bought by the Treasury. All the building societies that had demutualized went under and were bought up by more abstemious rivals.[77]

The collapse plumbed the most sensational depths in Iceland. In 1998–2003 all its state-owned banks had been privatized and deregulated. They expanded at incredible speed, purchasing assets all over the world, so that they became known as the 'Viking raiders'. By 2007 financial assets equalled 1,000 per cent of annual GDP. But then in 2008 all three major banks crashed, leaving Iceland the most indebted country in the world, at more than six times annual GDP.[78]

What this amounted to was a massive heart attack at the centre of inter-national finance. It was directly caused by the collapse of mutual trust. Banks and building societies found it difficult to realize the assets in their portfolios, since selling them drove down the price and degraded those assets. Alistair Darling, British Chancellor of the Exchequer, later recalled that, when faced with the imminent bankruptcy of the Royal Bank of Scotland, he realized, 'It was that stark: the banks didn't trust one another any more. . . . If we didn't act immediately, the bank's doors would close, cash machines would be switched off, cheques would not be honoured, people would not be paid.'[79] Mervyn King, Governor of the Bank of England, declared: 'We have been dealing with the greatest financial crisis since 1914. We have been on the precipice.'[80] He added, 'Never in the field of financial endeavour has so much money been owed by so few to so many.'[81]

In one respect, it should be noted, collapse did *not* happen. In September 2008 there were no queues of ordinary people desperate to withdraw their savings from endangered banks. That was because since the 1930s governments had guaranteed the deposits of savers up to a certain level. This was 'the dog that did not bark in the night'. If it had, the crash would have been far worse. Deposit insurance prevented an even more convulsive loss of trust among ordinary savers; on the

[77] Tett, *Fool's Gold*, chapter 15.
[78] Chang, *23 Things They Don't Tell You about Capitalism*, 232–5.
[79] Alistair Darling, *Back from the Brink*, London: Atlantic Books, 2011, 150, 154.
[80] Tett, *Fool's Gold*, 278, 282.
[81] *The Independent*, 21 October 2009: <www.independent.co.uk/news/business/news/mervyn-king-never-has-so-much-money-been-owed-by-so-few-to-so-many-1806247.html>.

other hand it also increased moral hazard by weakening the attention of both bankers and depositors to the soundness of individual banks.[82]

Shareholders, of course, were not protected. Stock markets round the world plunged, losing $600 billion in just 36 hours. Builders, retailers, and manufacturers all faced tighter markets and began laying off employees. House price falls accelerated, and with them sank owners' confidence in their own wealth, and their ability to raise loans with their homes as collateral. About one-third of US homeowners found that their debts now exceeded the market price of their real estate; some of them could no longer afford their monthly payments. Foreclosures began in earnest, converting some American suburbs into derelict zones.

This collapse was totally contrary to the concept of self-regulating markets, which had so long been an article of incontrovertible faith in economic theory. Testifying to a Congressional committee, Alan Greenspan, former chairman of the US Federal Reserve, confessed, 'Those of us who have looked to the self-interest of lending institutions to protect shareholders' equity—myself especially—are in a state of shocked disbelief.'[83]

No better illustration could be found of the crucial importance of trust to the functioning of our contemporary economies. It is like the heart which pumps life-giving blood round the economic system, enabling people to buy and sell goods and services with confidence. Fortunately, in autumn 2008 western governments' direct reaction was sensible: they turned away from classical economic theory and lightly regulated markets to the ideas of a theorist whose understanding of depression economics gave them the weapons they needed to surmount the immediate crisis: John Maynard Keynes.

He had pointed out that classical free-market theory ignored crucial features of the economy, and became especially misleading at times of depression. The defects he pointed out all turned on questions of trust and confidence. Theory posited that in investing and concluding contracts all economic actors had good information about the state of the economy as a whole, and could therefore take decisions with confidence. But in the real world information was often imperfect or worse, especially in the fast-changing circumstances of a serious market downturn, hence most economic actors had little confidence in the future. 'The fact that our knowledge of the future is fluctuating, vague and uncertain, renders wealth a peculiarly unsuitable subject for the methods of the classical political economy.' It followed that 'our desire to hold money as a store of wealth is a barometer of the degree of our distrust of our own calculations and conventions concerning the future'.[84]

Classical theory supposed that in a depression prices would fall; money would then flow to where goods were available at favourable prices, or where investment held out good prospects, and in that way market equilibrium would be restored. Keynes countered that in uncertain or unfavourable conditions,

---

[82] Coggan, *Paper Promises*, 159.   [83] *The Independent*, 24 October 2008, 43.

[84] Quoted in Peter F. Clarke, *Keynes: The Twentieth Century's Most Influential Economist*, London: Bloomsbury, 2009, 154–5.

people would lose overall confidence and would hoard money, as the best hedge against future risk. Thus, by providing individually against possible disaster, they would bring about real disaster in the economy as a whole. The individually rational would precipitate the socially ruinous.

Finally, theory prescribed that states should balance budgets in all circumstances, whereas Keynes recommended that, on the contrary, in an economic depression they should override short-term concerns about the budget and spend more heavily to inject both money and confidence into the economy. It is often forgotten that Keynes also believed that in good times governments should run a budget surplus and save up funds to inject into the economy in a downturn. In short, he favoured balanced budgets as a means of sustaining confidence, but only over long-term cycles. He knew capitalism was liable to cyclical crises, which at their height led to wasteful over-production and at their depth to mass unemployment and poverty. He therefore recommended that as an economy turned towards recession, the state should break normal budgetary rules by injecting extra spending, even at the cost of budget deficits. It would thus explicitly become the public risk manager, the upholder of generalized economic trust. In particular, it should keep up welfare payments, since they helped to preserve social peace and enabled the poor to make their contribution to the economy, at least as consumers. He did consider it important, though, that the surplus thus financed was spent on projects which would genuinely increase future wealth, since otherwise the result would eventually be uncontrolled inflation.[85]

Whether or not they were directly inspired by Keynes, in 2007–8 Western governments rightly overrode decades of free-market dogma and intervened directly, providing first aid in the form of subsidies, guarantees, share purchases, and the outright nationalization of financial institutions, in order to enable economic activity to continue at all. The British government, for example, poured some £600 billion into the economy. In doing so, it doubled the National Debt, bringing it up to approximately 80 per cent of annual GDP.[86]

The immediate crisis was overcome. But, as with a heart attack, the underlying problems did not go away. They simply shifted from one dimension to another. Governments' interventions in the financial markets were immensely costly, and left many of them with greatly increased debt. The bonds they issued to finance those debts became ever more expensive to service, and so they began to cut state expenditure on welfare, social services, and economic projects. National populations resented having their lives blighted by international institutions which seemed remote, heartless, and undemocratic. Nor were governments keen to surrender their economic sovereignty. As *The Economist* commented, 'Governments broadly welcome the benefits of global finance, yet they are not prepared to set up either a global financial regulator, which would interfere deep inside their markets, or a global lender of last resort. Instead, regulated financial firms are

---

[85] Robert Skidelsky, *Keynes: The Return of the Master*, London: Allen Lane, 2009.
[86] *The Guardian*, 20 January 2009, 8–9.

overseen by disparate national supervisors.'[87] The mismatch between the national and the international was particularly acute in the eurozone, where it soon became the arena of a conflict between national and international economic priorities.

That conflict merits separate consideration. Why in an era of globalized economics do we still place our trust in the nation-state, expecting it to provide the solutions to all serious problems? I began to answer this question in Chapter 5, showing how nations draw deeply on trust-generating symbolic systems. I consider it further in Chapter 7.

It is widely agreed, at least by non-bankers, that capitalism needs to reconnect with morality. This would not be the imposition of an alien external force: trust in the trustworthy is at the heart of capitalism. Capital cannot be created without investment, and investment is credit. No one will offer credit if they have no confidence in the future of the firm receiving their investment. In a recent report on the UK equity market, the economist John Kay noted that 'Trust in the financial sector is at an all-time low: only ten per cent of respondents to a recent ITN poll believed that bankers told the truth. That places bankers even lower than journalists and politicians. Yet trust is the essence of financial intermediation.'[88] It is clear that something has gone fundamentally wrong with our financial institutions, and at the heart of that degradation is the loss of trust.

Capitalism depends on its bankers, to provide the credit—packaged trust—without which trade and industry are crippled. This trust depends on their ability to act in a trustworthy manner and to spot untrustworthy behaviour in others. The snag, however, is that, while capitalism as a whole depends on trust in the trustworthy, the individual capitalist will often do better for himself by acting in an untrustworthy manner. Hence, to restrain untrustworthy behaviour we need a strong constitutional state, which in turn depends on (i) its politicians to make good laws and devise sensible policies; (ii) its media to keep the public well informed, made aware of problems, and supplied with ideas on how to cope with those problems; and (iii) the police and law courts to guarantee the basic underpinning of law and order. In Britain we have discovered in the last few years that our bankers, politicians, journalists, and police are all to some degree untrustworthy. In other western countries, though conditions vary, populations are drawing analogous conclusions. We have no choice, however, but to go on trusting them, otherwise our society cannot continue in recognizable form. We have our own brand of 'forced trust'—strong thin trust to which there seems to be no readily available alternative. Yet forced trust cannot be the best way of ensuring the survival of both capitalism and the constitutional political order. The central question, then, is how to restore genuine trust in the genuinely trustworthy.

---

[87] *The Economist*, 15 November 2008, 13.   [88] *Financial Times*, 23 July 2012, 11.

7

Why Trust the Nation-State?

In 1889 delegates from the socialist and labour parties of twenty countries met in Paris to set up the Socialist International. Its aim was to coordinate the efforts of workers of both genders and all ethnic origins to overthrow capitalism and end the hegemony of the nation-state; then ultimately to establish an international workers' state which would end war and promote social justice throughout the world. It unanimously passed a resolution proclaiming that the advent of socialism would end war between nations. In the meantime it called for the abolition of standing armies, presumed to be acting in the narrow interests of imperialists, and their replacement by people's militias, which, the resolution asserted, by their nature could not make war on other nations.[1] The ultimate aim, then, was to overcome the 'security dilemma', to replace nation-based negative-sum games with international positive-sum games.

How though was this project to be implemented? The International had no central decision-making body, and its constituent parties retained all their organizational autonomy. The Paris congress of 1900 created an International Socialist Bureau as a permanent office, one of whose main duties was 'to initiate and organise coordinated protest movements and anti-militarist agitation in all countries on all occasions of international importance'. There was no agreement, however, about how this was to be done. French delegates argued that, if governments declared war, workers in all potentially belligerent countries should respond with a general strike; but the Germans rejected this idea.[2]

By 1912 the largest party in the International, the German Social Democratic Party (SPD), seemed to be an outstanding success. It had nearly one million members. In the Reichstag elections of that year it gained 4,250,000 votes, some 35 per cent of those cast, and twice as many as those of the Centre Party, its nearest rival.[3] In the election campaign it had claimed that the stronger the party's showing in the Reichstag, 'the stronger the anchors of world peace'.[4] The party's

---

[1] James Joll, *The Second International*, London: Weidenfeld & Nicolson, 1955, 46–7.
[2] Georges Haupt, *Socialism and the Great War: The Collapse of the Second International*, Oxford: Clarendon Press, 1972, 15, 21–2.
[3] Thomas Nipperdey, *Deutsche Geschichte, 1866–1918*, ii: *Machtstaat vor der Demokratie*, Munich: C. H. Beck, 1993, 555–6.
[4] Francis L. Carsten, *August Bebel und die Organisation der Massen*, Berlin: Siedler Verlag, 1991, 215–16.

patriotic opponents took this claim seriously and warned the public that the SPD was 'treacherous and without fatherland'.[5]

The party made serious efforts to live up to its reputation and to avoid committing the German people to a war between nations. When an Austrian ultimatum was sent to Serbia on 23 July 1914, after the assassination of Franz Ferdinand, the heir to the Hapsburg throne, the German Social Democrats' newspaper, *Vorwärts*, reacted with a declaration calling the ultimatum a 'frivolous provocation' and a 'criminal action of the warmongers'. 'A grave hour has come,' the paper warned, 'graver than in many decades. Danger is on the march! The ruling classes, who in peacetime gag, despise and exploit you, want to use you as cannon fodder.... No drop of a German soldier's blood must be sacrificed to the Austrian despots' lust for power, to imperialist commercial interest.... Everywhere the ears of the autocrats must ring with the cries "We want no war! Down with war! Hurrah for the international brotherhood of peoples!"' Their call resonated in massive demonstrations held in Berlin and other cities.[6]

Yet less than two weeks later, on 4 August, the SPD voted in the Reichstag for the credits the German government was requesting in order to conduct the war precipitated by that very ultimatum. When it came to the crunch, the German Social Democrats turned their back on their internationalist pledges and decided to put their trust in their own fatherland and their own state led by the Kaiser, rather than in the workers of the world and the international socialist movement. One can see many reasons why they did this. They were naturally anxious to provide for the effective defence of their wives, children, and homes. General strike or not, the workers of the world were quite incapable of defending them against the Russian army, and most German socialists regarded rule by the Tsar as far worse than the Kaiser's regime. Social Democrats were also anxious to protect their large and complex party organization, which provided a social life as well as political support for millions of workers, and which would be completely destroyed if they chose illegality by opposing a war supported by the majority of the Reichstag. Their party organization, though regarded askance by the government, gave them a stake in the country, and in their own way they were therefore patriotic Germans. They reassured the German government on 29 July 1914 that if Germany declared war they would not call a general strike but would help to defend the homeland.[7] Whether the 1914 war was actually defensive was of course dubious; the immediate military violation of Belgian neutrality certainly looked aggressive, but it is not clear whether the SPD leaders knew about this in advance.

However that may be, their vote was a grave disappointment to many German socialists, and to socialists elsewhere in Europe, who had hoped that proletarian solidarity could prevent a war between nations. The socialist leaders in other countries had however already reached the same conclusions as the SPD and

---

[5] Carsten, *Bebel*, 227.

[6] Kenneth R. Calkins, *Hugo Haase: Democrat and Revolutionary*, Durham, NC: Carolina Academic Press, 1979, 45–6; Joll, *Second International*, 159–60; Haupt, *Socialism*, 210–11, 233.

[7] Haupt, *Socialism*, 211–12, 240.

voted for their own governments' war credits. When a delegate from the SPD met French socialists in Paris on 1 August, he discovered to his horror that they had not even considered voting against credits for a war in which they deemed Germany the aggressor. The only socialists to reject war credits were the Russians and Serbians, neither of whom felt they had a real stake in their own nations, because of their meagre representation in parliament.

The German Social Democrats' decision in 1914 set the tone for the twentieth century. Whenever war threatened, socialists—except a small radical minority—put their trust in their own national governments rather than in a shadowy international movement. Later, an initially even more radically internationalist movement, the Soviet Communist Party, whose predecessors had actually voted against war credits in 1914, became the bearer of Russian imperial nationalism from the 1930s to the end of the Soviet Union. Repeatedly the peoples of Europe, in a crisis, have looked to their own governments and armed forces to protect them rather than to international organizations, of whatever kind. They trust nations far more than international associations of any kind. We saw at the end of Chapter 6 that, in tackling the financial crisis of the early twenty-first century, international cooperation soon faltered and nation-states were left each to tackle its own crisis in its own way, even in areas where national egoism obviously threatened international disaster. Financial institutions and large companies can acquire property and move huge amounts of money across national boundaries at the touch of a computer mouse. Yet there is a widespread, semi-conscious assumption—strong everywhere and seemingly getting stronger—that when we get into trouble, it is the nation-state which should protect us.

For the same reason, we resist the subordination of the nation-state to international law, its deeper integration into structures such as the European Union, the International Monetary Fund, or the United Nations. All over the world, as empires retreated, formerly colonized peoples reached for the sovereign nation-state model. In the United Nations the number of nation-states shot up from 51 in 1945 to 117 in 1965 and 193 today. Why is it that in a major crisis most people still assume that their well-being and security is best guaranteed by the nation-state, even at the risk of wars, and even though most of the financial arrangements we make to secure our futures depend on the global economy?

The answer to this conundrum depends on understanding the way we place our trust. As we have seen in Chapter 5, the nation-state represents a powerful amalgam of trust-generating symbolic motifs, some of them quasi-religious in nature. During the late nineteenth and twentieth centuries financial arrangements added further reasons for placing trust in the nation-state.

THE FISCAL COVENANT

During the late nineteenth and early twentieth centuries most European nations drew on trust in financial institutions to create a major new load-bearing component of national solidarity. During that period, and most markedly after the

Second World War, the nation-state became a *fiscal covenant*. Parliaments created fiscal provisions designed specifically to enable states to mitigate the worst excesses of capitalism, which were threatening to intensify social inequality and thereby enfeeble generalized social trust. The state gradually assumed responsibility for protecting its own weaker or less fortunate citizens against the evils of sickness, accidents, unemployment, and old age. Precise arrangements differed from country to country, but the underlying principle was the same: during their active working life, all adults had to contribute through the tax or social insurance system in return for the confidence that in misfortune the state or local authority would protect them against absolute penury. In this way the fiscal system became an instrument of generalized social trust.

The provision of social insurance in urbanizing societies had actually begun much earlier, in England and the Netherlands as early as the sixteenth century, with parishes, guilds, and religious associations, then later friendly societies, trade unions, and other forms of mutual aid. These associations had the advantage of being local and personal, but the downside was that the risk was shared by relatively few people; as a result they could not always provide against large-scale misfortune, especially if it was concentrated locally, such as an epidemic. In any case, local and voluntary provision was haphazard, sometimes unprofessional or even corrupt, and liable to breakdowns.

Besides, in time older structures of trust and mutual aid broke down under the pressure of urbanization, industrialization, and mass migration. Neighbourhood and kinship trust structures no longer functioned adequately. Parish-based welfare weakened as rural parishes lost their younger, most energetic members. Urban parishes were often too large, raw, and anonymous, with numerous unassimilated immigrants arriving and departing. During the eighteenth and nineteenth centuries guilds were being abolished or at any rate losing their economic grip. Families became too scattered to assist their own members; in any case the decline in agricultural and artisanal labour weakened them as economic units. Family incomes were becoming more dependent on the fluctuating fortunes of capitalist markets.[8]

As traditional trust structures weakened, people also became aware of the need to provide against the new and broader risks large industrial cities posed even to their wealthier inhabitants: epidemics and urban disorder. In large industrial towns, whether or not poverty increased absolutely, it certainly became more conspicuous, and also more dangerous, since disease could spread more easily from the poor to the affluent. Besides, the concentration of the poor and disaffected close to major administrative centres—sometimes to the institutions of the capital city itself—posed a potential threat to social order.[9]

One of the first statesmen to rise to this challenge was Edwin Chadwick in Britain. In 1842, in his sanitary report, he wrote: 'Such is the absence of civic

---

[8] Charles Tilly, *Trust and Rule*, Cambridge University Press, 2005, 120–4.

[9] Geoffrey Finlayson, *Citizen, State and Social Welfare in Britain, 1830–1990*, Oxford: Clarendon Press, 1994; Abram de Swaan, *In the Care of the State: Health Care, Education and Welfare in Europe and the USA in the Modern Era*, New York: Oxford University Press, 1988.

economy in some of our towns that their condition in respect of cleanliness is almost as bad as that of an encamped horde or an undisciplined soldiery.' Tackling the problem even in one city was extremely difficult, for it required him, in the words of his biographer, to 'cut through the tangle of vestries, paving boards, water companies, and replace them by one single Crown-appointed Commission'.[10] In the crabbed style of his memoranda Chadwick persuaded government and parliament to take a broader vision, to override the closely knit and cliquish local bodies which had made collective provision in the past and replace them with overarching, more impersonal institutions on a city-wide or even national scale. He and his successors also had to persuade middle-class voters and their parliamentary representatives to approve taxes, local and central, from which they would benefit only indirectly. His success marked a clear example of the progression from thick to thin modes of trust, more reliable but less personal.

In the later nineteenth and early twentieth centuries further motives contributed to the growth of social protection. Britain was losing its economic domination in world trade and was beginning to face a potential military challenge from Germany. The promotion of national solidarity, productivity, and efficiency began to seem crucial to the country's security, the flourishing of its empire, and continuing great-power status. One direct result was the introduction in 1907 of medical inspections in schools, and the provision of free school meals for poor children; these measures were motivated by the discovery that many of the recruits who volunteered for the Boer War were not medically fit for military service.[11] Social welfare was intended, among other aims, to strengthen the nation's military potential.

In raising the state itself to the role of public risk manager, Germany was probably the pioneer. Already from the seventeenth century the ideal of the *Rechtstaat* had included the Cameralist concept of 'police', which implied not only supervision of the population, but also the provision of welfare for those who needed it in order to serve the state. Since the army was crucial to Prussia's survival, the state always recognized a duty to take care of the health and physical condition of soldiers and their families. Guilds also played their part in managing risk, as did mutual funds such as those of the coal-miners, while in the Catholic regions of Germany, monasteries, parishes, and brotherhoods were accustomed to relieving the needs of the poor and sick. When during the eighteenth century economic development also became an object of Prussian state policy, so too did the welfare of those who would promote it: farmers, artisans, factory workers, merchant seamen. On the other hand, the burden of poor relief tended to fall mainly on local government, which found it increasingly difficult to cope with. After the unification of Germany, in the later nineteenth century, university economists and sociologists, such as Adolf Wagner and Werner Sombart, who became known as *Kathedersozialisten* (lecture-hall socialists), recommended that the German state itself should take over from local and segmented associations the task

[10] S. E. Finer, *The Life and Times of Sir Edwin Chadwick*, London: Methuen, 1952, 218–19, 309.
[11] Geoffrey Searle, *The Quest for National Efficiency, 1899–1914*, Oxford: Blackwell, 1971; Gerhard A. Ritter, *Social Welfare in Germany and Britain*, Leamington Spa: Berg, 1983, 147–52.

of protecting workers and the poor against risk and adversity. They considered that only central state provision would prove effective enough to accomplish this, and thereby to improve industrial productivity and strengthen the social fabric, essential if Germany were to become a major world power.[12]

Bismarck augmented and consolidated the responsibilities of the state in his legislation of the 1880s. His efforts should be seen in the context of a new nation-state, powerful and even menacing from the viewpoint of outsiders, but still from an internal perspective raw, untested, undergoing the strains of rapid industrialization, threatened by other European powers, and weakened by long-standing regional, religious, and class loyalties. Bismarck hoped by means of social insurance to ease these potential conflicts, strengthen national loyalty, and give workers especially a stake in the new nation. He intended also to undercut the Social Democrats; they were popular among the workers, but he considered their political influence seditious and dangerous, and he banned them between 1878 and 1890. The Kaiser proclaimed frankly in a proclamation of 17 November 1881: 'The redress of social problems is not simply to be sought by repressing Social Democrat excesses, but equally by positively promoting the workers' welfare.'[13] By 1914, then, many workers had a stake in the German state, not only through their Reichstag vote, but through the social security system.

Similar policies were implemented in all European countries during the twentieth century. After the Second World War these powers were usually extended to cover the entire population: this was the 'welfare state'. The nation-state (or in a federal state its constituent members) gradually took over the functions of lower-level trust networks, and integrated them into national-level social security systems. Because these systems absorbed risk at the highest practicable level, they were far more reliable than the segmented or localized networks they replaced. There was a downside to this beneficial development, however: they forfeited the warmth and personal knowledge which those networks offered.[14]

In creating the welfare state and assuming the role of universal public risk manager, the nation-state was pursuing three main aims: to mitigate the socially damaging effects of unregulated capitalism, to strengthen the sense of belonging to a national community, and to ensure the nation was as fully prepared as possible for war. For all these purposes generalized social trust was essential. If it broke down, then segments of society would seek to provide against risk in their own way, while evading their responsibility to the wider community. This transition marked part of the path to today's characteristic mode of strong thin trust.

The fiscal covenant supplemented the creation of a national framework for public credit (see Chapter 4) through the sharing of tax burdens: together they have proved to be powerful factors in cementing nationhood. The central bank underpins confidence in the currency. The national treasury (plus the treasuries of

---

[12] Gerhard A. Ritter, *Der Sozialstaat: Entstehung und Entwicklung im internationalen Vergleich*, Munich: Oldenbourg, 1989, 66–82.

[13] Ritter, *Social Welfare*, 33–5.

[14] Finlayson, *Citizen, State and Social Welfare*; de Swaan, *In the Care of the State*, chapter 5.

component states in federal systems) becomes the clearing-house through which the whole nation shares the costs of providing mutual security and well-being: defence, communications, education, health services, pensions, and other forms of social welfare. For that very reason, after 1945 the weakening or surrender of aspects of fiscal sovereignty has been one of the toughest battle lines in creating international economic institutions. The nation is our public risk manager, and we are very loath to surrender any part of that management to outside forces.[15]

MONOPOLY OF LEGITIMATE VIOLENCE

Another crucial attribute of the nation-state is that it claims, and usually enforces, a monopoly of legitimate violence. It deals with illegitimate violence through the criminal law. If it cannot do so, we begin to see signs of a failed state. Max Weber considered this monopoly the defining characteristic of the modern state. A German analyst of trust, Jan Philipp Reemtsma, considers that the key benefit provided by the nation-state is an extensive zone of uncontested peace, maintained by this monopoly. He calls 'the renunciation of violence' practised by individuals and groups within the nation 'the decisive factor in social cohesion'.[16] The state's monopoly enables ordinary individuals, groups, and economic enterprises to go about their business without having to provide for their own protection. In that way it generates the confidence without which all economic activities would be far more risky, complicated, and expensive. It is true that this benefit comes at a cost: the individual must restrain his or her aggressive tendencies. Moreover, one can no longer place all or most of one's trust in a traditional collective of people whom one knows well. Trust becomes thinner.

In addition, as we saw in Chapter 1, the state's monopoly of violence can be grossly abused. It can impose horrifying levels of coercion and violence on its own people, or in war on other peoples, without encountering serious resistance. Auschwitz, the Gulag, the Chinese famine under Mao, the Cambodian 'killing fields' were possible only because the state had deprived its own citizens of the right to armed self-defence.[17]

The only restraint ordinary people have over the monopoly state is democracy: the rule of law and the ballot box—but they are crucial. Through voting systems we entrust our political choices to our elected representatives and the governments they create and sustain. The population can on the whole trust governments because—eventually—it can remove them. Between elections, though, trust requires some monitoring. That is another function of those elected representatives: they are expected to monitor the performance of the government and to hold it to

---

[15] The term 'public risk manager' derives from Hilton L. Root, *Capital and Collusion: The Political Logic of Global Economic Development*, Princeton University Press, 2006, chapter 10.

[16] Jan Philipp Reemtsma, *Vertrauen und Gewalt: Versuch über eine besondere Konstellation der Moderne*, Hamburg: Hamburger Edition, 2008, 99.

[17] This is the more general theme of Reemtsma's book.

account when it fails or transgresses the law. The media exist to make these processes widely known, and law courts to ensure they are upheld. This is the normative coherence, openness, and accountability which Sztompka considers so important to a 'culture of trust'. When any of these mechanisms fail, the culture of trust is weakened.

To appreciate how important are the nation-state's functions, consider what happens when it is unable to provide backing for one or more of these trust-inducing systems. If it cannot ensure the integrity of its own territory and frontiers, it becomes vulnerable to predatory neighbours or to the intrigues of internal war-lords. If it cannot satisfy popular aspirations for identity and community, it is liable to be fragmented by discontented ethnic or religious groups on its own territory, as happened in Yugoslavia after 1990.[18] If it cannot guarantee the parameters of the market economy, economic operators face far more risk in conducting each transaction, productivity declines, and most people become more impoverished. Then, in the absence of social security as well, they may fall ill and become sources of epidemic disease; they may seek their fortune by emigration or by criminal activities such as smuggling or banditry which they protect by gang warfare. The stronger economic actors will defend their property by hiring private armies, threatening or even murdering their opponents, and ransacking their property. We saw these consequences of a weak state in post-Soviet Russia in the 1990s.[19]

Nations dominated the twentieth century, and continue to do so in the twenty-first, in spite of the globalized economy. They revealed the full force of the dichotomy of trust and distrust. In the huge twentieth-century wars combatant nations displayed a solidarity and stamina beyond even that anticipated by many of their leaders, and also a furiously destructive attitude towards enemies. That was almost as true of nations under democratic leadership as it was of those under totalitarians; democratic nations also considered it legitimate to conduct mass bombing campaigns against civilians.

The most vicious and purposeful destructiveness was displayed by the Germans under the Nazis, whose mass murder of the Jews and 'war of annihilation' against the Soviet Union were only the most terrible of their crimes. As with the Soviet Union in Chapter 1, here we can observe the terrible results of breakdowns of trust. The Germans were a nation whose foundations of generalized social trust had been weakened or destroyed during the two decades before they gave the Nazis enough votes to propel them into power. Germans had long relied on a large and well-organized army, inherited from Prussia, to defend themselves from enemies to east and west. The symbols, rituals, and local connections of that army had become a focal part of their national identity.[20] Yet the army was defeated in the First World War and reduced to a mere shadow in the subsequent peace settlement. At the same

---

[18] See below, 'Internationalism—an Alternative'.   [19] See Chapter 6, 'Post-Soviet Russia'.
[20] Ute Frevert, *A Nation in Barracks: Modern Germany, Military Conscription and Civil Society*, trans. Andrew Boreham with Daniel Brückenhaus, Oxford: Berg, 2004.

time the Prussian monarchy, which had created a united Germany and then presided over it for several decades, was discredited and abolished.

As if these disasters were not enough, during the following fifteen years further trust-eroding developments took place. The Russian Revolution and the rise of a strong Communist Party in Germany aroused fears of subversion and possible revolution, with expropriation of property and subservience to a foreign power. The inflation of 1922–3 undermined confidence in money and rendered the savings of the thriftiest worthless.[21] The crash of 1929 then reduced industrial output by around 40 per cent over three years, raising unemployment and poverty to new levels. State social security funds could no longer cope. People sought protection and solidarity at lower levels of cohesion. Communists and Nazis formed paramilitary bands and fought each other on the streets and at public meetings.

The extent of their mutual detestation is conveyed in the memoirs of a Communist, who declared he had been carried away 'into an intense hatred of those I thought responsible for mass suffering and oppression. Policemen were enemies. God was a lie, invented by the rich to make the poor content with their yoke. . . . Every employer was a hyena in human form, malevolent, eternally gluttonous, disloyal and pitiless.' Such intense distrust and fear required as their counterpart undying trust in one's own comrades: 'I believed that a man who fought alone could never win; men must stand together and fight together and make life better for all engaged in useful work.'[22] The solidarity of the fearful and desperate ignited the street battles which accompanied the end of the Weimar Republic.

In this atmosphere of economic devastation, national humiliation, and intense mutual distrust, Nazi propaganda seemed very attractive to many. The Nazis offered a revitalized version of the united and harmonious nation-state in which most Germans had grown up to put their faith. They promised to restore military might, law and order, guarantee property, and revive a strong German economy not dependent on international capital, which they identified with the Jews. By comparison, the Communists' programme of expropriating property, nationalizing industry, and allying with, even becoming subservient to, the Soviet Union appeared threatening rather than reassuring to most Germans outside the organized working class (and even to many within it). In the elections of 1930–2 the Nazis won votes disproportionately from those likely to feel most threatened by Communism and working-class militancy: women, older voters, civil servants, the self-employed, those living in small towns and villages. In short, against the background of degraded trust structures, many Germans turned to the Nazis as a political party—or self-proclaimed national movement—which would restore both their economic fortunes and their national pride. Those who gave the Nazis fewest votes were those who could put their trust in alternative forms of symbolic and social solidarity: the Catholics and the organized working class.[23]

---

[21] See Canetti's comments in Chapter 4, 'Money'.

[22] Richard Krebs, quoted in Richard J. Evans, *The Coming of the Third Reich*, London: Allen Lane, 2003, 239–40.

[23] Evans, *Coming*, chapter 4.

The Second World War impelled Germans to refocus their distrust and fear and project it across their borders. Both trust and distrust were radicalized in the army, and Nazi policies lent a harder edge to both, giving rise to the most terrible atrocities. In the past German commanders had been reluctant to tolerate their soldiers running amok among civilians, killing or raping, since such behaviour undermined military discipline and tended to degrade armies into criminal gangs of violent youths. But Nazi political leadership withdrew that restraint: already during the Polish campaign of 1939 Hitler pardoned soldiers found guilty of abuses against civilians.[24] This sent a clear message which was further amplified by the aims and conditions of the war against the Soviet Union from 1941. Army commanders had orders to eliminate the 'Jewish-Bolshevik intelligentsia'; most of them agreed with such orders as necessary to destroy the leaders of the enemy's resistance. Initially the task was entrusted to extra-military formations such as the SS, SD, and the Order Police (*Ordnungspolizei*), but in the disarray of war, especially after the emergence of a widespread Soviet partisan movement, ordinary Wehrmacht soldiers often got caught up in their operations, and it transpired that most of them were prepared to accept those operations as a perhaps regrettable but natural component of a brutal and harsh war.[25]

The human feelings aroused among the perpetrators of such atrocities have been much illuminated by the work of the German historian Thomas Kühne.[26] The focus of his account is 'comradeship', the emotion which bound together the men of the small military unit and enabled them to sustain morale through the terrifying and potentially demoralizing experiences of total war. Members of the unit demonstrated their manliness and mutual solidarity to each other in communal drinking, fighting, sexual excess, and the readiness to kill or be killed. Behaviour that is common among inner city gangs, but would normally be regarded as dangerously anti-social, was not only tolerated but encouraged in the Nazi style of warfare. Each member of any army unit was desperately anxious to be seen—and in case of death remembered—as a hero, as one who was hard and unflinching in combat. He was fiercely loyal to his comrades, ready to risk life and limb to rescue one who was wounded. Such small-group combatant loyalty and mutual trust were certainly not unique to the Wehrmacht: many soldiers, in whatever army, recall this compelling sense of comradeship as the most powerful experience of their lives.[27]

In the circumstances of the *Vernichtungskrieg* (war of extermination) against the Soviet Union these characteristics were amplified many times over. Soldiers whose comrades had been killed by partisans felt justified in exterminating a whole village

---

[24] Jürgen Förster, 'The Relationship between Operation Barbarossa as an Ideological War of Extermination and the Final Solution', in David Cesarani (ed), *The Final Solution: Origins and Implementation*, London: Routledge, 1994, 85–102.

[25] Omer Bartov, 'Operation Barbarossa and the Origins of the Final Solution', in David Cesarani (ed), *The Final Solution*, 119–36.

[26] Thomas Kühne, *Kameradschaft: Die Soldaten des nationalsozialistischen Krieges und das 20-e Jahrhundert*, Göttingen: Vandenhoeck & Ruprecht, 2006.

[27] John Keegan and Richard Holmes, *Soldiers: A History of Men in Battle*, London: Hamish Hamilton, 1985, 52–3.

in revenge, to sustain their 'honour' and their mutual solidarity. Not every soldier delighted in such atrocities, but those who felt repelled or sickened by them often played their part or at best unobtrusively abstained in order not to undermine comradely morale. They had been told that this was total war, conducted for the survival of the German people, and most of them accepted that Jews, Bolsheviks, and partisans were mortal enemies, against whom all methods were legitimate.[28]

Some of the same motives could be found among perpetrators who were from neither the SS nor the Wehrmacht, but from the Order Police. On 13 July 1942 the men of police Reserve Battalion 101 were told by their commander, the 53-year-old Major Trapp, that they were to participate in the round-up of 1,800 Jews from the Polish village of Józefów. Able-bodied male Jews were to be sent to labour camps; the remainder—women, children, the elderly—were to be shot on the spot by the members of the battalion. Trapp admitted that he was distressed by the obligation to carry out this action, but the orders came from the very top. Moreover, he reminded them, the Jews had inspired the war and were active among the partisans, while enemy bombs were falling on German cities. All the same, he made an offer that no SS or army commander was in a position to make: any member of the battalion who felt unable to participate in this action should say so forthwith and fall out. After some hesitation one man did so and his example was followed by ten or twelve others (out of some 500). Unknown to them, one platoon leader had already refused to participate in an action 'in which defenceless women and children are shot'. During the following day, in the course of the operation several dozen others (exact numbers are impossible to establish) dropped out, physically repelled by the reality of doing so.[29]

At the most, then, 15–20 per cent of these middle-aged, middle- or lower-middle-class men from Hamburg (one of the least Nazified cities) declined at some stage to have a hand in mass murder. What impelled the rest to go along with such a monstrous violation of normal social morality, especially since most of them had been brought up and socialized before the Nazis took over? Although police discipline was less harsh than military, many of the same considerations applied: habitual conformity, the feeling that 'orders are orders' especially in wartime, the desire to trust one's leaders, not to be a coward or shirker, not to 'lose face' or be a bad comrade. Views generally accepted in the society around them doubtless influenced them subconsciously. Besides, at the outset the Jews were unknown to them, faceless and threatening 'others', scarcely human. Significantly, those who had some personal contact with their victims during the operation were the most likely to pull out; but even they did so inconspicuously, with the result that their withdrawal did not challenge group norms but rather upheld them. Besides, some of the abstainers did take part in later operations of the same kind.[30] In situations

---

[28] Kühne, *Kameradschaft*.
[29] Christopher R. Browning, *Ordinary Men: Reserve Police Battalion 101 and the Final Solution in Poland*, London: HarperCollins, 1992, 1–2, 55–70.
[30] Browning, *Ordinary Men*, chapters 8 and 18.

of great danger and uncertainty trust in one's immediate comrades and in one's nation overrode all other considerations.

INTERNATIONALISM—AN ALTERNATIVE?

The Second World War had presented horrific evidence of the damage unrestrained nation-states, each with its own monopoly of violence, could inflict on each other. After 1945 statesmen were determined to prevent any subsequent repeat of the disaster. They set about creating international institutions which would enable nations to share risk, to consult and take action collectively to preserve peace, to face crises together rather than individually, and to provide some degree of global governance to underpin global commerce. In other words, they worked to maximize the possibility of positive-sum games and to broaden the radius of trust to the global level required by economic developments.

The keystone of the arch was the United Nations, set up, as its Charter proclaimed, 'to maintain international peace and security, and to that end: to take effective collective measures for the prevention and removal of threats to the peace . . .', 'to develop friendly relations among nations . . .', and 'to achieve international cooperation in solving international problems'.[31] It sponsored institutions which would make it easier for nation-states to tackle common problems together: the World Health Organization, the World Food Programme, the United Nations' Children's Fund, and the International Atomic Energy Agency. During its life, it has focused special attention on problems which threatened peace and which required concerted international action; it thereby endeavoured to replace relationships of hostility and mutual suspicion with ones of mutual trust sufficiently strong to sustain such common action.

As we saw in Chapter 6, some of its organizations exist to tackle problems in the field of economics and finance, which in the 1930s caused fatal rifts through mutual distrust and the consequent playing of negative-sum games.[32] The new organizations were intended to pool risk and offer an arena for negotiation, so that positive-sum games could be generated instead.

The record of the United Nations, inevitably, has been mixed. Its formation was a contest between those who believed in the primacy of international law as a trust-generating symbolic system and those who held that sovereign nation-states should be paramount.[33] On the whole the latter triumphed: as we have seen, from 51 nation-states in 1945, it grew to 193 by 2011, largely as a result of the independence declarations of former European colonies, a process which was scarcely foreseen when the UN was launched.[34] It has become clear that nation-states

---

[31] UN Charter, chapter 1, article 1; Paul Kennedy, *The Parliament of Man: The United Nations and the Quest for World Government*, London: Penguin Books, 2007, 29–45.

[32] See Chapter 6, 'Money and Commercial Trust'.

[33] Mark Mazower, *No Enchanted Palace: The End of Empire and the Ideological Origins of the United Nations*, Princeton University Press, 2009, chapter 3.

[34] Mazower, *No Enchanted Palace*, 145–6.

still claim the primary and often exclusive loyalty of their citizens. The great powers, especially the USA, China, and the USSR/Russia, have accorded especial priority to sovereignty and have frequently given their own interests precedence over international ones, since they have been in a position to do that. The original aim of establishing a UN army to keep the peace was abandoned: nations were reluctant to contribute their soldiers to it, and in any case feared that such an army might be deployed against their individual national interests. Nation-states wished to conserve their own monopoly on legitimate violence, and their citizens have overwhelmingly supported them in this.[35]

The consequences of the fixation on nationality were horrifyingly revealed in the early 1990s in the violent break-up of the Communist system in Yugoslavia, which for nearly half a century had been a relatively peaceful multi-ethnic federation. The coming of multi-party democracy led to the rise of separatist nationalist parties, especially in the two largest republics, Serbia and Croatia, which aimed to dissolve the multi-ethnic federation and set up their own nation-states. In June 1991 Croatia declared independence without making any special provisions to protect the Serbs who formed 12 per cent of the country's population against discrimination or even arbitrary violence. Many of these Serbs were concentrated in areas which had formed part of the old Hapsburg Military Frontier, the Voina Krajina, imbued with military traditions rather similar to those of Russian Cossacks. Those traditions had been renewed during the Second World War, when the German-backed Croatian Ustaše launched a campaign of what later became known as 'ethnic cleansing', and the Serbs of Krajina conducted partisan warfare to resist them. Memories of that war and fears of Ustaše-type violence were abruptly revived when Croatia declared independence with evident international approval and without guaranteeing minorities' rights. When a British journalist had trouble at a Serbian road block at that time, one of its soldiers told him: 'You must understand that we no longer trust anyone here any more. We know that we will all probably die fighting to defend our village, but we will never let the Ustaše take it.'[36]

This feeling of being abandoned by the world, of being able to trust only one's own comrades and having to rely entirely on them, generated among Serbs of the Krajina a grim determination to fight to the end and, if they thought it necessary, to inflict humiliation and death on all opponents. As the newly independent Croatian authorities dismissed Serbs from official posts and began to discriminate against them in other ways, the Krajina Serbs announced their determination to break away from Croatia and rejoin Yugoslavia, which by that time was ruled over by Slobodan Milošević and his Serbian Socialist Party (SPS). The Yugoslav Army (JNA)—by that time largely manned by Serbs—was sent in to defend them.

Immediately the emblems of exclusive nationhood began to dominate the streets. In Croatia large red and white chequered national flags appeared everywhere in the capital, Zagreb. In Belgrade more and more signs appeared in Cyrillic

---

[35] Kennedy, *Parliament*, chapter 3.
[36] Misha Glenny, *The Fall of Yugoslavia: The Third Balkan War*, 3rd edition, London: Penguin Books, 1996, 111.

rather than Latin script.[37] A Croatian writer observed with horrified amazement 'the terrifying speed with which all colleagues change colour, flag, symbols, the genres of oral and written confession with which they cleanse themselves of Communism and Yugoslavism' in order to take on their new identity of Serbs and Croats, denouncing each other. To be called Petar Petrović was not enough: political manipulators were standing behind everyone, shouting 'Petar Petrović the Serb is radically different from Petar Petrović the Croat. Make up your mind which you are!'[38]

As the suddenness of the transformation suggests, it represented not simply the resurgence of age-old ethnic loyalties submerged for several decades under an artificial Communist federation. Serbs and Croats had long lived side by side, if not wholly peacefully, at least without chronic feuding. Even now many Serbs, especially in Belgrade and the larger towns, did not share the ethnic paranoia of their Krajina compatriots. Nevertheless ethnic sentiment was strong enough to form a reservoir of feeling which could be manipulated by Communist politicians struggling to retain public support now that their party faced effective rivals for the first time. That was the path taken by Slobodan Milošević, president of the League of Communists in what was then called the Socialist Republic of Serbia (within federal Yugoslavia). As the break-up of the country approached, he defeated more federally minded rivals in the League by agitating on behalf of Serbs in Kosovo, where the majority of the population was Albanian. He then fought off a challenge from a new Serbian nationalist party in order to refit his Communist clothing in Serbian nationalist colours and rename the Serbian branch of the League of Communists the Serbian Socialist Party.[39]

He then made use of the fact that Serbs, more than other nationalities, lived scattered throughout Yugoslavia, and endeavoured to reconstitute most of the federation's former territory as a kind of 'Greater Serbia'. In the summer of 1991 Serb forces began a process of ethnic cleansing, driving out civilians of alien ethnicity and murdering them if they resisted. In doing so, they received the support of the JNA, now more or less openly a Serb army, which was well armed. A ceasefire was negotiated in January 1992 and a UN peacekeeping force was deployed, but all the same the war dragged on, with intermittent bouts of fighting, until 1995.

Serbs repeated the strategy in the former republic of Bosnia–Herzegovina, where they feared falling under the rule of political Islam. Already in September 1991, as Yugoslavia fell apart, Bosnian Serbs were marking out 'Serbian Autonomous Regions'. One Serb later recalled 'I knew there was going to be a war, but I didn't want to admit it to myself. Coming home from a cafe, I was stopped by

---

[37] Glenny, *Fall*, 43, 82–3. The Croat and Serbian languages are very similar, but Croat is written in Latin, Serbian in Cyrillic, script.

[38] Dubravka Ugrešić, *The Culture of Lies*, trans. Celia Hawkesworth, Philadelphia: Pennsylvania State University Press, 1998, 36, 42.

[39] V. P. Gagnon, Jr, *The Myth of Ethnic War: Serbia and Croatia in the 1990s*, Ithaca, NY: Cornell University Press, 2004, esp. 96–8.

SDS[40] people I knew from before. They said "We've all got to take up arms or we'll all disappear from here. It's 80% Muslim." [41] When, following a popular referendum, Bosnian President Izetbegović declared an independent Republic of Bosnia–Herzegovina in March 1992, Serb paramilitaries set about driving Muslims from those 'Regions', again with the support of the JNA. They would harass and intimidate Muslim citizens, urging them to leave, then bombard Muslim villages and urban precincts, and finally drive out Muslims who remained. By June 1992 800,000 Bosnian Muslims were refugees—a fifth of their population.[42] The Serbs' most ambitious target was the capital city of Sarajevo, with a population of half a million. After the Serbs failed to take it, their artillery surrounded it in the hills and sporadically bombarded it for four years, without ever being able to achieve final victory.

The Bosnian Muslim Army (ABiH) was poorly placed to resist effectively, since it had no regular access to weapons. The UN had imposed an arms embargo which usually only the Serbs were able to circumvent. The AbiH followed a deliberate strategy of launching limited military actions to tie up as much of the Bosnian Serb army as possible and prevent it from heading in full force for Sarajevo. During 1992 Bosnian Muslim fighters succeeded in taking the town of Srebrenica and surrounding areas, driving out some 8,000–9,000 Serbs.[43] The UN subsequently declared Srebrenica a 'safe area' for Muslims, but all the same Serb forces refused to withdraw from around the town, while the Muslims within it remained armed. Eventually the Serbs were able to impose a siege, which rendered life inside the town impossible, and finally in July 1995 they launched an all-out assault to capture it. In the course of deporting its inhabitants, they separated men from women and children, then took the men to isolated sites and shot them en masse. It is estimated that at least 6,500 Muslim men, civilians as well as soldiers, were murdered during this operation alone.[44]

The impotence of international organizations in such polarized situations was dramatically revealed. Lightly armed Dutch troops were deployed in the Srebrenica 'safe area' under a UN mandate which authorized them to 'deter' attacks and to use their weapons 'in self-defence', but nothing more. This mandate was appropriate to a *peacekeeping* mission, that is, one agreed to by the parties to the conflict. Yet neither the Serbs nor the Muslims had given full agreement to the mission; hence what the Dutch troops were endeavouring to implement was essentially peace *enforcement*. For this they were hopelessly under-equipped; moreover, they were themselves endangered and dependent on the Serbs for their supply lines. As a result, during the operation of mass murder, they stood helplessly by,

---

[40] A Serbian ultra-nationalist party.

[41] Tim Judah, *The Serbs: History, Myth and the Destruction of Yugoslavia*, 3rd edition, New Haven: Yale University Press, 2009, 195.

[42] Jan Willem Honig and Norbert Both, *Srebrenica: Record of a War Crime*, London: Penguin Books, 1996, 71–7.

[43] Honig and Both, *Srebrenica*, 77–81. See also the subsequent Dutch report, at <www.srebrenica.nl/Content/NIOD/English/srebrenicareportniod_en_part01.pdf> (accessed 12 October 2013), 602–4.

[44] Honig and Both, *Srebrenica*, chapter 3.

understanding in broad terms what was happening but unable to prevent it.[45] The United Nations, plagued by great-power disagreements, diplomatic circumlocutions, and a confused authority structure, showed itself in this instance to be completely untrustworthy.

The descent of former Yugoslavia into civil war, in which its citizens inflicted on each other torture and murder, is a terrible reminder of the way in which, even in apparently civilized and tolerant societies, trust structures can change with bewildering speed under the pressure of political change, the appearance of new and unfamiliar threats to an old-established way of life, and the absence of any overarching authority. Trust networks which have long functioned pretty reliably suddenly come under mortal threat or disappear altogether. People lose their confidence in the regularities of life around them. They become convinced that they can rely only on themselves and their immediate colleagues, and are ready to seize upon any possible means of surviving in what now seems a harsh, unforgiving, and desperate world. The scene is set for atrocities to break out. The speed with which this can happen is something we should constantly bear in mind.

It is indeed difficult to imagine citizens placing their primary confidence in an organization as complex, contested, and (so far) lightly armed as the United Nations.[46] One cannot imagine it enforcing a monopoly of legitimate violence. Neither has it developed the symbolic repertoire which arouses loyalty. If we consent to its claiming some of our resources, that is from rational considerations—but trust and distrust dwell at a deeper place in the human heart than reason.

THE EUROPEAN UNION

Another attempt to transcend the exclusive and dangerous nation-state was the creation of the European Economic Community (EEC). Jean Monnet, one of its founders, outlined the problem it was designed to solve in a memorandum written in early 1945: 'There will be no peace in Europe if its states reconstitute themselves on the basis of national sovereignty, with everything that entails in the way of prestige politics and economic protectionism. If the countries of Europe protect themselves once more against each other, they will again have to create huge armies. . . . Alliances will once again be formed: we know their value. Social reforms will be prevented or retarded by the weight of military budgets. Europe will once more recreate itself in fear.'[47] Two world wars had provided overwhelming evidence of the truth of his warning.

After it was set up in 1957 initially the EEC was extremely successful. Its member states ceased to plan for war against each other, because in a remarkably

---

[45] Honig and Both, *Srebrenica*,180–5; chapters 5–6.
[46] It depends on member nations to provide, voluntarily, the troops and weapons for its missions.
[47] Jean Monnet, *Mémoires*, Paris: Fayard, 1976, 263–4.

short time such wars had become literally unthinkable. This was proof that sometimes disasters can, through the heartfelt desire to avoid them in future, lead to rapid expansions of areas of mutual trust. France and Germany, which had made war on each other three times in the previous seventy years, saw their economic and political interests indissolubly intertwined in the EEC. To reinforce this interdependence symbolically, they enacted a ceremony of reconciliation in 1962 when their leaders, Charles de Gaulle and Konrad Adenauer, celebrated mass together in Rheims cathedral.[48] The EEC not only avoided wars: economically too, it was a resounding success. Trade between the six founding members quadrupled between 1957 and 1968, while per capita incomes typically trebled or quadrupled from 1950 to the early 1970s.[49]

At a more modest level these achievements continued during the following decades, as the EEC became the European Community, then the European Union (EU). Its economic success also proved a powerful force for the democratization of European politics. Recently authoritarian countries queued up to join it—Greece, Spain, and Portugal in the 1970s, former Warsaw Pact countries in the 2000s—and they accepted the conditions of entry in order to gain the advantages to trade, security, and peace afforded by a broadened radius of trust. Under the Single European Act of 1986 the Union strengthened its international features at the expense of nation-states by instituting majority voting procedures for many issues, overriding the national veto and thus weakening national sovereignty. It also obliged members to work towards a completely free market in goods, capital, labour, and services by 1992. This was not fully achieved, but constitutional political systems, market economies, and the observation of human rights were still very attractive to potential members when combined with the promise of a booming economy. The aim of all the enactments was to create broader trust structures and positive-sum games over as extensive an area as possible. The result was, as intended, a huge further expansion of trade between member states in the 1990s and 2000s.[50]

Yet in political terms these benefits did not look so impressive. Their strength was also their weakness: they were not firmly yoked to nation-states. From an early stage there was a disconnection between the populations and the elites who were designing the new edifice. A European Parliament was created in 1979 to strengthen the Community's democratic relationship with its own voters, but after a relatively high turn-out in the first elections to it (65 per cent), the vote fell off with each succeeding ballot, suggesting that national populations were indifferent to the European Union. Even worse was the fate of the Constitutional Treaty of 2004. Made necessary by the cumulative enlargement of the Union, it was designed to centralize procedures and allow majority voting for a greater range of

[48] Gesa Blum, 'Vertrauensarbeit: Deutsch-französische Beziehungen nach 1945', in Ute Frevert (ed), *Vertrauen: Historische Annäherungen*, Göttingen: Vandenhoeck & Ruprecht, 2003, 365–93.

[49] Tony Judt, *Postwar: A History of Europe since 1945*, London: Heinemann, 2005, 324–6; Barry Eichengreen, *The European Economy since 1945: Coordinated Capitalism and beyond*, chapter 2.

[50] Ivan T. Berend, *Europe in Crisis: Bolt from the Blue?* London: Routledge, 2013.

issues. All the governments supported it, but to their horror the populations of both France and the Netherlands rejected it in referendums. These were not recent entrants, but founder members of the Union, who had done well out of it and whose loyalty to it had hitherto been unquestioned.[51] Evidently, however, they now found the prospect of surrendering more national powers to it repugnant. They continued doggedly to place their primary trust in their own nation-states. A damaging gap was opening up between democracy at the national level and the requirements of an international union.

This mismatch was symptom of a growing distrust of globalization, which many people felt was taking power away from them and putting it in the hands of financiers, EU administrators, and international business tycoons over whom they had no influence and whom they certainly could not remove and replace. This fear was closely connected in their minds with immigration. Many incomers from former European colonies, North Africa, and the Middle East had been arriving in EU countries since the 1950s, then had stayed in their host countries long after the industrial boom which initially attracted them had faltered. Moreover, they invited their families to join them—something which states that honoured human rights could not easily forbid. Muslims were prominent among the immigrants. In many large European cities mosques and halal butchers became part of the scenery; some urban quarters became virtual Islamic ghettos. Religious distrust was superimposed on ethnic distrust. Many of the natives felt that the incomers were unfairly outstripping them in the hunt for jobs and housing, and that they were drawing social security benefits without paying taxes, in short, that they were breaching the tacit fiscal covenant of the nation-state. Such stories, dramatized for effect, became the staple of the right-wing nationalist media and blogosphere, fuelling public distrust of immigrants.

Feelings intensified after the 9/11 destruction of the New York World Trade Center in 2001. Already in 2002, in the first round of the French presidential elections, the National Front came second, defeating the Socialists. The Front's programme called for resistance to further immigration, especially of Muslims from Africa and the Middle East. In many people's eyes Islam became associated with terrorist conspiracies, with prejudice against women, and also with fanatical, bigoted, and dictatorial politics. Even innocuous symbols of Islam, such as the hijab (headscarf), attracted vehement distrust. In 2004 France outlawed it from state schools, along with the Jewish *yarmulka* and large Christian crosses.[52] Religious symbols had become such mediators of generalized distrust that it was thought prudent to ban all of them, including Christian ones, from public places.

Anti-immigrant parties were also nationalist in their economic programmes. They articulated the public's growing distrust of globalization and recommended reclaiming some or all of the powers nations had ceded to the EU. The French National Front, for instance, called for revocation of most of the EU's open market treaties in

[51] David Marquand, *The End of the West: The Once and Future Europe*, Princeton University Press, 2011, 45–6.
[52] Marquand, *End of the West*, 85–91.

order to protect French jobs. As the economic situation deteriorated from 2008, such parties performed even better. In the Netherlands in June 2010, the Freedom Party headed by Geert Wilders gained 15 per cent of the vote and 24 seats (out of 150) in the national parliament. Its programme included restricting the powers of the EU, and a moratorium on the immigration of non-western foreigners and on the construction of new mosques and Islamic schools. Wilders's views bore the marks of Al-Qaeda: he asserted that Islam is essentially a terrorist religion and that the Koran should be banned as a book which incites hatred. In his opinion Muslims should be offered incentives to leave the country, otherwise Europe will soon become 'Eurabia'. 'Take a walk down the street and see how things are going. You no longer feel you are living in your own country. There is a battle going on, and we have to defend ourselves. Before you know it there will be more mosques than churches!'[53] Intense ethnic and religious distrust was erecting new borders in the middle of European cities.

This rise of anti-EU and anti-immigrant sentiment was taking place in countries which had been founding members of the EU, and had stable constitutional political systems and a reputation for tolerance. They were paralleled in later joiners. In Britain UKIP (the United Kingdom Independence Party) advocated withdrawing from the EU and reclaiming for the Westminster parliament all the powers it had ceded to the EU. At the European Parliament elections of 2009 UKIP won 12 out of 75 UK seats, and in local government elections of 2013 it picked up 23 per cent of the votes in the constituencies it contested.[54] In Finland the True Finns won 39 seats and became the third largest party in parliament on a programme of opposition to the EU, of limiting immigration, and deporting immigrants convicted of serious crimes. In Hungary Jobbik won 16.7 per cent of the votes in calling for a 'struggle against the EU which colonises and enslaves Hungarians'.[55] It described itself as a 'principled, conservative and radically patriotic Christian party . . . protecting Hungarian values and interests', and resisting 'ever more blatant attempts to eradicate the nation as the foundation of human community'.[56]

It should be stressed that all these parties, right-wing on ethnic policy, tend to the left on economic policy. They all envisage weakening the influence of international financial markets, restoring state welfare expenditure on disadvantaged members of the indigenous nation, and boosting state investment in infrastructure and jobs for their benefit. The parties' principal aim is the restoration of the nation's economic and ethnic integrity against the global economy in all its manifestations. When a serious crisis erupts, then, many citizens rediscover their primary trust in the nation-state.

---

[53] *Expatica*, 13 February 2007: <www.expatica.com/actual/article.asp?subchannel_id=1&story_id=36456>, accessed 8 August 2012.
[54] *Keesing's Contemporary Archives*, 2009, 49273; 2013, 52696.
[55] <www.jobbik.com/jobbik-news/jobbik-announcements/3245.html?>, accessed 8 August 2012.
[56] <www.jobbik.com/about_jobbik/3207.html>, accessed 8 August 2012.

THE EURO CRISIS

The second stage of the post-2007 global economic crisis (see Chapter 6, 'The Western Financial Crisis') was the turbulence which hit Europe's single currency, the euro, from 2009. In the generally optimistic mood of the 1990s, after the fall of the Berlin Wall and the end of Europe's division, the EU had aimed to complement its achievements by setting up the single currency to match and reinforce the single market. During its first decade the euro had proved extremely successful. It had brought its members the significant benefits of broadened trust structures. Risks caused by potential currency fluctuations were eliminated; weaker nations were able to benefit from both currency stability and the low interest rates justified by the stronger economies. In a book published in 2008, Othmar Issing, a founding member of the European Central Bank's executive board, felt able to say that 'over nine years that have passed since its birth on 1 January 1999, the euro has been a striking success'. A few months later he would no longer have been able to express such confidence. It is true, he also warned, 'The fact remains that for sovereign states to cede their authority in the monetary sphere to a supranational institution, while retaining a greater or lesser degree of autonomy in other policy areas, is historically unprecedented.'[57]

His encomium was premature, but his warning was fully justified. The establishment of the euro had intensified the mismatch between global risks and national risk managers. Since member nations clung to their budgetary sovereignty, the euro was launched without several of the preconditions I noted in Chapter 4 for creating confidence in a currency: a common fiscal policy, a single finance ministry, central financial supervision, or a central bank able to act as lender of last resort. Hence ultimately the euro lacked the full and credible commitment of all its members, an essential prerequisite for mutual trust. Its founders were aware of the problem, and tried to maintain confidence through a 'Stability and Growth Pact' (1997), which committed member states to keep their annual budget deficits under 3 per cent of GDP, and their total national debt lower than 60 per cent of GDP. Governments continued, however, to bridle at having their budgets controlled by an international institution, and in 2003, having breached the prescribed limits, France and Germany agreed not to enforce the Pact, so that they could promote economic growth in their own ways. Most of the other members followed suit.[58]

Therewith the one tangible restraint on the expenditure of member governments was removed. Henceforth they could continue to pile up debt uninhibited by the disciplines normally imposed on a national currency. That was a recipe for untrustworthy and destabilizing behaviour. The problem was exacerbated by the fact that among some of the more recent entrants the state had never really been trusted as public risk manager, since many people regarded it, with some justification, as

[57] Othmar Issing, *The Birth of the Euro*, trans. Nigel Hulbert, Cambridge University Press, 2008, 2.
[58] Berend, *Europe in Crisis*, 86–7; David Marsh, *The Euro: The Politics of the New Global Currency*, New Haven: Yale University Press, 2009, 196, 212, 234.

staffed by employees looking primarily after their own interests and finding jobs for their cronies. This suspicion fuelled a reluctance to pay taxes, of the kind I highlighted in the Introduction. As a result, tax proved difficult to collect, welfare difficult to finance, and people sought risk mitigation in traditional patron–client networks, at local or national level.[59]

As noted, these newer and less competitive members had initially gained from the stable currency: they were able to borrow as if their economies were as sound as Germany's. The drawback was that they could no longer cope with financial crises by devaluing their currency; they had to bear the entire brunt inside their own national economy. That meant that when the international financial crisis burst in 2008–9, trust in their economies turned abruptly to toxic distrust. Individual nation-states had to bail out their own banks, even though some of those banks were huge international players, with assets which exceeded the entire annual GDP of their home countries. As a result national treasuries fell deep into debt: 137 per cent of annual GDP in Greece, 119 per cent in Italy, 85 per cent in Portugal, all well above the prescribed EU maximum of 60 per cent. To start reducing these debts governments introduced stringent austerity programmes, raising taxes, cutting investment and welfare spending. The result was a loss of economic confidence throughout the eurozone. In Greece and Spain tens of thousands took to the streets to protest against mass unemployment and the degradation of their education, health care, and welfare systems. The weaker governments, Greece, Spain, Portugal, Ireland, even Italy, began to find it difficult to sell the bonds they routinely issued to finance their debts. Large banks which had purchased such bonds earlier had to write down their assets and faced their own crises. By the autumn of 2011, loss of confidence had reached the stage where serious economic commentators were beginning to discuss the possibility of the euro collapsing altogether.[60] Lazy and uninquisitive trust had turned into convulsive distrust.

The crisis hit Greece especially hard. Its government had gained entry to the eurozone by misrepresenting its fiscal position, then had used the advantages of the single currency to buy huge quantities of arms, play lavish host to the Olympic Games, support a bloated and corrupt state sector, turn a blind eye to tax evasion, and put off reform designed to make the economy more competitive. Early in 2010 the recently elected government of George Papandreou published more honest budgetary figures. The international impact was spectacular: Greek debt was downgraded to junk status in April 2010, making it almost impossible for the Greek government to raise funds by selling its bonds. The eurozone and IMF reacted with two large bailouts, in May 2010 and October 2011, but only on condition of tax rises, privatization of many state-owned enterprises, and huge cuts in state expenditure. These conditions were so onerous that after the second bailout Papandreou announced there would be a referendum on whether the population was prepared to accept them. The other euro countries' leaders reacted

---

[59] Berend, *Europe in Crisis*, 29–30.   [60] Berend, *Europe in Crisis*, 52–9.

with horror at this democratic 'interference' with financial markets. Under pressure Papandreou withdrew his announcement and resigned.[61]

But the crucial question had been posed: should one give priority to (national) democracy or to (international) financial markets? The two now seemed incompatible, indeed on collision course. The answer might appear obvious: the West preaches democracy to the rest of the world, hence surely democracy should have priority. It should be remembered, though, that the financial markets are not alien invaders: they contain the mortgages which enable many of us to buy our own homes, as well as all our pensions and insurance policies—in short, our confidence in the future, which we would not wish to see degraded. So the choice is not straightforward. The question should be rephrased, though: which kind of confidence is more important, in the nation-state or in global markets? Meanwhile, politicians are on the horns of a dilemma: they are less trusted because they promise benefits to a national electorate which they are then unable to fulfil because of pressures from the international economy.

In Greece the austerity measures, as expected, inflicted most suffering on the majority of the population which had not benefited from their elites' financial irresponsibility. The cuts undermined social welfare, depressed incomes, and led to unemployment of 50 per cent or more among young people. The number of Greeks made homeless, sleeping on streets and dependent on soup kitchens, rose sharply. Meanwhile the economy went into a vicious downward spiral: austerity causing economic decline causing more austerity. By 2012 GDP had fallen by about 20 per cent since 2008, and was approaching the levels of decline experienced in the US economy in the early years of the 1930s Great Depression. Following huge public sector strikes, tens of thousands demonstrated in Athens's Syntagma Square and attempted to attack the Finance Ministry building before being dispersed by riot police using tear-gas. In the elections of May 2012, the radical left-wing movement Syriza called on voters to reject EU–IMF bailout conditions; it won 16.8 per cent of the vote in the first round, and 26.9 per cent in the second. Some Greeks blamed immigrants for their plight: the anti-immigrant and openly fascist party Golden Dawn paraded the slogan 'So that we can rid this country of filth'. It won 7 per cent of the vote and gained entry to parliament for the first time.[62] International investors had lost confidence in Greece; the population had lost confidence in its own government.

Yet leaving the euro did not seem an attractive option for Greece either. The new/old currency, the drachma, would inevitably be much devalued, probably by at least a half. Consequently either the debts would double in size or Greece would have to renounce them and forfeit the confidence of foreign investors completely. Either way the economy would plummet even further, certainly in the short term. European banks that had bought Greek bonds would lose heavily, and some of them might face insolvency. Moreover the contagious tendencies of distrust would seriously damage confidence in other eurozone countries which were in economic difficulties: Portugal,

---

[61] Berend, *Europe in Crisis*, 13–22.   [62] *Keesing's Contemporary Archives*, 2012, 52007–8.

Spain, Ireland, and Italy, possibly even France. The result could be a catastrophic loss of trust in the euro as a whole, and therefore in the European Union itself. Only after a second Greek election could a government (just) be put together which was prepared to sign up to the bailout conditions.[63]

The only country which could stave off the collapse of the euro was Germany, as the EU's largest and most prosperous member. But Germany continued to be haunted by its own national memories: the destruction of its currency after both the First and Second World Wars. Besides, it had built its enviable post-war economic reputation on the foundation of balanced budgets and a productive, export-oriented economy. Germans were not prepared to squander (as they saw it) the fruits of their discipline on 'feckless' nations which had not observed that discipline. This was an understandable but short-sighted view, since Germany had benefited hugely from being able to export its products to a very large single-currency area. Others' profligacy had been Germany's boon.[64]

Few Germans saw it that way, however. Germany refused to support a European banking union which could absorb individual banks' losses at a higher level, since such a union would in practice have required Germany to become the major lender of last resort to its fellow euro members. Chancellor Angela Merkel repeatedly insisted that Germany would not support attempts to share the burden of Greek, Spanish, and Italian debt among all the euro members, since Germany would have to shell out the lion's share of that debt. She demanded that first the euro countries accept draconian controls over all their national budgets.[65]

The demand that nations should consent to the mutual discipline needed by the common currency was reasonable in itself, but did not seem to take account of the looming immediate crisis, the danger of a sudden loss of trust in the euro as a whole. That, after all, is how distrust works. Germans' refusal to act in solidarity with their weaker euro partners contrasted conspicuously with the huge financial burden willingly shouldered by all West Germans two decades earlier as the price of reuniting their nation: they then had accepted a special tax in order to make transfers of between 5 and 8 per cent of GDP annually for several years to keep the economy of the former GDR afloat.[66] National trust structures have proved generous and robust, international ones stingy and fragile.

One EU institution did step in to shore up the euro's tottering edifice. In July 2012 Mario Draghi, governor of the European Central Bank, announced that 'the ECB is ready to do whatever it takes to preserve the euro. And believe me, it will be enough.'[67] This was the soundbite that saved the euro. Although it was doubtful whether the Bank's constitution allowed him to disburse the huge sums buying

[63] *Keesing's Contemporary Archives*, 2011, 50516–17; 2012, 52007–8, 52076–7.

[64] *The Economist*, supplement on Germany, 15 June 2013.

[65] *Keesing's Contemporary Archives*, 2011, 50784.

[66] Christopher Flockton, 'The German Economy since 1989–90: Problems and Prospects', in Klaus Larres (ed), *Germany since Unification: The Development of the Berlin Republic*, 2nd edition, Basingstoke: Palgrave, 2001, 70–1.

[67] Alan Crawford and Tony Czuczka, *Angela Merkel: A Chancellorship Forged in Crisis*, Chichester: Wiley, 2013, 123; *Keesing's Contemporary Archives*, 2012, 52170–1.

sovereign debt which would be required to keep his promise, his declaration did have the effect of provisionally restoring international confidence in the euro. Such are the trust-generating properties of the pronouncements of a central banker! On their own, however, they did not create the prerequisites of a sound currency.

Altogether the euro crisis is an object lesson in the mismatch between international economics and national politics, in the effects of misplaced trust and its sudden transformation into herd-like distrust. It also reminds us of the need for all members of a trusted organization to behave in a trustworthy manner.

We are now in a better position to answer the question: why trust the nation-state? A nation is an eclectic bundle of symbolic systems which fortify social solidarity. Ethnic nationhood strengthens trust by offering uncertainty reduction in dealing with strangers. Civic nationhood buttresses the prerequisites which Sztompka considers conducive to generalized social trust: normative coherence, stability, openness, and accountability. The nation-state is also a fiscal covenant designed to spread risk, guarantee the financial system, and moderate economic inequality. Its monopoly of violence ensures internal peace and security. In all these ways it underpins generalized social trust. The nation-state is a reliable public risk manager, or at least the most reliable we have yet discovered. No international organization has ever come within miles of providing the same benefits. That is not to deny the importance of finding ways to enable nations to cooperate in devising positive-sum games and overcoming security dilemmas. But we must probably expect the nation-state to outbid all rivals in providing a focus for different kinds of trust for the foreseeable future.

8

The Lessons of Studying Trust

In all times and places human beings have been concerned about the future, about how they should live, cope with problems, take decisions and act, in matters both major and trivial. As I have shown, the concepts of 'trust' and 'distrust', though vague and used in diverse and sometimes incompatible ways, can be deployed as a means of analysing the way humans do this, especially when they act in solidarity with their fellows. It is important we do use these concepts, for they help us to understand crucial aspects of society which are not readily captured with our other conceptual tools. In different societies people trust or distrust each other for different reasons, and those reasons always have a social context, which differs according to time and place. Social scientists have studied trust, but, as I have suggested, they have not been able to create suitable terminology or an agreed methodology for doing so, and in any case much of their work has a minimal historical context, proposing a simple dichotomy between 'modern' and 'pre-modern' societies.[1]

To provide a firmer historical context, I have suggested that trust is mediated through symbolic systems and their corresponding institutions, and that those systems and institutions change over time. I have given especial attention to two systems, religion and money, and to the institution of the nation-state, which has proved remarkably adept at absorbing a variety of trust-generating symbolic systems and enabling trust—very thin trust—to operate within very large collectivities.

Religion is the most all-embracing trust-generating system. It provides trust in a deity or supreme principle which is benevolent and powerful, and under whose canopy we can define our own identity and form mutually trusting communities. Religion offers believers a secure knowledge of the world and of their place within it; it also underwrites a congregation or community of some kind, within which mutual trust is taken for granted, as well as specialized institutions which foster trustworthy relationships. Religion propounds a moral ideal to guide personal conduct. It usually projects the model of a person in the past who exemplifies that moral ideal, as well as congregational leaders or guides in the present who continue this tradition and can therefore be especially trusted. Religion promises believers a way of avoiding evil, or at least radical contamination by it, and a path to salvation, in this life or the next. All of these influences make it easier for believers to trust themselves, those around them, and the universe in which they find

---

[1] See for example a work which has many useful and interesting things to say about trust: Anthony Giddens, *The Consequences of Modernity*, Cambridge: Polity Press, 1991.

themselves. That is why, as we have seen, in a great variety of societies, believers have recourse to religious symbols when faced with danger or about to undertake a difficult or dangerous task.

At the same time religions display to the full the tendency of trust collectives to form round themselves a boundary across which they project distrust towards adherents of other religions and, perhaps even more vehemently, towards their own members who are considered to have abandoned or betrayed the faith. Protestants and Catholics were prepared to go to war with each other to affirm their own unique rectitude; the same can be said of Sunni and Shia Muslims. Islam created the category of the *jihad*, which has often meant holy war against unbelievers. Christianity responded with the crusades, while conducting its own internal wars against heretics and 'witches'.

There is another danger about religion: it has links to most other symbolic systems, and it is so powerful that it constantly threatens to take them over and bend them to its own purposes, or the purposes of its institutions.

In this respect it stands at the opposite end of the symbolic scale from money. Money and financial institutions underpin the minimal trust necessary to the never ceasing human activity of trade in goods and services. Money fixes the inborn human inclination to trust and makes it economically effective. It gains further credibility when associated with authoritative political institutions, whose symbolic representations it usually bears. When coupled with the trust-generating symbolic system of law it facilitates the conclusion of contracts and the creation of large-scale companies to produce goods and conduct trade on a broad basis. In the modern world the potentialities of trust are deployed on an even larger scale through institutions of credit and investment, which enable economic actors to benefit from *future* production and trade. This is the basis of capitalism.

At the same time, the value-neutrality which makes money so adaptable to an infinite variety of situations can make it a dangerous symbolic system. It can easily become isolated from other systems and even threatening to them. It can invade them, injecting into them its own ethical anarchy and eroding the values which normally uphold trustworthiness. This is especially the case when credit institutions become complex and poorly understood, as is the case today. Money and its institutions are a double-edged tool. Capitalism's mobilization of presumed future wealth in the present makes it a sophisticated form of betting. This betting can get out of hand, as can be vividly seen in the successive phases of boom and bust, powerful waves of exaggerated trust succeeded by convulsive episodes of distrust, in which fortunes are created at breakneck speed and then even more swiftly destroyed. In the process ordinary people's livelihoods can easily be shredded, as we saw in the South Sea Bubble and the financial crises following 1929 and 2007. That is why capitalism needs a moderator and regulator to smooth out its extremes, stabilize finance, and enable us to maintain confidence in our economic life.

Today that moderator is likely to be the nation-state, which at first sight appears incongruous in a world of globalized trade and finance. But the nation-state is unlikely to relinquish its hold on our trust in the foreseeable future, since it fulfils so many of the symbolic prerequisites for generalized social trust. Most nation-states have an ethnic core, with its own *Leitkultur* (dominant culture). Ethnicity offers a range of complexity-reducing mechanisms which simplify social interaction and facilitate social trust: language, culture, traditions, shared history, and the range of meanings communicated through gesture, clothing, food, and drink. Sometimes ethnicity includes a common religion, but even without that it takes over some of the functions of religion: shared ceremonies, a feeling of togetherness, a traditional ethical code, in many cases a generally accepted leader. But a nation-state is far more than an ethnie: it provides armed forces to defend our borders, police to secure peaceful civil life, and law to define the framework of all social interaction.

Moreover, a nation-state is a fiscal covenant in a way which is unlikely to be matched by any supranational institution. Through its taxation system it finances the provision of physical safety, communications infrastructure, health and education systems, and social security for those who suffer from the instability of capitalism. It also guarantees the soundness of the national currency and of financial networks through the operations of a central bank, a single treasury, and a single governmental fiscal policy. Much of the recent economic crisis is attributable to an earlier weakening of the state's role in upholding the fiscal covenant. At the moment of most acute danger in 2008, nation-states had to step back in to restore trust, by recapitalizing the banks and guaranteeing their loans when they were no longer able to provide the credit which normally lubricates the market economy. Since then, however, governments have proved strangely passive in the face of over-mighty financiers who have forgotten their obligation to remain trustworthy. Meanwhile, the recent travails of the euro, a currency designed without some of the nation-state's stabilizers, demonstrate the tension between supranational finance and national regulation. Our trust in the institutions and symbolic systems of the nation is thin trust, but none the less tenacious for that. Capitalism and the nation-state belong together. They are associated frameworks for the deployment of strong thin trust.

For several generations now, as I showed in Chapter 6, financial institutions have played a vital role in satisfying our need for security and confidence in the future. But now, since those institutions' own leaders have behaved in a blatantly untrustworthy manner, we are no longer sure if we can trust them. We face the possibility that our insurance policies and pension funds are worth far less than we were assured, and that the state can no longer act effectively as provider of social security.

It is not at all clear how we can find a way out of this crisis. Most politicians take as their lodestar the pursuit of economic growth, as measured by GDP. As Robert and Edward Skidelsky have pointed out, however, this by itself is an unsatisfactory and in some respects even harmful goal. They propose instead that 'the long-term goal of economic policy should henceforth not be growth, but the structuring of our collective existence so as to facilitate the good life'.[2] The 'good life' implies promoting for as many people as possible health, security, respect (being taken seriously), personality (the ability to shape one's life in one's own way), harmony

---

[2] Robert and Edward Skidelsky, *How Much is Enough: The Love of Money and the Case for the Good Life*, London: Allen Lane, 2012, 179.

with nature, friendship, and leisure. I agree with their proposals, but would add the facilitation of trust in the trustworthy. It harmonizes with their recommendations, but adds an essential extra element: it runs with the grain of what capitalism ought to be. Our contemporary economic system is unimaginable without capitalism (or at least it *can* be imagined: remember the Soviet Union and think of North Korea), but we need a guiding light to bring out its best features and restrain its worst.

What should that guiding light be? I suggest that, in searching for solutions, we need to place the concept of trust in the trustworthy at the centre of our rethinking. The reason capitalism is in crisis is that it has betrayed its own fundamental principles, which rest on trust in the trustworthy. The greedy and irresponsible behaviour of financial leaders has undermined the credit which is capitalism's indispensable lubricant. We have all aided and abetted the process by seizing at proffered loans to buy consumer durables, foreign holidays, and real estate; but in the latter case at least we had little choice if we wanted a roof over our heads. Governments were able briefly to restore a measure of confidence by providing replacement capital—but that is an option which can be exercised only once, since it has swollen state debt to levels which threaten to become unsustainable and has thus generated acute fiscal crises. Cutting expenditure and raising tax levels can only be pursued up to a certain point. Beyond that, austerity, especially if it is accompanied by growing inequality and social injustice, becomes unacceptable to the people. It breaches the tacit contract involved in democracy, which is itself a prerequisite of modern trust structures, as Sztompka has shown. It is also self-defeating, since it downgrades the economy as a whole.

How can we get back to the basic principles of trust and trustworthiness? Surveys suggest that in western societies, long before recent crises, generalized trust had been declining since the 1950s. In the UK in 1959, when asked, 'Would you say that most people can be trusted?', 56 per cent replied 'Yes'. In 1998 the equivalent figure was 30 per cent. In the USA, over a similar period the decline was from 55 per cent to 35 per cent. In Western Europe the fall was similar, though less marked.[3] In a book published in 1999, Francis Fukuyama suggested that the decline was the result of the transition from an industrial to a knowledge society, in which trust reconfigured itself in different but not necessarily more detrimental patterns. Specifically, he argued that trust tended increasingly to be focused more informally, personally, and on a smaller radius, through what he called 'the miniaturisation of community'. There were more associations, but they were narrower in focus, while the authority of large organizations had waned.[4]

This change may have been occurring in places, but Fukuyama's diagnosis misses the broader context. I have suggested the very opposite, that we tend to entrust ever more consequential resources to larger, more impersonal organizations. Moreover,

---

[3] Richard Layard, *Happiness: Lessons from a New Science*, London: Allen Lane, 2005, 80–2, 226; Robert D. Putnam, *Bowling Alone: The Collapse and Revival of American Community*, New York: Simon & Schuster, 2000, 138–42.

[4] Francis Fukuyama, *The Great Disruption: Human Nature and the Reconstitution of Social Order*, London: Profile Books, 1999, especially 88–91.

I believe Fukuyama was seriously over-optimistic about the capacity of capitalism by itself to generate and sustain trusting relationships. Insofar as it has been able to do so, that is only because it has been structured by nation-states and international financial institutions which maximized the radius of trust and sought high-level positive-sum games. On the whole this arrangement worked well till recently, but its downside is that the institutions in which we place our trust have become much more distant from us and also more opaque. We know little about them and have no close relationship with them.

As a result, the nature of trust has been changing, away from thick towards thin trust, even to meet our most significant needs. That is why I assert that strong thin trust has become the dominant mode in our society. The banks where we deposit our money and the insurance companies which bear our risk deploy our funds to trade across the world, acquiring shares in enterprises we know nothing at all about. We trust systems of knowledge of which we understand little or nothing, and we entrust our fate to institutions whose reliability we can often monitor only by hearsay. There is no real alternative: we cannot opt out of the legal or monetary system. The law still provides protection for our routine dealings. In spite of everything, our savings are more secure in a bank than anywhere else. We risk our lives if we reject all medical knowledge or refuse to submit ourselves to the treatment of medical experts.[5] In this sense—in defiance of most social science theory on the subject—it makes sense to talk of 'forced trust', or at least trust under pressure.

The 'thinning' of trust relationships is part of a process which the sociologist Anthony Giddens has called 'disembedding', in which social relations are lifted out of local and temporal contexts and restructured across indefinite spans of time and space.[6] When I receive an e-mail nowadays, it is not immediately apparent whether it comes from next door or from Vladivostok. E-mails are very convenient, but they do not represent a direct response to another person, as in a conversation, even one conducted over the telephone. The result is a 'thin' relationship, in which we may know little about even the location, let alone the background, capabilities, or personal character—hence trustworthiness—of our interlocutor. Identity fraud, rare in pre-internet days, is now rampant. Yet often we have to rely on information our interlocutor supplies and, on even less evidence than usual, trust him or her to cooperate with us.

In all these cases trust has become more impersonal, more fragmentary, and more instrumental. That is to say, it is based less on close personal relationships, it encompasses less of our life, and it is directed more at particular rather than general ends. In addition, because we entrust so many of our risk avoidance strategies to government and to large financial institutions, the practices of bureaucrats, accountants, and lawyers determine much of the routine of our lives, imposing on us forms to fill in, reports to write, and targets to meet. Those officials also tend to

[5] Anthony Giddens, *The Consequences of Modernity*, Cambridge: Polity Press, 1991; Onora O'Neill, *A Question of Trust: The BBC Reith Lectures 2002*, Cambridge University Press, 2002.
[6] Giddens, *Consequences*, 21–9.

impose very intrusive levels of monitoring, designed to eliminate all risk; in doing so, they arouse resentment and probably deepen distrust.[7]

In recent years, in the West in general (and the UK in particular), we have become aware that our systems of trust are in serious jeopardy—not yet terminal, but certainly precarious.

This is dangerous, since if we cannot learn to build more robust trust structures into our politics, economics, and society, then our way of life cannot be sustained. In 2009 Anthony Seldon addressed the problem of declining trust in a thought-provoking book. He diagnosed many of the same ills that I have traced above, and came to the conclusion that the pace of modern life and its 'disembedding' effects have created a milieu where 'we lose touch not only with others, which is the essential prerequisite for trust, but with ourselves'.[8] This self is naturally trusting: 'In our core natures we are trusting. It is our cores which, as Donne wrote, are connected one with another.' But because of the pressures of modern life, 'we lose touch with our centres.... The path back to sanity begins with getting back in touch with our centres. To achieve this, personally and professionally, we should adopt a "presumption to trust". This has to begin with trusting ourselves, so we can be the change we wish to see in the world.' Hence his recommendation that we should all spend ten minutes a day just being with ourselves, whether 'reading poetry, meditating, praying, breathing deeply or just being'.[9] Likewise, Marek Kohn concludes his book on trust with a chapter entitled 'Leaving the Door Unlocked', restoring thick trust within families and communities, and putting thin trust, essential though it is in the modern world, firmly back in its place.[10]

Seldon's practical suggestions to achieve greater trust are all well worth serious debate. And I agree with his assertion that human beings are naturally trusting. But to leave it at that is to miss the historical context, which is crucial. We have an authentic self, but it is shaped by the history of our society and the way it is currently structured. We grow up trusting and distrusting in ways we learn from those around us. We have to find solutions which will work in our society, which has committed so much of its trust to financial, professional, scientific, and governmental institutions. Besides, trust in itself is not always beneficial, as Kohn implies. Trust in the untrustworthy is at best unrewarding, at worst pernicious. It is true, though, that thin trust, however beneficial for large-scale positive-sum games, needs to be supplemented by a partial revival of thick trust, as both Seldon and Kohn point out.

One great strength of Seldon's book is that it refocuses our attention on trust. Social commentators and historians have given too much attention to power, not enough to trust. Or rather, we have not been sufficiently aware that the exercise of power needs to work along with the vectors of trust. Even Machiavelli, who was obsessed

---

[7] This is a principal theme in O'Neill, *A Question of Trust.*
[8] Anthony Seldon, *Trust: How We Lost it and How to Get it Back*, London: Biteback, 2009, 46.
[9] Seldon, *Trust*, 214–15.
[10] Marek Kohn, *Trust: Self-Interest and the Common Good*, Oxford University Press, 2008, chapter 7.

with power, did not make that mistake. The same is self-evidently true of economic systems.

The work of re-instilling trust in the trustworthy into our media, politics, and economics has to be a conscious one. We all know there is a 'crisis of trust', but without understanding *why* generalized social trust has become endangered, we cannot begin the task of restoring it.

To what principles, then, should we refer when working to strengthen trust in the trustworthy? Here are some general observations and recommendations to help us with the gradual but systematic reinforcement of trust structures:

- Trust and distrust are basic human dispositions, necessary to both our cognitive and our decision-making capacities. We all seek, even in apparently desperate situations, to have confidence in the world and in other people.

- Human beings are by nature trusting, though not infinitely so. In seeking to strengthen trust, we are working *with* the grain of human nature. But we also need to recognize that, once trust is broken, distrust takes over forcefully and cumulatively. When it becomes widespread, it is extremely destructive, as I showed in my account of witch-hunting and of various financial crises.

- Social trust creates communities with a strong sense of mutual interdependence, such as the medieval parish, the monastery, the city-state, or the fighting unit in an army. This trust is mediated through symbolic systems and the institutions attached to them. The social frameworks associated with those institutions harbour the bonds of trust on which most of us rely in taking decisions and acting. They have their own boundaries, within which mutual trust is strong, but across which virulent distrust may be projected on outsiders, especially in a crisis. In the 1930s Germans projected their own internal disorders onto outsiders, Slavs and Jews in particular; in the late twentieth and early twenty-first centuries many European populations have done so, less murderously but still forcefully, against immigrants.

- Trust is closely linked to identity. We tend to trust those who most resemble us, because they are using symbolic systems similar to our own. Hence we feel a sense of community with them, and to trust them requires little conscious effort. Even when we distrust them, to discover the causes of that distrust and resolve the conflict is easier. This is one of the reasons why nations are strong, and why they seek to expand and acquire their own statehood. It is also why minority ethnic or religious communities may seek to break away.

- When social trust breaks down, it tends to reconfigure in a lower-level collective, which then erects rigid boundaries around itself. Thus when trust in the state is weakened, it tends to refocus on a political party, a religious movement, an ethnic group, a regional or tribal leader, a military strong man, or on an economically powerful figure. In a crisis of trust, political leaders will often try to draw tighter boundaries around the community and project distrust across them. Trust is easier to generate within a community when it is threatened or thought to be threatened. Post-revolutionary France found in patriotism a cohesion which it had not found in the cult of the Supreme Being. When Yugoslavia broke up in the early 1990s, social trust sought refuge in lower-level ethnicities, each with its own paramilitary bands.

- All the same, in a crisis of trust, the optimal response is usually the opposite one: to attempt to broaden the radius of trust by seeking higher-level positive-sum games, reaching across boundaries to solve common problems and discover common interests, hoping in the process to create the first links of mutual trust, which can then be strengthened. This is, ideally, how diplomats operate in dealing with crises. It is how Muhammad united fractious Arabian tribes in preaching and practising his new religion, Islam; indeed this is the function of all universal religions. It is how European statesmen dealt with the catastrophic results of war after 1945, creating international institutions under the United Nations and also what later became the European Union.

- One of the benefits of seeking higher-level integration is the pooling of risk, so that individuals and collectives can cope with misfortunes which could devastate them on their own. This is the principle on which banks and insurance companies were built, and it is why commercial risk is usually handled by companies rather than individual entrepreneurs. The nation-state, as public risk manager, supplies this benefit for all its citizens.

- As the world has become more complicated and societies more interdependent, we tend to move from thick trust to thin trust. We have to place ever more trust in persons and institutions about whom/which we know very little in the direct and personal sense. On the whole this tendency is beneficial, but we need to recognize its dangers, and do what we can to mitigate them and to reconstruct forums for thick trust.

These observations suggest some practical moral guidelines for everyday life (along the lines suggested by Sztompka and O'Neill).

- In collectives and institutions, mutual trust should be presumed as a starting point. Systematic distrust, if exercised as a norm, for example by constant oversight through league tables and performance indicators, generates perverse behaviour designed to boost performance indicators rather than restore trust. Then distrust reproduces itself and degrades human social interaction. But when things seem to be going wrong, there must be *some* monitoring of performance, since carelessness about outcomes also creates distrust. Balancing these requirements is tricky, and should be recognized as an essential skill of management.

- Similarly, in a polity, total trust in government is likely to be dysfunctional, as it can easily be abused. Here a certain level of distrust is a prerequisite of trust! Monitoring government and holding it to account remains crucial to political trust. That is the function of the media and of parliament, especially the opposition.

- We all need information about what is going on around us, in a form which we can understand. When things go wrong, we also need ideas about how to put it right. Communicating information and allowing ideas to circulate is an important task of the media and of anyone running a collective, or indeed a political system. On the other hand, some advice and some dialogues, both official and personal, need to remain confidential if trust is to be preserved. An unrestrained Wikileaks-type flood constrains such exchanges and reduces trust: no adviser can always be candid if he suspects that his advice will feature in tomorrow's headlines. Again, this is a tricky balance. To cultivate the skills necessary to maintain it, we need to recognize the overriding importance of trust in the trustworthy.

- Personal trust is easier to create and sustain than impersonal trust. This is true even in today's world of long-distance automatic communications, indeed perhaps especially so—which partly explains why religions retain their attractiveness. All organizations need to help their members get to know each other, though for large organizations this may be in sub-units. And when dealing with outsiders, they should arrange for at least some contact to be through persons rather than impersonal agencies. In today's world of strong thin trust, reintroducing a personal element into trust relationships is more difficult than ever before. But we should aim at it whenever we can.

For us as individuals, the starting point must be a moral one: doing one's best to be trustworthy oneself, in the workplace, at home, and in social life. Observing professional standards, keeping one's word, being loyal to family and friends sound a long way from the all-encompassing global processes I have been describing, but in fact they are the bedrock. Social conditions may change, but 'trust in the trustworthy' remains the key. It is time it became a guiding focus of public debate.

Index

Since trust and distrust are the theme of the whole book, there are no separate entries for these two terms. See associated entries, e.g. financial trust, reflective trust.